RELIGIOUS FUNDAMENTALISM
IN THE MIDDLE EAST

Studies in Critical Social Sciences Book Series

Haymarket Books is proud to be working with Brill Academic Publishers (www.brill.nl) to republish the *Studies in Critical Social Sciences* book series in paperback editions. This peer-reviewed book series offers insights into our current reality by exploring the content and consequences of power relationships under capitalism, and by considering the spaces of opposition and resistance to these changes that have been defining our new age. Our full catalog of *SCSS* volumes can be viewed at www.haymarketbooks.org/category/scss-series.

RELIGIOUS FUNDAMENTALISM IN THE MIDDLE EAST

A Cross-National, Inter-Faith, and Inter-Ethnic Analysis

MANSOOR MOADDEL
STUART A. KARABENICK

Haymarket
Books
Chicago, IL

First published in 2013 by Brill Academic Publishers, The Netherlands.
© 2013 Koninklijke Brill NV, Leiden, The Netherlands

Published in paperback in 2014 by
Haymarket Books
P.O. Box 180165
Chicago, IL 60618
773-583-7884
www.haymarketbooks.org

ISBN: 978-1-60846-380-0

Trade distribution:
In the US, Consortium Book Sales, www.cbsd.com
In Canada, Publishers Group Canada, www.pgcbooks.ca
In the UK, Turnaround Publisher Services, www.turnaround-psl.com
In Australia, Palgrave Macmillan, www.palgravemacmillan.com.au
In all other countries, Publishers Group Worldwide, www.pgw.com

Cover design by Ragina Johnson.

This book was published with the generous support of Lannan Foundation
and the Wallace Action Fund.

Printed in Canada by union labor.

10 9 8 7 6 5 4 3 2 1

Library of Congress Cataloging-in-Publication Data is available.

For our wives and children
Marjan S. Moaddel
Armin, Nilufar, Payvand
and
Julie Karabenick
Robin, Scott, Rachel, Leah

CONTENTS

LIST OF TABLES AND FIGURES

TABLES

FIGURES

FOREWORD

There has been the misperception that critical and quantitative research are intrinsically at odds with each other. This is misfortunate. The problem is the way in which survey research and data analysis are often conducted. Critical research on religion needs to make use of all tools available to it including quantitative research. It is none other than quantitative researchers who are most acutely aware of the limitations of their own data and their analysis of it. A bit of cross-fertilization between critical research and quantitative data analysis would be mutually beneficial.

Mansoor Moaddel and Stuart Karabenick in *Religious Fundamentalism in the Middle East* do precisely this. They tackle important theoretical and empirical issues in the study of religious fundamentalism. They engage in a historical and quantitative comparative analysis of fundamentalism in Egypt, Iran, Lebanon, and Saudi Arabia. The quantitative component focuses "on fundamentalist beliefs and attitudes." Although they concentrate on Islamic fundamentalism, they also include fundamentalism among Lebanese Christian sects.

Moaddel and Karabenick integrate religious fundamentalism both as a movement organized in terms of positions on a set of historically significant issues and as a set of attitudes into a single theoretical framework. They first examine a host of historical, sociological, and social psychological factors which have shaped the fundamentalist movements. They then operationalize the concept of fundamentalism not simply as particular religious beliefs but rather as distinctive attitudes toward whatever religious beliefs one has. Next, they identify a series of psychological and sociological factors that predict fundamentalist attitudes at both macro and micro levels. Religious fundamentalism is a highly complex issue. There are variations in fundamentalist beliefs across nations, faiths, and ethnicities. Their analysis is keenly aware of these differences.

Fundamentalist beliefs have four different elements, which is true for both Islam and Christianity. These are: (1) an image of God/Allah as disciplinarian (2) a literalist belief in the scriptures as inerrant (3) believing that one's own religion is superior and (4) being intolerant of other religious traditions. Moaddel and Karabenick use several different variables related to fundamentalism. People who are fundamentalist tend to be more religious. They rely more on religious authorities as a source of information, have more frequent mosque attendance, support *shari'a*, have a stronger in-group solidarity, and are less likely to use computers.

Moaddel and Karabenick discuss the conditions that both strengthen or weaken fundamentalism. Among these is whether the cultural environment is pluralistic or monolithic and whether the state is democratic or authoritarian. Cultural pluralism leads to a tolerance of beliefs. In contrast, cultural environments that are monolithic create favorable conditions for the emergence of religious fundamentalism. Secular authoritarian states, through the suppression of political dissent, create the conditions for the rise of religious fundamentalism, which is a response to it. Likewise, religious authoritarianism is the breeding grounds for secularism. These are both situations of "oppositional identities.".

The authors introduce a new set of concepts to more effectively understand religious fundamentalism. Among them are "sacred and secular spirituality," "discursive space," "besieged spirituality," and "epistemic authority."

Moaddel and Karabenick make a distinction between sacred and secular spirituality. They frame the relationship between them in terms of a "cycle of spirituality." This cycle, which began in the 18th century, is from fundamentalism to modernism and back to fundamentalism again. Their study analyzes reformist fundamentalism in the eighteenth century, modernist movements, and the religious fundamentalism of the more recent era. They seek to understand "the causes and processes of these movements."

The authors of this book do not reduce "religious ideas to objective social conditions." Instead, they attempt to make sense of "historical anomalies." For instance, how does one make sense of the Iranian Constitutional Revolution, which was led by two ayatollahs? After a long period of modernization and secularization, how does one understand Iran's return to theocracy? To do so, they argue that human beings have spiritual needs, which may be provided for by either sacred or secular sources. Spiritual needs arise out of people's search for meaning, longing for security, and desire for empowerment. While sacred and secular spirituality may coexist, "the rise of one is often associated with the decline of the other." This has led to a cyclical pattern of alternations between sacred and secular spirituality in the Islamic world.

Modernization may not only produce conditions that are favorable to secularization; some of its negative by products (anomie, alienation, etc.) may also give rise to religious revival. Part of the process of secularization may entail traditional religions being replaced by secular ones. This is what they mean by "secular spirituality" as opposed to a "sacred spirituality." Depending on the conditions under which secularization occurs (i.e. religious monopoly or forced secularization), it may spawn reactions against it.

The recognition of anomalies and formulation of innovative ideas in any system of thought, including religious belief system, depends on "the availability of a discursive space." Systems of sociopolitical thought have different degrees of flexibility in making room for new ideas. For example, the ideology of the current Iranian regime has a very "limited discursive space." Depending on the cultural context, there may be an expansion or contraction of discursive space. This also influences the development of alternative religious discourses, which includes religious fundamentalism.

Under monolithic cultural conditions, spirituality is besieged whether it is sacred or secular. "Besieged spirituality" is a product specific historical conditions- the perception that it is under attack. Religions that are under siege are more likely to be intolerant. The more a religion is repressed, the more its members are likely to adhere to fundamentalist beliefs and attitudes. Religious fundamentalism arises from feelings of insecurity and powerlessness.

To understand religious fundamentalism, one also needs to take into consideration sources of "epistemic authority." These are sources of information, which individuals perceive to be valid—whether they are from parents, teachers, clergy, peers, or the mass media.

Religious fundamentalism is a predictor of several different attitudes including those on westernization, secularization and gender roles. Fundamentalism is a proponent of traditional gender roles, and its adherents express these attitudes. Those with stronger fundamentalist beliefs have a more negative perception of Western culture and secularism. They have a strong Islamic identity, support Islamic government, and believe that women are not equal to men.

Moaddel and Karabenick do us a great service in this book. In doing this analysis, they provide us with a better understanding of the social, political, and economics conditions that give rise to religious fundamentalism, provide us with a tool by which we can measure fundamentalist beliefs, and therefore provide us with the information needed to help counteract the vicissitudes that stem from them. It is this approach to the study of Islamic fundamentalism that provides a common link between critical and positivistic research.

Warren S. Goldstein, Ph.D.
Center for Critical Research on Religion
www.criticaltheoryofreligion.org

PREFACE

Since the 1960s, a dominant trend among intellectual leaders in Muslim majority countries has been to use religion in their attempts to resolve the sociopolitical and cultural issues their countries have encountered; hence the creation of religious discourses that gave rise to diverse religious movements. These movements then took an increasingly radical turn in the form of either revolutionary Shi'ism spearheaded by the clerics in Iran or Sunni extremism led by al-Qaeda. The fanaticism of the ruling clerics in Iran, on the one hand, and the Sunni extremists, on the other, resulted in the fixation of the attention span of both the public and the pundits in many Western democracies, the U.S. in particular, on a presumed conflict between "Islam" and "the West." The term "Islam versus the West," however, is nothing but a simplistic expression of a complex yet comprehensible phenomenon at the core of which is a clash between two sets of attitudes, one being religious fundamentalist and the other liberal. Confounding this complexity is the pervasiveness of political correctness in certain academic circles epitomized by discomfort with the concept of Islamic fundamentalism. The result has been the eclipse of a systematic scientific evidence-based analysis of religious fundamentalism.

This book is a modest attempt to provide an account of historical and cross-national variations of religious fundamentalism in terms of a series of scientific concepts and theories. It brings historical materials and survey data to bear in support of the conceptual and theoretical framework presented herein. Its validity thus rests on the logical consistency of its theoretical statements and the adequacy of the supporting empirical data. This book is not intended to pass judgment on religion in general or Islam in particular. Rather, its intention is to specify the parameters of the social context that prompt a group of people or intellectual leaders to develop a disciplinarian conception of deity, espouse literalist interpretation of the scriptures, develop alarmist attitudes toward the followers of the faiths other than their own, and consider their faith to be superior to and closer to God than those of others.

We are grateful to the National Science Foundation, the United States Institute of Peace, Bank of Sweden Tercentenary Foundation, Office of Naval Research, Rodney Stark, Eastern Michigan University, and the University of Michigan for sponsoring data collection and supporting the time for data analysis and writing this book. We are also grateful to Arland Thornton for his financial and intellectual contributions to youth surveys in Egypt and Saudi Arabia and to Julie de Jong and Linda Young-DeMarco for their invaluable assistance in the questionnaire design and the management of the surveys. This appreciation is also extended to Judy Baughn for her administrative assistance and many staffs working at the University of Michigan's Population Studies Center, including N.E. Barr, Mark R. Sandstrom, Ricardo Ramon Rodriguiz, and David Sasaki, for invaluable technical assistance. We would also like to extend our appreciation of Caryn Charter, acting director, Susan Campbell, and Margie Dargo from the Office of Research Development, and Anthony Valdez from Grant Accounting at Eastern Michigan University.

We especially appreciate comments by Albert J. Bergesen, Roger Finke, and Robert Robinson on chapters of this book. The comments from Warren S. Goldstein, editor of the book series, and anonymous reviewers for Brill, are also gratefully acknowledged. Finally, we appreciate the meticulous editorial work by Glen Marian and the assistance of Pat Cotter. This acknowledgement by no means indicates that any of these individuals, institutions, or foundations are responsible for the ideas expressed or errors made in this book.

Mansoor Moaddel & Stuart A. Karabenick, Ann Arbor, Michigan

THEORETICAL ISSUES IN THE STUDY OF RELIGIOUS FUNDAMENTALISM

As anyone who has attempted to study the subject is likely to confess, what has been conceptualized as religious fundamentalism in the Muslim world, and elsewhere, is a complex phenomenon. This complexity, while requiring a correspondingly complex framework to understand it, is not simply due to its periodic historical emergence or cross-national variability. Rather, Islamic fundamentalism in particular represents a marked historical discontinuity with the Islamic modernism of the last decades of the nineteenth century and the early twentieth. That is, Muslim theologians-cum-intellectual leaders had taken positions on some of the significant issues facing their faith that were cross-nationally similar under a recognizable set of concurrent historical conditions but diametrically opposed to positions taken by a similar group of thinkers decades later. Complexity is also revealed by the variation in fundamentalist beliefs and attitudes among the public that has been documented by survey research in recent years. The basic challenge is thus to construct a theoretical frame work that captures both the historical diversity and cross-national variability of religious fundamentalism as well as one that accounts for the relationship between fundamentalism as a discourse produced by its harbingers to address historically significant issues and fundamentalism as a set of beliefs about and attitudes toward religion.

To address this complexity, this book proposes a theoretical framework to address three sets of empirical questions related to religious fundamentalism. First, how do we incorporate the reformist fundamentalism of the eighteenth century, Islamic modernism of the late nineteenth century and early twentieth, and Islamic fundamentalism of the second half of the twentieth century into a broader historical narrative of the relationship between Islamic movements and varying social contexts? How do we conceptualize this sequence of fundamentalism-modernism-fundamentalism? Is it possible to explain this sequence in terms of variation in the same set of historical variables or does it reflect a broader change in people's spiritual needs? Second, how does the knowledge about the dynamic of this sequence help to understand cross-national

variation in fundamentalist beliefs and attitudes among the ordinary publics and vice versa? To what extent do the historical variables proposed to
account for change in Islamic movements also enhance our understanding of variation in fundamentalist beliefs and attitudes across countries,
religious faiths, and ethnicities? Third, what is the relationship between
fundamentalism as a discourse on issues and fundamentalism as a set of
beliefs and attitudes?

In this chapter we introduce the concept of "cycle of spirituality" as a
heuristic device to describe the sequence of fundamentalism-modernism-
fundamentalism that marked the history of the Islamic movement from
the eighteenth through the twentieth century. We then suggest a series of
variables related to the structure of intellectual markets, the political
structure and form of the ruling regimes, the role of the state in culture
production, discursive space, besieged spirituality, and dysphoric emotions as instances of social and psychological processes that may shape
religious discourses as well as beliefs about and attitudes toward religion.
We also attempt to empirically demonstrate that fundamentalist beliefs
and attitudes predict people's orientations toward the sociopolitical and
cultural issues that were also the concerns of the leaders and activists of
the fundamentalist movements in their historical contexts.

Two Approaches to the Study of Religious Fundamentalism

The vast and sprawling literature on religious fundamentalism in the contemporary Middle East has almost exclusively focused on the sociopolitical and religious discourses of the leaders of the fundamentalist
movements, their organizations and sociopolitical behavior. There has
been very little attention given to the fundamentalist beliefs and attitudes
among the ordinary public. Until recently, we knew little about how widespread such beliefs and attitudes are and their linkages with people's
socioeconomic backgrounds, other beliefs and attitudes as well as the
broader religious, ethnic, and national contexts in which they live. Related
to these questions are the connections between people's fundamentalist
beliefs and attitudes and their orientations toward the religious discourses
advanced by leaders of the fundamentalist movements.

Considerable information is available on the discourses, organizations, behaviors, and backgrounds of the leaders and activists of the past
Islamic fundamentalist movements. Yet this empirical knowledge may
not reflect the religious orientations and attitudes of the people who live

contemporaneously in the social contexts in which the fundamentalist movements have emerged. On a more general level, we know that in contemporary Middle Eastern societies religious fundamentalism was preceded by such other religious and cultural movements as Islamic modernism, liberalism, anti-clerical secularism, and Arab nationalism. We do not know, however, whether the opinions of the public at large during those periods corresponded to the views expressed by the intellectual leaders and activists of the movements in those societies.

Can one argue, for example, that the emergence and remarkable expansion of the Society of the Muslim Brothers and the decline of the Wafd nationalist party in Egypt in the 1930s and 1940s signified a shift in cultural orientations primarily among the country's intellectual leaders and political activists, or was it possibly preceded by a change in public attitudes from territorial nationalism to Islamic fundamentalism? Or, alternately, can one argue that there was no such shift but rather a change that resulted from the politicization and mobilization of only the conservative section of the Egyptian public and the demobilization of the more liberal or secular section? To what extent did the rise of revolutionary Shi'ism in the late seventies and the decline of secular politics among activists represent a corresponding turn in attitudes toward religious subjects among Iranians? Were Iranians mobilized for the establishment of a religious regime in the country in 1979, or was this demand vociferously being advocated by only a relatively small but more organized and better financed section of the population?

Of course, the absence of data precludes answering such questions regarding past historical periods. The present study, however, attempts to shed light on these historical questions. It also analyzes the contemporary status of fundamentalism in the Middle East by focusing on fundamentalist beliefs and attitudes in Egypt, Iran, Lebanon, and Saudi Arabia. Although our focus is on Islamic fundamentalism, religious fundamentalism among major Christian sects in Lebanon is included as well.

Fundamentalism as a Discourse and as a Set of Attitudes

We approach the study of religious fundamentalism from two complementary perspectives. The first approach takes into consideration the social, political and historical context in which fundamentalist beliefs and attitudes are embedded; here, the religious and cultural movements that Muslim-majority countries have experienced in the modern period. According to this approach, religious fundamentalism constitutes a

religious discourse on a set of historically significant issues. These issues
are related to forms of government, the relationship between religion and
politics, the basis of individual identity, the nature of the Western world,
the social status of women, and the proper methods of political action—
revolutionary or radical versus reformist or moderate. Diverse cultural
movements in the Middle East may be identified in terms of the movements' positions on these issues.

In terms of positions on issues, Islamic fundamentalism is thus identified as religious discourses in which Western culture is portrayed as decadent, constitutionalism is abandoned in favor of the unity of religion and
politics in an Islamic government, the institutions of male domination
and gender segregation are prescribed and rigorously defended, and often
the revolutionary methods of change are encouraged. Islamic modernism, by contrast, is represented by those who had taken positions on these
issues that were quite different, if not diametrically opposed to, the positions taken by the leaders of Islamic fundamentalism. In Islamic modernism, Western culture is acknowledged favorably, Islamic political theory
and the idea of constitutionalism are reconciled, the construction of the
modern state is endorsed, an Islamic feminism is advanced in order to
defend women's rights, and moderate and peaceful political action
isendorsed.

The second approach views fundamentalism as a distinctive orientation toward religion (Altemeyer 2003; Altemeyer & Hunsberger 1992,
2002). It is not a set of specific religious beliefs, or about the contents of
such beliefs per se. Rather, religious fundamentalism is defined as *a set of
beliefs about and attitudes toward* whatever religious beliefs one has. For
example, the belief in God is a general religious belief. The belief in the
unity of God, however, is an Islamic belief, and the belief in the Trinity of
God, Christ, and the Holy Ghost (or the Father, the Son, and the Holy
Spirit) is a Christian belief. On the other hand, the belief that God severely
punishes people even though they had engaged in only a minor infraction
of His laws, that one's religion is closer to God than the religions of others,
or that only the followers of one's faith will go to heaven are examples of
fundamentalist beliefs and orientations.

We propose, and will elaborate subsequently in more detail, that fundamentalist beliefs and attitudes include four interrelated components
that are applicable across the different religious traditions that are considered in this book: Christianity and Islam. These components are (1) a disciplinarian image of the deity, which embraces an etiology of good and
evil that is derived strictly from God versus Satan duality; (2) a vigorous

defense of construing the scriptures as literal, inerrant, and infallible; (3) bestowing a standing to one's religion that is superior to and closer to God than other religions; and (4) being intolerant of other religions. This approach implies that these components are present, although in varying degrees, among fundamentalists across specific religious traditions being discussed in this book, whether they are Christians, Sunni Muslims, Shi'i Muslims, or Druze Muslims.

We begin by presenting an overview of religious fundamentalist movements in the contemporary period. We then focus on fundamentalism as a set of belief and attitudes toward religion by introducing and discussing its different components. Next, we assess religious fundamentalism and conduct a series of macro and micro analyses within the context of Egypt, Iran, Lebanon, and Saudi Arabia, based on data collected in surveys of youth in Egypt and Saudi Arabia in 2005, adults in Iran in 2005, and Lebanon in 2008. These data allow both cross-national comparisons, comparisons between Christians and Muslims, and comparisons between different religious sects and ethnic groups.

FUNDAMENTALISM AND THE CONTEXT OF RELIGIOUS DIVERSITY

We can gain a fuller understanding of religious fundamentalism by integrating the existing empirical knowledge of the phenomenon into a broader narrative that captures the historical diversity of people's religious and spiritual experiences, including the attitudes and behaviors of religious actors that, out of context, may appear anachronistic. This broader narrative covers the nature of the historical circumstances that shape the spiritual and religious options that were available to both Muslim intellectual leaders and the ordinary publics. The conventional approach to the social-scientific study of religion may not be adequately equipped to account for diverse religious experiences. The conventional approach relates the reformist fundamentalism of the eighteenth century, the modernist movements that emerged over a century later, and the religious fundamentalism of late to the contemporaneously existing social forces. In other words, if one knows the type of events that triggered these movements, the demographic characteristics as well as the socio-cultural and political outlooks of the participants, the sources and flow of information, the people or institutions who provided the resources, and the type of network these movements used, one may be able to advance reasonable explanations about the causes and processes of these movements. The conventional approach is by no means a minor accomplishment in the sociology of religion. Nonetheless, considering the broader historical framework that has informed these movements, and from the perspective of irreducibility of religious ideas to objective social conditions, one is seriously confronted not only by cases that are left unexplained but by serious historical anomalies as well.

One prominent example of such anomalies is the movement against monarchical absolutism and the demand for democratic rule made during the Iranian Constitutional Revolution of 1905–1911. In the first decade of the twentieth century, Iran was far behind Egypt, Lebanon, and Turkey in terms of the level of economic development, industrialization, and the rise of modern education. Yet, it was the first Middle Eastern country to experience a major revolution for democratic constitutional change. What is more, the revolution was led by two ayatollahs. Even more surprising, the revolutionary movement was actually sparked by the action of a group of five theology students and merchants who staged a sit-in at the British legation, demanding from the reigning monarch the ratification of the Constitution, a political tactic that is unfathomable today given the prevalence of anti-Western attitudes in the region. The sanctuary started on July 19, 1906, and by August 2, their number soared to fourteen thousand, representing nearly one-third of the labor force of Tehran. The sit-in ended on August 10, 1906, when the monarch capitulated to collective public pressure for change, signed the Fundamental Law of the Constitution, and consented to the formation of a parliament (Afary 1996). The astonishing fact is that the Constitutional Revolution occurred against a background that Iran had barely experienced in terms of economic development—commercialization, industrialization, the expansion of a modern educated elite, and the rise of new social classes.

Iran in 1979, by contrast, had about a three-quarter century of modernization highlighted by an impressive rate of economic development, a remarkable expansion in modern education, and the rise of the middle class, particularly in the 1960s and 1970s. By objective economic measures, it was somewhat more developed than Egypt, Lebanon and Turkey. Again, it was the first country to experience a major revolution that brought religious extremists to power. Like the Constitutional Revolution, religious leaders led the revolution. While in the previous Constitutional Revolution a foreign (i.e., the British) embassy was used to stage a sit-in at its site in order to force the Shah to consent to constitutional change, in the 1979 revolution a foreign (i.e., the American) embassy was seized by a group of religious zealots in order to mobilize the public against the U.S., defeat their liberal opponents within the ruling power block, and pass a constitution that gave absolutist power to the ruling cleric.

How did an underdeveloped country with no colonial experience manage to support a fairly liberal constitution in the ulama-led 1906 revolution? And how did the same country, after experiencing decades-long episodes of impressive secularization and economic development, give rise to a revolutionary movement that overthrew a dictatorial monarch and enthusiastically endorsed a constitution that installed religious absolutism? How can one explain such diametrically opposed political behaviors and attitudes between the ayatollahs who led the Constitutional Revolution and those who led the revolution of 1979?

Certainly, Iran was not the only country that experienced Islamic modernism and fundamentalism in the modern period. Such other countries as Algeria, Egypt, India, Indonesia, and Syria have also experienced the rise of Islamic modernist movements in the late nineteenth century and early twentieth, where prominent Muslim intellectual leaders and theologians examined the methodological principles of the Islamic orthodoxy and revised sociopolitical thought in Islam in light of the standards of the Enlightenment. In Algeria, Muslim reformers, in order to undermine the French control of the religious institutions, went so far as to demand the separation of religion and politics. Decades later, however, virtually all Muslim-majority countries experienced the rise of Islamic fundamentalism. This movement rejected the Western political model and forcefully promoted the unity of religion and politics in an Islamic government. However, it has been in the Iranian historical context that these anomalies are so conspicuously played out and the inadequacy of the conventional sociological approach in explaining religious behaviors is strikingly marked.

HUMAN SPIRITUAL NEEDS, CYCLE OF SPIRITUALTIES, AND RELIGIOUS FUNDAMENTALISM

The anomaly raised by the contrasting revolutions in Iran has dual features. One refers to the very selection of the divergent political options by leading Shi'i theologians in the two different historical occasions. The other is that the selected political options appear to have occurred at the "wrong" times, that is, contrary to what one would have expected from a sociological perspective. If Iran were to experience political modernity, one would reasonably expect the Constitutional Revolution to have occurred in 1979, and the 1979 revolution in the early twentieth century.

We do not question the significance of the sociological and historical factors shaping the two revolutions. Nor is our objective here to advance alternative explanations of these events. Rather, if we start from the premise that prosperity, security, happiness, and empowerment were the invariant forecasts of the two revolutions, then an explanation of why the religious activists and the majority of the people involved were resolute in zealously defending a constitutional system in one revolution, but exhibited alarmist attitudes against secular forces while fervently trying to establish purportedly the rule of God on earth in the other, must be explained at least in part in terms of the difference in the broader historical context that had given meanings to such opposing mechanisms for the realization of the same set of objectives. We employ the concepts of spiritual needs and the distinction between sacred and secular spirituality to capture this broader historical context. We propose that sacred and secular spirituality are two opposing providers of meaning, security, and empowerment. While they may coexist, the rise of one is often associated with the decline of the other. Thus, we suggest a cyclical pattern of spiritual alternations between the sacred and secular in the Muslim world in the modern period.

Spirituality is concerned with the human search for security, happiness, empowerment, and the meaning and teleology of life. Weber was among the first to emphasize that humans have spiritual needs. While conceding the importance of such social conditions in shaping religion (e.g., those of the underprivileged or the rationalism of the middle classes), he pointed to "the metaphysical needs of the human mind as it is driven to reflect on ethical and religious questions, driven not by material need but by an inner compulsion to understand the world as a meaningful cosmos and to take up a position toward it" (Weber 1964, 117). In addition to the broader quest for meaning, people become spiritual as they seek help and guidance from supreme beings in order to stay healthy and happy, succeed in business, prosper in life, and enjoy other earthly benefits (Maehr and Karabenick 2005). They thus yearn for a savior who could protect them and their loved ones from capricious harms and treacherous evils, and a broader universe in which the tension between the inevitability of death and the desire for an eternal life and salvation is reconciled— hence continuity between this and the other world is established.

We thus expand the concept of spiritual needs to also cover such other areas of human concerns as the need for complete security, perpetual happiness, empowerment, and comfort in order to cope with hard-to-bear unpredictable losses. A comprehensive empirical knowledge about reality is not possible. A complete security and deliverance from harm can only be imagined but not experienced. The feeling of total empowerment even for the most conceded absolutist ruler in search for eternal presence is always negated by either a mighty revolutionary force from below or the inevitability of death. However, the need and yearning for a comprehensive meaning, perfect security, and total power are always present in people's lives. *We thus define spiritual needs as that residual component of people's quests for meaning, security, and empowerment that remain unfulfilled by the available sources.*

Religion is one of the most important purveyors of spiritual fulfillment, where people strive to satisfy their spiritual needs from sacred or supernatural sources. They pray to God, revere the saints, pay tribute to places of worship, and contribute to religious institutions and various religious causes in return for these deliverances. For many, religion is indeed the only plausible source of rewards such as these (Stark and Finke 2000, Chapter 4). Religion also provides people with spiritual support to cope with unsettling emotions. "As a religious problem," says Geertz (1973, 104), "the problem of suffering is, paradoxically, not how to avoid suffering but how to suffer, how to make of physical pain, personal loss, wordly [sic], or the helpless contemplation of others' agony something bearable, supportable—something, as we say, sufferable." In Sewell's (1997, 45) explication, "what religious symbolism does is not to deny the existence of the uncanny, of suffering, or of evil, but to provide concepts that make them thinkable (such as divine mystery, imitation of Christ, or original sin) and ritual practices that give them an experiential reality (such as the Eucharist, extreme unction, or penance)."[1]

---

[1] Others have also offered somewhat similar conceptions of spirituality. Du Toit (2006: 1252, 1254), for example, argues that historically, spiritual needs are believed to be rooted in such diverse human experiences as those related to the wonderment and mystique of nature in the pre-modern period and those arising from encountering the complexity of a techno-scientific world in which the magic of progress has turned into a runaway train that can no longer be stopped. "Spirituality," for Sri Aurobindo, "is something else than intellectuality; its appearance is the sign that a Power greater than mind is striving to emerge in its turn" (cited in Lyden 1995: 186). For Kourie (2006: 19), it "refers to the *raison-d'être* of one's existence, the meaning and values to which one ascribes." Finally, for Wuthnow (1998: viii), "at its core, spirituality consists of all the beliefs and activities by which individuals attempt to relate their lives to God or to a divine being or some other conception of a transcendent reality." It is also "an assortment of activities and interpretations that reflect the past, that include new ways of understanding the past, and that envision on the horizon something distinctly different from the past" (p. 8).

To be sure, socialization plays a significant role in shaping people's religiosity and attachment to the sacred beings. However, sacred spirituality in people's life is reinforced by and through their purported "spiritual experiences" (Smith 1998, 173–177; Wuthnow 1998, 123), or through what Norris and Inglehart (2011, 5, 18) describe as "ego-tropic risks" (those that pose direct threats to people themselves and their families) and "sociotropic risks" (those threatening their community). Further, religious symbols and rituals not only enhance collective solidarity and group empowerment (Durkheim 1965); they also entertain, generate enthusiasm, boost collective joy, and reduce in-group tensions. Participations in collective rituals and ceremonial practices that are organized in places of worship and religious festivals that are often accompanied by food, dance, and music illuminate the horizontal dimensions of social relationships and enhance the feeling of communal belonging.

At the same time, ritualistic practices break down the monotony of daily lives and transform, as Victor Turner (1967, 30) aptly stated, "the irksomeness of moral constraint... into the 'love of virtue'" (see also Stark and Finke 2000, Chapter 6). Finally, even under the pluralistic religious tradition of the contemporary American society, where the uncertainties associated with changes in communities, families, and education are said to have weakened the ability of structured dwelling-oriented spiritual reliefs to meet people's spiritual demands, other spiritual venues have opened up. People are no longer attached to specific places of worship for regular visitation; rather, they engage in seeking-oriented and practice-oriented spiritualities (Wuthnow 1998), and as a result the sacred remains their chief source of spiritual fulfillment.

However, under certain circumstances, people's religious beliefs may be shaken. Loved ones die; floods, tornadoes, and other natural catastrophes destroy homes; accidents and serious illnesses shatter the illusion of invulnerability; acts of abuse steal childhood innocence. Experiencing such life-altering events, people sometimes feel that God deliberately harmed them, failed to heed their requests, or passively allowed their undeserved sufferings. People may thus develop intense anger and mistrust toward God (Exline and Rose 2005, 317). Beyond individual experience, an entire people may become subject to long, unjustified, and horrific experience that leaves unbearable sorrows. This may prompt them to abandon religion or adopt such alternative visions of the deity as a hidden or absent God that is less relevant to their daily lives. According to Katz (cited in Wolpe 1997, 26; Katz 1985, 280):

> In light of the Holocaust, it becomes necessary not only to advocate this thesis but also to ask anew, how and when is God's restraint of His omnipotence to be interpreted differently from His lack of omnipotence? How in *fact* and in *logic* do we know there really is an omnipotent God who is exercising self restraint—at a staggering human cost—rather than allowing this evidence of "self-restraint" to be construed as data for either the nonexistence of god or at least God's non-omnipotence as advocated, for example, by a Platonic-Whiteheadian "process" theism?
>
> If the non-presence, non-power, non-involvement of God proves his presence, then by a similar demonstration we could "prove" all sorts of entities and attributes into existence.

All these processes and events may thus give rise to the realization that religion has failed to deliver its spiritual goods. In addition, large-scale social processes associated with modernization may also undermine the function and significance of religion in society. As pointed out by proponents of secularization theory, religion may decline as a result of new scientific discoveries. Such discoveries provide fresh explanations about the working of the universe, the causes and processes of human health and happiness, and the cycle of life in general, calming the anxious mind. Impressive technological inventions are said to enhance human safety and security, which make the urgency of seeking spiritual guidance from a greater power redundant. Inventions in communication technology, by facilitating the dissemination of knowledge and information about events across the globe, are believed to cause the breakdown of religious dogma and weaken the relevance of the local priest or mullah for speculative understanding.

Modern means of transportation render travel less costly, make the movement of people to faraway places possible, and bring people closer to one another, contributing to what Harvey has termed "time-space compression" (Harvey 1990). When people of different localities and provinces in a country become aware of each other's problems, this knowledge may not only increase the possibility of mutual assistance but also enhance broader collective consciousness and even nationalist awareness. International exchange of ideas and transfer of meaning introduces people across the globe to different modalities of social life and politics. Reorganization of production processes made possible by technological invention may also bring about new occupational positions and hence expand social differentiation, generate new social actors, and thus create a novel basis for rethinking the role of culture and religion in social life.

Although scholars have abandoned the teleological reading of the changes brought by modernization in which the decline of religion was forecasted, they have instead recognized that the secularization process varies cross-nationally, is historically contingent (Martin 1969), and has different patterns (Goldstein 2009). They have also pointed to such additional conditions as individualism, pluralism, egalitarianism, and rationalism as factors in religious decline (Bruce 2002, 2006). For Norris and Inglehart (2011), the key factor contributing to the decline of religion revolves on the extent to which modernization affects people's well-being and security. They argue that the demand for spirituality varies and is inversely related to the amount of security provided by modernization. Thus, "greater protection and control, longevity, and health found in postindustrial nations mean that fewer people in these societies regard traditional spiritual values, beliefs, and practices as vital to their lives, or the lives of their community" (p. 18).

For the nemeses of the secularization theory, on the other hand, a decline in religiosity has little to do with modernization. Rather, this decline is a direct function of the quality of religious services provided to the faithful. The quality of such services is diminished when the structure of religious markets deviates from its natural pluralistic state and is transformed into a religious monopoly regulated and subsidized by the state. Assured of steady income, the priest becomes complacent, priesthood lethargic, and the entire religious congregation moribund (Stark and Bainbridge 1985; Stark and Finke 2000). From this perspective, one may conclude that "any spirituality that does not produce service is false" (Grassow 1991, 53, cited in Du Toit 2006, 1255), leading people to seek alternative sources to satisfy their spiritual needs.

The decline of religion may thus become particularly dramatic when a society with a long experience of ecclesiastical domination in which the high priests or ayatollahs are closely tied to a despotic ruling elite or allied with self-serving members of the upper classes faces a major revolutionary change. In such a society, the revolutionary ideology may display a strong anti-religious orientation. "A clerical society," says Marty (1969, 18–19), "bred anti-clericalism: a Christian dogmatic skin evoked an anti-Christian one." It has been suggested that the decline in the established religion either prompts the emergence of a new sect in the same religion or a brand new religion that tries to meet more effectively the spiritual needs of its followers (Stark and Finke 2000; see also Goldstein [2011] for an alternative interpretation). In the modern period, however, where the production, dissemination, and consumption of ideas are liberated from the tight grips of organized religion, secular ideologies and institutions may take over many of the functions of religion and in some notable cases emulate religion. According to Marty:

> Post-Revolutionary France did not differ from Revolutionary France in one important respect: its citizens were not able to be de-Christianized without having the crutch of some alternative faith. French intellectuals who wanted to extricate themselves from the embrace of the Church and to shrug off the dreams of the old Christendom often gravitated, as had the philosophers before them, to new schemes for organizing society and synthesizing all of life into neat systems. These systems were paratheological in nature. They have often been called secular religions. Many of these cosmic schemes provided an answer for everything and a ceremony for every occasion. In each, Christianity was either to be displaced or transformed beyond recognition (Marty 1969, 30).

However, one need not follow the secularization theory in order to accept the premise that certain historical processes that are often associated with modernization may contribute to a decline of religion. A combination of such factors as the imposition of a monolithic religious discourse from above under a religious state-alliance, awareness of alternative modalities of politics, expansion of modern education, scientific breakthrough and technological innovation, and the emergence of nationalist and women's movements—all may give rise to the awareness that through intellectual exertions, organization of collective action, and the reorganization of sociopolitical life humans may enhance their economic prosperity, happiness, and power to predict and control events. This awareness that humans can understand and change the world constitutes the essence of secular spirituality.

Secular spirituality in turn provides a broad intellectual context for the development of various secular ideologies, each projecting a distinctive pathway to prosperity, security, happiness, and human empowerment. For the harbingers of the Enlightenment, for example, this pathway was through provision of political equality and democratic government; in Marxism, through socialization of the means of production; in various forms of nationalism, through struggle against foreign domination and the achievement of national sovereignty. Such anticipated benefits—acquired freedom, attained equality, and the joy of being liberated—in a new sociopolitical order have been quite effective in further reinforcing secular spirituality, attracting passionate followers.

All these ideologies, in our view, furnish a new type of spirituality that is secular, which in essence appears to play the same function as sacred spirituality. As will be argued in the following chapter, without under-standing the significance of the secular spirituality in the intellectual cli-mate of a country, it would be hard to understand why Muslim intellectual leaders in the late nineteenth and early twentieth centuries predomi-nantly supported the formation of a constitutional national government.

Secular spirituality, however, has limits; scientific explanations are essentially provisional, contingent, and inadequate. New technology goes so far in controlling the unforeseen effects of life-changing events and the unpredictability and inevitability of death. Likewise, this-worldly deliver-ances of secular ideologies are almost always imperfect. Hence, they are no competition for the untested other-worldly promises of religions that rely on the unlimited power of God and other supernatural forces. As Aldridge (2000, 96) stated, "naturalistic belief-systems, however well-grounded in science, simply cannot compete with super-naturalist reli-gion when it comes to the provision of [ostensibly] credible compensators for such rewards." Science and secular discourses are thus unsatisfactory for the seekers of spirituality who yearn for certainty, guaranteed happi-ness, and secured salvation. Furthermore, the scientific insufficiencies, on the one hand, and the unsatisfying outcomes of secular ideologies, on the other, contribute to the subjective mindset that not only allows religion to persist even in a most secular social context but also protects religious beliefs against the onslaught of science and other secular discourses.

More crucially, however, is the fact that in the same way that the condi-tion of religious monopoly or religious authoritarianism contributes to a decline in religion and that a clerical society breeds anti-clerical opposi-tional discourse, secular authoritarian regimes or generally the domina-tion of authoritarian secular institutions in society, where secular ideas are used to serve particularistic political and economic interests, may also delegitimize secular discourses, contributing to a crisis of secularism. In particular this crisis may be deepened, when the ruling elites of an author-itarian regime become the spokespeople of secularism, when the domi-nant classes monopolize secular politics, when secular intellectual leaders and policy makers engage in frontal assaults on the prerogatives and privi-leges of religious institutions, or when secular institutions are incapable of effectively addressing and resolving social problems.

As a result, a shift may occur in people's orientations in searching for meaning, happiness, security, and empowerment toward the sacred sources. The people's move away from the secular and toward the religious subjects may be reinforced by the outbreak of such varied historically significant events as a brutal act of repression by a secular government, a sudden economic downturn, a major climatic catastrophe, the outbreak of a war or foreign invasion, or the upsurge of religious movements in neighboring countries.

All these may in turn generate a new cycle of religious activism with the objective of bringing the forces of religion and almighty God to the forefront of struggle against the ineffectual secular institutions, organizations, and individuals. For sure, people for whom it is an important spiritual resource and a motivational factor in pursuit of personal happiness and success in life, religion does not necessarily require God's discipline and punishment. These individuals benefit by worshiping God, which makes them feel happy, protected, purposeful, and delivered from the evil forces. The belief that one is connected to, loved and protected by a supreme being is comforting. And when people are reassured of love and kindness, they tend to be less ethnocentric, aggressive, or exclusivist (Adorno et al 1950; Allport 1954; Talbott 1997; Mikulincer and Shaver 2007). From this perspective, therefore, being religious does not necessarily encourage a seeker of spirituality to adopt a stronger fundamentalist orientation than would a seeker of spirituality who is not religious.

Nonetheless, the newly activated seekers of sacred spirituality, under certain conditions, may become unconditionally convinced regarding the righteousness of their creed and the certainty of the spiritual deliverances of the sacred, categorically reject secular ideologies as well as other religions, demand a total commitment to their group norms, and insist on the urgent need to mobilize the faithful against the unbelievers and outsiders. They may resort to group pressure and violence in order to ensure conformity and obedience to religious norms. At the same time, they may inject the fear of the wrath of God in the followers that they will be severely punished should they deviate from the true path and violate God's instructions. The image of God as a disciplinarian thus gains significance in their perception as a deity. A religious movement that insists on rejecting other faiths may also heighten in-group solidarity and diminish inter-faith trust. One that stresses the purity of the faith may also foster intolerant attitudes toward, and advocate segregation from, the followers of other religions.

These tendencies toward religious fundamentalism may be manifestations of the social context where secular spirituality is in decline and sacred spirituality is on the rise. For the seekers of spirituality, religious fundamentalism is one way of protecting the newly acquired conviction in unsurpassed quality of sacred spirituality provided by their religion. At the same time, as will be explained below, there are also intellectual, social, and psychological factors that reinforce or weaken fundamentalist attitudes and beliefs.

CORRELATES OF RELIGIOUS FUNDAMENTALISM

We use the notion of the cycle of spirituality as a heuristic device in order to more effectively comprehend the changes in the form, content, and orientationof religious movements the Muslim world experienced in the period between the decline of the Islamic empires beginning in the early eighteenth century and the crisis of secular authoritarian regimes in the Middle East in the second half of the twentieth. These changes are manifested in the rise of reformist fundamentalism of the eighteenth century, then Islamic modernism of the late nineteenth century and early twentieth, and then the Islamic fundamentalism of the second half of the twentieth century (the secular turn among Iranians in recent decades and the Arab Spring may still indicate another shift in people's spiritual orientations; see the concluding chapter). Because of the presence of dramatic differences in form, content, and orientation between Islamic fundamentalism and modernism, the historical sequence of these diverse religious movements, we propose, is a reflection of a sequential rise and demise of sacred and secular spirituality in the Muslim world, as the predominance of one meaning system gave way to the other.

Conceptualizing the broader historical context in terms of this cycle will serve for a more effective interpretation of the linkages between various sociological and social-psychological factors and religious fundamentalism. This cycle will thus illuminate the specific parameter of the historical context whose changes explain, for example, the diametrically opposed political behaviors of Iranian religious leaders in the Constitutional Revolution of 1905–1911 and the Iranian Revolution of 1977–1979. Considering this context as the background, we then move forward by introducing the variety of the sociological and social psychological factors that not only explain the social conditions in which Islamic fundamentalism and modernism originated, but also inform a more effective empirical quantitative evaluation of religious fundamentalist beliefs and attitudes among ordinary individuals in Egypt, Iran, Lebanon, and Saudi Arabia. This exercise also provides a way to link findings from comparative historical studies of religious fundamentalist movements to findings from the surveys of fundamentalist beliefs and attitudes.

In other words, because the rise of sacred spirituality in a society maynot necessarily be manifested in fairly strong religious fundamentalist movements in that society, the sociological and social psychological factors specified below may attenuate or intensify support for such movements. We suggest that these factors may shape the belief system and values orientations of both intellectual leaders and the public at large. Some of these factors operate on the macro while others on the micro levels.

Discursive Space

Whether or not the social context is characterized by the rise or decline of sacred spirituality, the availability of a discursive space is important in shaping the production of religious discourse among intellectual leaders in society. To elaborate our understanding of the concept, we start with the premise that any system of sociopolitical thought shaping human behavior—be it rooted in religion, Marxism, or various nationalist worldviews—may display a degree of rigidity or flexibility in incorporating or accommodating new ideas. We conceptualize this flexibility as a discursive space: an interstitial capacity or opening in the conceptual system that enables its practitioners to detect, recognize, discuss, and even reconcile inconsistencies. Although therelationship between discursive space and flexibility may not be linear, to some degree the wider the discursive space, the more flexible the system of thought. By sociopolitical thought we do not mean something that is formally constructed based on a reading of the text relevant to that system. For example, in assessing the relationship between Islamic political thought and the behavior of Muslim intellectual leaders and activists in different historical periods, we do not mean the general Islamic theory of caliphate that may be reconstructed by analyzing the religious text or the tradition of the early pioneers of the Islamic movement. Rather, we mean the discursive framework that these individuals were actually using at the time they were addressing the sociopolitical issues facing their faith and community. Although Muslim intellectual leaders have always claimed that their discourses were essentially Islamic, these discourses varied in different places and historical periods. We suggest that these discursive frameworks also varied in terms of the degree of flexibility.

The discursive space consists of the space that is occupied by the number of elements in a system of sociopolitical thought that can be removed without essentially causing the collapse, or undermining the integrity,

of that system. Marxism, for example, may accommodate different socialist political parties, without these parties subscribing to the principles of
democratic centralism or the role of the Communist party as the van-
guard of the working class. Leninism, on the other hand, may collapse if
one questions these principles. Thus, the discursive space is much wider
in Marxism than it is in Leninism. As will be further illuminated in Chapter
One, Muslim intellectual leaders and activists in the late nineteenth century recognized that one may reject the currently existing Islamic theory
of government or question some of the pillars of Islamic jurisprudence
without questioning the basic tenets of the faith. This very recognition,
we argue, enabled these intellectual leaders to formulate a modernist religious discourse that also accommodated some of the principles of the
eighteenth-century Enlightenment. By contrast, the religious ideology of
the current Islamic regime in Iran displays a limited discursive space. The
entire political system is likely to collapse if one successfully challenges
the principleof the governance of Islamic jurisprudence that gave absolute power to the leader of the Islamic Republic. In sum, whereas the
expansion of discursive space may promote a moderate and transcendental religious discourse, the contraction of this space may contribute to
intellectual rigidity and religious or secular fundamentalism.

Pluralistic versus Monolithic Cultural Context

Broader cultural context shape not only the discursive space but also
directly the manner in which culture producers formulate religious ideas.
We propose that variation in the *cultural context*—whether it is pluralistic
or monolithic—contributes to the expansion or contraction of the discursive space and the development of alternative religious discourses in society, including religious fundamentalism (Moaddel 2005). The production
of sociopolitical and religious ideas takes place within the dynamic context of debates and argumentations among intellectual leaders. This
context varies not only in terms of being pluralistic or monolithic, but also
in terms of the extent of state intervention, which ranges from being minimal to extensive. In the latter case, the state is directly involved in controlling and manipulating the process of cultural debates and religious
disputation. We propose that there is a higher likelihood that moderate
and transcendental discourses are produced in a pluralistic cultural context where the state plays a minimal role in culture. Cultural pluralism
that is reflected in the presence of diverse religious and cultural groups
may provoke an awareness of inconsistencies and anomalies in one's

thought and the recognition of dispensability of some of its elements to resolve the inconsistencies and account for the anomalies.

Cultural pluralism is conducive to the idea of liberating the faith and the faithful from the shackles of religious authoritarianism and monolithic domination, revising the norms and rules of a bygone era, and expanding the opportunity for individual spiritual fulfillment. Under such conditions the guardians of religious authoritarianism and its theologians may find it difficult to mobilize the forces of God against the agents of change—whether it is the ruling elite, secular intellectuals and critics of religion, or an opposition movement within the existing religious establishment. This context may be favorable to the rise of religious modernism. By contrast, a monolithic cultural environment, particularly where this environment has been controlled and manipulated by the state, creates a favorable condition for the rise of religious fundamentalism (Moaddel 2005). In sum, the cultural environment in a society attenuates religious fundamentalism when it is pluralistic, but intensifies religious fundamentalism when it is monolithic.

Besieged Spirituality

The above argument may be framed differently in order to more clearly spell out a mechanism that connects the broader social, political and cultural context to a particular individual mindset that is receptive to fundamentalist beliefs and attitudes. One factor that affects people's attachments to and solidarity with their religious denomination is the quality of the religious benefits they receive from it. At the societal level, this quality is a function of the level of religious pluralism and the degree to which diverse religious organizations (i.e., religious firms) are free to market their services and compete for followers. When the state supports religious institutions or promotes a particular religion, religious sect, or denomination in society, the priests and other religious workers are assured a steady income, and as a result, the quality of the services offered by the official religion declines and its capacity to satisfy people's spiritual needs is diminished (Finke and Stark 1988; Bainbridge 1995; Stark and Finke 2000). This condition may either promote religious heterodoxy, where people seek spiritual advice from religious sources outside the mainstream religion (Sufism in Islam, for example), or secular spirituality (Sharp 2006), as people seek alternative secular sources as a way to satisfy their spiritual needs (e.g., cultural clubs, romantic socialist movements, humanitarian cultural movements, etc.).

If, on the other hand, in a more restricted context, the range of religious activities is limited and monitored by the state, or the ruling elites promote secular ideas, policies, and institutions at the expense of the existing religious institutions, such actions may undermine the spiritual function of religion and block a source of spiritual fulfillment. For the seekers of sacred spirituality, this may in turn give rise to the perception that their faith is under siege, that is, the state of *besieged spirituality*, and hence necessitate mobilizing the forces of God in defense of His dominion and against the unbelievers. Perceiving one's faith besieged by secular and/or irreligious forces, the faithful may develop alarmist attitudes toward outsiders, who are viewed with suspicion. Such attitudes are reflected in the faithful growing as described in Smith's (1998, 8) description of the post-1925 Christian fundamentalism in the U.S., "hypersensitive even to the slightest hint of theological corruption within their own ranks." Alarmist attitudes toward and suspicions of outsiders may in turn promote and be reinforced by conspiratorial thinking.

The conception of besieged spirituality is exemplified by the reaction of Egyptian Hassan al-Banna, the founder and leader of the Society of Muslim Brothers, to what he perceived as the secularist onslaught on religion in the 1920s. Reacting to the Egyptian University's secularism, for example, al-Banna denounced the university for its "non-Islamic" currents and for acting as though it "could not be a lay university unless it revolted against religion and fought the social tradition which derived from it" (Cited in Mitchell 1993 [1969], 4). Similarly, Rashid Rida, a prominent Muslim scholar, assailed the university as "a haven for heretics and a breeding ground for atheism," and a Muslim Brother member, Muhammad al-Ghazali, said the liberals were "puppets and slaves of the European and serving the cause of Christian imperialism" (Reid 1990, 149). This picture was traumatic for al-Banna and his fellow Muslim activists. He once reported that "no one but God knows how many nights we spent reviewing the state of the nation...analyzing the sickness, and thinking of the possible remedies. So disturbed were we that we reached the point of tears" (cited in Mitchell 1993 [1969], 5).

In a comparative context, a religious sect, such as Shi'i Islam, may have a larger repertoire of disturbing historical memories than such other religious sects as Sunni Islam. It may thus lend greater textual support for the notion that the faith is under siege. Generally, however, besieged spirituality is primarily a product of the specific historical conditions of a lived religion, the distinctive manner that a religion is experienced by the ordinary public that has shaped the perception that it is being under attack or undermined by the machinations of outsiders. Under such conditions, seekers of spirituality may consider as an appropriate option to mobilize the supernatural forces of God (e.g., God's wrath) to combat secular attacks on religion. As a result, the disciplinarian conception of the deity and the invocation of God's wrath become the key features of the religion. When a religion is perceived to be under siege, we propose that exclusivity and intolerance are more likely to become accepted features of the movement for the liberation of the faith. Thus, the more intensive and/or the longer religious activists experience repression by the secular state, or the more they experience that their faith is being undermined by the followers of other religions, the stronger is their perception of besieged spirituality, and the stronger their adherence to fundamentalist beliefs and attitudes.

State Culture and National Identity

State structures (whether authoritarian or democratic) and state cultures (whether religious or secular) may shape religious fundamentalism or the generation of secular discourse in different ways. One is through the control of the channel and content of the system of mass communication. Because of this control a secular authoritarian state may undermine the public perception of the validity of the secular sources of information, thus prompting the public to use religious media as their favored sources of news and knowledge (more on this in the following section). Thus, the more people rely on such sources, the more fundamentalist they tend to become. Moreover, the secular authoritarian state, by disrupting the organizations of secular oppositions—political parties and civic associations—may channel oppositional politics through the medium of religion, generating yet another favorable context for the rise of religious fundamentalism.

Religious authoritarianism, on the other hand, may prompt the public to seek information from non-religious and secular sources. In other words, religious authoritarianism may inadvertently promote liberal values as, for example, seems to be the case in Iran under the current Islamic regime (Moaddel 2009). Another manner in which authoritarianism promotes religious extremism is through heightening the feeling of powerlessness and fatalism among the public (promoting dysphoric emotions), as will be discussed subsequently.

Finally, the state also shapes people's identities. In an authoritarian context, people's identity is often shaped in oppositional relations to the identity of the state. That is, secular identity emerges in opposition to the identity of an Islamic regime, while religious identity becomes popular in opposition to the secularism of an authoritarian state. The rise in religious identity may in turn strengthen fundamentalist beliefs and attitudes.

Sources of Epistemic Authorities as Shortcuts to Religious Knowledge

While the extent of the availability of the sacred or secular sources of spirituality matters, people's spiritual orientations are also a function of the sources of information that they consider valid. To be sure, most people simply adopt the spiritual style of their parents. In the US approximately two-thirds of children do so. In the cultural context of the contemporary Middle East, this proportion is much higher. However, even in the democratic Western culture, where the freedom of religion is recognized and people have the right to choose their own religion as they see fit, people may not have the time or intellectual resources to engage in a prolonged quest for a most desirable religion. It may not be possible for many to systematically study various aspects of different religions to decide which religion or aspects thereof best suit their spiritual needs, which includes limited access to all the necessary information that is required for such an assessment. Moreover, the cost of learning about religion may outweigh the instrumental benefit of an enlightened religious choice. Thus, if some people adopt fundamentalist beliefs and attitudes, this may not be a result of their rational assessments of diverse trends within their faith.

How do people then decide to follow religious fundamentalism? The clue may lay in the fact that rational ignorance, to use Downs' (1957) expression, is compensated for by the availability of alternative venues for making a reasonable religious choice. Investigators of public opinion have pointed out that people form opinions on important issues by relying on a variety of sensible and mostly adaptive shortcuts (Popkin 1991, Sniderman et al 1991; Kinder 1998). Reliance on shortcuts to knowledge may also be relevant to people's decisions regarding religious issues via religious authorities.

Understanding religious fundamentalism thus involves examining the sources of information about religion that people rely on. Kruglanski (1989, 1990) employed the concept of *epistemic authority* to capture the process of knowledge formation according to which people perceive the information they have received as valid and, consequently, rely less on alternative sources. This process begins in infancy, when children accept the epistemic authority of parents and other proximal caregivers to comprehend objects and events they encounter. Then, in the course of subsequent socio-psychological development, one's peer group and, still later, broader social institutions serve as the individual's primary epistemic authorities (Ellis and Kruglanski 1992; Kruglanski et al. 2006; Raviv, Bar-Tal, Raviv, Biran and Sela 2003).

There are five general sources of knowledge that people use in learning about a wide variety of issues such as (a) education and career choice; (b) evolution: explanation of how plants and animals have evolved; (c) the role of women in society and politics; (d) Western societies and foreign culture; (e) politics and forms of government; and (f) the role of religion in politics and society. These sources include (1) parents, (2) peers, (3) teachers, (4) religious leaders, and (5) the media. Predictions regarding some epistemic sources may not be straightforward, given the variability in the sources themselves. It is difficult to predict the impact of parents or peers on one's religious attitudes, for example, without knowledge of their own beliefs regarding religious orthodoxy and fundamentalism, which may either reinforce or counter the prevailing societal norms in these countries. Fundamentalist or secular parents may promote corresponding attitudes among their children. The same would hold for friends— one's religious orientation is reinforced or weakened, depending on whether one's friends are fundamentalist or secular.

Predictions regarding the effects of religious leaders are more straightforward. Among Islamicists, a group of scholars connects Islamic religious tradition to contemporary fundamentalism. According to their thesis, fundamentalism is the logical outcome of the survival of the traditional religious institutions in the modern period. Fundamentalism thus reflects the resistance of these institutions to the modernization policies implemented by the modern state in Muslim countries. Although not always explicitly stated, this presumed continuity between Islamic religious tradition and fundamentalism has led the proponents of this perspective to conclude that Islam is in essence a fundamentalist religion. These scholars have employed a reductive text-based understanding of the religion in order to arrive at the unity of religion and politics, the scripturally sanctioned gender inequality, and the non-recognition of individuality in historical Islam, claiming that the distinctive view of Muslim fundamentalists on gender, politics, culture, and science are derived from these principles (e.g., Gibb 1947; von Grunebaum 1954; Lambton 1962; Lapidus 1992; Lewis 1993a, 1993b, 1988).

Islam-cum-fundamentalism was also the dominant view of religion among the nineteenth-century European colonial administrators in

Muslim countries. For example, William Wilson Hunter (1876, 136), a rank-
ing member of the British civil service in India, predicted that "no young
man, whether Hindu or Muhammadan, passes through our Anglo-Indian
schools without learning to disbelieve the faith of his fathers. The luxuri-
ant religions of Asia shrivel into dry sticks when brought into contact with
the icy realities of Western Science." Likewise, Lord Cromer (1908, 229),
the British consul general in Egypt, believed that "Islam cannot be
reformed . . . reformed Islam is Islam no longer; it is something else."
Echoing the view of his colleagues in India, he was convinced that
educated Egyptians were "demoslemised Moslems and invertebrate
Europeans" (p. 228). This is because "in passing through the European
educational mill, the young Egyptian Moslem loses his Islamism, or, at all
events, he loses the best part of it" (p. 230).[2]

Thus, reliance on the religious leaders representing the Islamic cultural
institution may promote religious fundamentalism among individuals.
Reliance on secular teachers (i.e., those teaching non-religious subjects), on the other hand, may have negative effects on fundamentalism.
By offering alternative explanations of social and physical phenomena,
secular teachers may project an image of the world that is less rigid,
more revealing of its complexity, and thus less committed to an
all-encompassing and uniform perspective on the universe that is portrayed by religious fundamentalism. Ideally, the contrasting ideas embod-
ied in secular learning and transmitted by teachers to students would
undermine fundamentalist attitudes to the degree that they alter the consistent schema in which such attitudes flourish. The media, including
radio, TV and the Internet, may also have varied effects on fundamentalist
beliefs and attitudes. Someone who relies exclusively on religious chan-
nels or uses the websites sympathetic to fundamentalist ideas may adopt
fundamentalist attitudes more readily than someone who relies on secular media. Nonetheless, it may be argued that satellite TV and the Internet,

---

[2] This approach rests on several assumptions about how religion shapes people's lives:
(a) that the normative injunctions and beliefs recorded in religious texts are adequate
descriptions of religion; (b) that these injunctions and beliefs correspond to people's
understanding of their religion, including their fundamentalist attitudes and behavior;
and (c) that religion is identified with the normative practices and rulings prescribed by
organized religion. The concept of lived religion (Hall 1997) departs from these assumptions. It captures the complexity of the role of religion in the lives of the great majority of
people in all religious traditions and attempts to understand how people make sense
of their religion. Lived religion is not just ordinary people's understanding of their religion,
which may or may not conform to religious norms. It is also the manner in which they
practice, market, negotiate, blend, and in short, live their religion.

by delivering a wide variety of sources of information to the users, may have a pluralistic effect on the users' religious view, weakening religious fundamentalism.

Religiosity

Does being religious make a person fundamentalist-prone? This may depend on the religion and whether the dominant orientation within a religious tradition is toward modernism or fundamentalism. There are two ways in which religiosity may shape fundamentalist beliefs and attitudes among individuals. One is that religious persons more often than non-religious persons may seek guidance in life from religious leaders and institutions. This reliance may in turn contribute to fundamentalism if such leaders and institutions have fundamentalist tendencies themselves. In addition to the extent of reliance on religious authorities as a source of knowledge about the sociopolitical role of religion, adherence to religious orthodoxy by individuals, in contrast to religious modernism, may also correlate with fundamentalist beliefs and attitudes.

Religious orthodoxy emphasizes the importance of religious laws for the faithful to follow. For the orthodox, the observance and the implementation of such laws are necessary for the creation and maintenance of a virtuous society. Considering Davis and Robinson's (2006, 170) conceptualization, religious "orthodoxy... does not refer to 'doctrinal' orthodoxy or belief in the specific tenets of a faith tradition.... In other words, as with fundamentalism, orthodox Catholics, Jews..., Muslims, and Protestants adhere to different religious tenets, but they share the broad worldview that the locus of moral authority is God and that legal codes should reflect absolute and timeless divine law." Modernists, on the other hand, are theologically individualistic in that they see individuals as largely responsible for their own moral decisions and fates. Because, for them, faith is a matter of one's choice, they tend to be less inclined to hold fundamentalist worldviews, favoring religious diversity and equality of all faiths before God.

Fundamentalists may share the views of religious orthodoxy, as they have also expressed support for Islamic laws. Nonetheless, it is crucial to emphasize that, in addition to orthodoxy, fundamentalists have often interpreted such laws as their political projects dictate. For example, many of the views espoused by Hasan al-Banna, the founder of Muslim Brothers, or Ayatollah Khomeini were not consistent with the notion of the *shari'a,* as was developed in historical Islam and understood by their orthodox colleagues who accepted the traditional formula that separated religious and political authority (al-Banna 1978; Moaddel 2005). While it may be said that the fundamentalists support the *shari'a,* not all those who do so are necessarily fundamentalists. At any rate, given the definition of fundamentalism as a set of beliefs and attitudes toward one's religion, it is conceptually distinct from an orientation toward Islamic laws.

Participation in religious services and individual religiosity may also be associated with fundamentalist beliefs and attitudes. When religious institutions are under the control of the orthodox clerics, and as a result the modernists have limited access to these institutions, participation in religious services that exposes the faithful to the conservative/orthodox views of the preacher may also enhance people's orientations toward Islamic fundamentalism. Moreover, in a society dominated by a single religion, or one experiencing an upsurge of Islamic fundamentalism, individual religiosity may reinforce the dominant monolithic view of religion and promote religious fundamentalism.

There is, however, some empirical evidence on the religiosity-fundamentalism nexus. In the Christian context, researchers have shown connections between religiosity and fundamentalism (Peshkin 1986; Ammerman 1987; Kellstedt and Smidt 1991). Likewise, among Muslims, analyzing the values surveys data, Blaydes and Linzer (2008, 577) have operationalized fundamentalism as a composite belief system that spans two broad areas: (a) preference consistent with a traditionalist worldview that systematically favors men over women and (b) personal piety and support for the confluence of politics and religion consistent with conservative Islamic values. If such a linkage exists, then the more people consider themselves religious, support religious orthodoxy, engage in religious services, and pray regularly, the more they should adhere to religious fundamentalism.

Social-Psychological Factors

Emotional experiences may also be linked to fundamentalism. Just as besieged spirituality shapes people's perception of the necessity to mobilize the forces of God against the unbelievers and the enemies of the faith, the feelings of insecurity, powerlessness, and fatalism, where people feel their situation is hopeless and that they are incapable of changing the unbearable circumstances in which they live, may also shape fundamentalist beliefs and attitudes.

We propose that life under authoritarian regimes is stressful, contributing to the feelings of powerlessness, pessimism about the future, and fatalism, which some under those conditions experience more than others. A sociological tradition relates pathological mental states to dysfunctional social structure and how this mental state in turn renders individuals receptive to extremist ideas (Arendt 1958; Johnson 1964, 1966; Davies 1969; Gurr 1970). Pioneering this tradition, Durkheim argued that fatalism, like anomie, is related to the problem of social regulations. While anomie is a result of societal normlessness and deregulation, fatalism is a type of subjective orientation produced by "excessive regulations," such that, as Durkheim noted, "futures [are] pitilessly blocked and passions violently choked by oppressive discipline" (cited in Dohrenwend 1959, 467). Sociologists have recently recovered Durkheim's conception of fatalism and stressed its importance for understanding the influence of an oppressive social environment on the individual's subjective orientation (Lukes 1967; Lockwood 1992; Besnard 1993; Acevedo 2005; Moaddel and Karabenick 2008).

Another key factor that may be associated with religious fundamentalism is the feeling of insecurity. This feeling enhances in-group solidarity and the mistrust of outsiders (Inglehart, Moaddel and Tessler 2006; Maehr and Karabenick 2005), which may in turn promote religious centrism and fundamentalism. Thus, in addition to holding such fatalistic attitudes about life as being full of suffering and unhappiness, the feeling of insecurity may resonate with the fundamentalist belief that religion is the only source of happiness and that happiness may only be realized after death in heaven.

In engendering the feelings of powerlessness, fatalism, and insecurity, authoritarian states, whether secular or religious, contribute to the rise of religious fundamentalism.

Demographic Factors

Religious fundamentalism may also vary as a function of education and socioeconomic background. As an indicator of cognitive ability (Stimson 1975), education is proposed to strengthen the information-processing efficiency of citizens and encourage certain values among individuals, including "openness of mind, a respect for science and empirical knowledge, an awareness of complexity and possibilities for change, and tolerance, not only of people but of points of view" (Sniderman, Brody and Tetlock 1991, 9; Tetlock 1986). Education may thus undermine or moderate religious fundamentalism. While this linkage is suggested in the liberal context of Western democracies, we expect that religious fundamentalism in Egypt and Saudi Arabia will also be weaker with increased levels of educational attainment. We also examine whether religious fundamentalism would vary as a function of socioeconomic background. The extant literature suggests that members of Islamic fundamentalist movements are predominantly drawn from the middle class (Mitchell 1969, Moaddel 2002b). Because Islam has been primarily an urban phenomenon, having stronger sociopolitical and cultural influence in major cities, we assess the effect of urban and rural environments on fundamentalist attitudes. Finally, while in the United States women tend to be more religious than are men, no matter how religiosity is measured, in Islamic countries the relationship between gender and religiosity may vary by country (Moaddel 2006). Thus we assess the relation of gender to fundamentalist attitudes without advancing an *a priori* hypothesis.

SUMMARY OF HYPOTHESES AND PREDICTIONS

This chapter provides the conceptual foundation for the analysis of fundamentalism by first defining religious fundamentalism as a set of beliefs about and attitudes toward religion. We distinguished this definition from the one that considers religious fundamentalism as a discourse produced by intellectual leaders of the fundamentalist movements in the Middle East to address and resolve historically significant issues. While sociological and psychological factors are important in shaping people's orientation toward religious fundamentalism, to more effectively single out the key features of the historical conditions leading to the rise or demise of this movement, we focused on the concept of spirituality. This concept was intended to capture humans' perpetual needs for understanding the meaning of life, search for security and empowerment, and desire for eternal salvation. We also discussed the difference between sacred and secular spirituality and proposed the notion of the cycle of spirituality.

Within the broader context of this cycle, this chapter discussed the conditions that are expected to strengthen or weaken religious fundamentalism. Included among these factors are discursive space, the nature of the intellectual environment and whether this environment is pluralistic or monolithic, state structures and cultures, the sources of epistemic authorities, besieged spirituality, religiosity, support for religious orthodoxy and religious authority, social psychological factors, religious identity, and demographics. The bulk part of this book discusses, measures and analyzes these concepts, and assesses their linkages with religious fundamentalism on what we will classify as macro and micro levels.

For a better comprehension of religious fundamentalist movement, in Chapter One religious fundamentalism is discussed within the broader historical context of the cycle of spirituality in the Middle East and among Indian Muslims in the contemporary period. In that chapter, religious fundamentalism is viewed as a discourse—a distinctive way of resolving a set of sociopolitical, cultural, and religious issues facing Muslim communities and their faith. The chapter begins with a discussion of the challenges to Islamic orthodoxy by harbingers of eighteenth-century reformist fundamentalist movements, then the rise of Islamic modernism in the nineteenth century within the context of secular spirituality, and then the decline of secular spirituality and the rise of religious fundamentalism in the twentieth century.

Chapter Two introduces macro level qualitative variables for a cross-national, inter-faith, and inter-ethnic comparative analysis of religious fundamentalism. It introduces readers to variations in the national context (Egypt, Iran, Lebanon, and Saudi Arabia), religion (Christianity and Islam), religious sects (among Muslims: The Druze, Shi'is, and Sunnis; among Christians: the Maronites, Catholics, and Orthodox), and ethnicity (the Azeri Turks, Lurs, Kurds, Gilakis, and Persians). Chapter Two is not intended to be a comprehensive description of national history, all the religions and religious sects, and various ethnic groups that exist in these societies. Rather, it provides the necessary information to better understand and interpret more fully the survey results. For example, while in Iran there are more than a dozen ethnic groups, we discuss only the Azeri Turks, Gilaki, Kurds, Lurs, and Persians because their numbers in the sample were sufficient for statistical analysis. The same is true for Lebanon where only the Sunnis, Shi'is, and Druze among Muslims and the Maronites, Orthodox, and Catholics among Christians were discussed.

In Chapter Three, the four proposed components of religious fundamentalism are elaborated and measured. Our position is that religious fundamentalism is not confined to a single dimension, such as inerrancy (e.g., Antoun 2008), but is rather a multifaceted concept that is comprised of several interrelated and logically consistent belief and attitudinal components. These components by and large cover the principle aspects of religion, including views on the nature of the deity, humanity, and punishment; the inerrancy and historical accuracy of the scriptures; exclusivity and religious centrism; and intolerance of other religions. We describe these components and how they collectively provide the conceptual rationale for measuring the degree of people's beliefs and attitudes that constitute religious fundamentalism.

Then, using the survey data collected in Egypt, Iran, Lebanon, and Saudi Arabia, religious fundamentalism is analyzed on the macro level, focusing on such factors as cross-national variations in the cultural context, state structures and cultures, the authoritarianism of the state, and variations in religion, religious sect, and ethnicity. Chapter Three evaluates the hypothesized linkages of pluralistic versus monolithic cultural environment, heterogeneity versus homogeneity of the ruling elite, the authoritarianism or democratic orientation of the state, the religiosity of the state, religion and religious sect, and ethnicity with religious fundamentalism. A central premise of this chapter is that adherence to fundamentalist beliefs and attitudes depends on social conditions.

The following two chapters provide micro analyses of fundamentalism. Chapter Four focuses on the data from the survey of youth in Egypt and Saudi Arabia, and Chapter Five on the adult survey data from Iran and Lebanon. Based on theoretical considerations and previous empirical findings, we predict that religious fundamentalism would be higher for respondents who: rely more on religious authorities as the source of information about religion; attend mosque more frequently; self-report being more religious; more strongly support the *shari'a* (religious orthodoxy); report being more fatalistic; express a higher level of powerlessness; report being more insecure; subscribe more strongly to conspiracy theories (i.e., display a stronger feeling of besieged spirituality); and have an Islamic identity. Religious fundamentalism, among Lebanese, is tied positively to in-group solidarity (negatively to inter-ethnic trust) and favorable attitudes toward the Iranian and Syrian regimes among the Shi'is and favorable attitudes toward the Kingdom of Saudi Arabia among the Sunnis. The connection between religious fundamentalism and attitudes toward government performance is mediated by the religiosity of the state. We thus propose that in confessional states of Iran, Lebanon, and Saudi Arabia the relationship would be positive, but negative in secular Egypt. By contrast, religious fundamentalism is predicted to be lower for those who rely more on secular teachers, domestic media and newspapers, or satellite TV and the Internet as sources of information about religion, and have more advanced levels of education. It should be noted that surveys from Egypt and Saudi Arabia provide information on all the specified variables, whereas information from Iran and Lebanon is not as comprehensive.

In Chapter Six, we attempt to connect empirically the two conceptions of fundamentalism discussed in this book: as a set of attitudes and beliefs and as a discourse on historically significant issues. We argue that religious fundamentalism conceptualized and assessed here will predict attitudes toward social individualism, gender equality, secular politics, secular politicians, secular identity, and Western culture.

In sum, based on the theoretical considerations discussed in this chapter and past empirical analyses, the present study advances a number of theses. They are:

Thesis 1: Fundamentalism conceptualized as a distinctive religious orientation has several components: views on the nature of the deity, humanity, and punishment; the inerrancy and historical accuracy of the scriptures; exclusivity and religious centrism; and intolerance of other religions.

Thesis 2: Those with stronger fundamentalist beliefs and attitudes would be related to negative attitudes toward Western culture—the notion that Western culture is decadent—and positively to beliefs in gender inequality, Islamic government and Islamic identity.

Thesis 3: Democratic political environments are less supportive of fundamentalism on the aggregate level than are authoritarian political conditions.

Thesis 4: Pluralistic religious environments are less supportive of fundamentalism on the aggregate level than are monolithic environments.

Thesis 5: Regional ties may shape fundamentalist attitudes: A minority ethnic group or religious sect that has ties with religious governments outside its country may be more supportive of fundamentalism than those that are tied to or take cues from secular governments.

Thesis 6: Fundamentalism is positively related to ethnic solidarity. The higher is one's ethnic solidarity, the higher is the support for fundamentalist beliefs and attitudes.

Thesis 7: People who rely more on others for knowledge or information tend to have a stronger fundamentalist orientation than those less reliant.

Thesis 8: Individuals who rely more on religious authorities/teachers tend to have a stronger fundamentalist orientation than those who rely less on such authorities or teachers.

Thesis 9: Individuals who rely more on the satellite and the Internet as sources of information tend to have a weaker fundamentalist orientation than those who do not rely on such sources.

Thesis 10: Religiosity may be linked to fundamentalism. This link may vary according to how religiosity is assessed and the social context.

Thesis 11: Social psychological variables consisting of fatalism, the feeling of insecurity, and pessimism about the future are positively linked to fundamentalism.

Thesis 12: The perception of besieged spirituality is positively linked to fundamentalism.

Finally, the concluding chapter summarizes the results and discusses both secular and sacred fundamentalism and suggests broadening the study of fundamentalism by examining different forms of secular fundamentalism. It also briefly discusses the Arab Spring.

CHAPTER ONE

CYCLES OF SPIRITUALITY AND DISCURSIVE SPACE: RELIGIOUS FUNDAMENTALISM IN HISTORICAL PERSPECTIVE

There have been three pivotal episodes in the history of ideological movements in the Muslim world in the period between the mid-eighteenth century and the end of the twentieth. Each of these episodes had far-reaching impact on the cultures and religions in Muslim-majority countries in the immediate subsequent period and beyond. The first was the reformist fundamentalism of the eighteenth century, which transformed into militant movements in the first of part of the nineteenth. The second was the rise of secular ideologies in the second half of the nineteenth century. These ideologies were institutionalized in the secular authoritarian interventionist states in the twentieth century. The third was the rise of religious fundamentalism, which began in Egypt in 1928, then spread to the rest of the Arab world in the second half of the twentieth century. Among the Iranian Shi'is, religious fundamentalism first emerged in the mid-1940s. Later in the sixties and seventies, religion constituted a key element of the cultural opposition to the state. Islamic fundamentalism also produced its own extremist offshoots, branching out into religious violence and al-Qaeda among the Sunnis, and clerical fanaticism and the Islamic regime in Iran among the Shi'is.

As proposed in the previous chapter, beyond economic or political interests, a critical factor that shaped all these movements are people's yearnings and search for meaning, security, empowerment, and a comprehensive understanding of life. At their core, these movements thus represented a sequence that first reflected the rise of sacred spirituality, then the popularity of secular spirituality and Islamic modernism, and finally again, the upsurge of sacred spirituality. The variation in the style and symbolism, organizational form, and religious or secular discourses that were associated with different trends in this sequence was undoubtedly shaped by a host of sociological and social psychological factors.

In this chapter, we begin with a discussion of the controversy over the concept of Islamic fundamentalism. We then provide an overview of the historical sequence described above by discussing Islamic orthodoxy, modernism, and fundamentalism. To specify the distinctly religious factors contributing to the generation of Islamic fundamentalism and modernism in the contemporary period, this chapter presents analyses of the effect of social processes on spiritual experiences as presented in the expressions of Muslim intellectual leaders of these movements. We also expand on the concept of discursive space, which we defined in the previous chapter as a cognitive mechanism that promotes the development of tolerant, moderate, and transcendental discourse, and which we proposed helps to understand the relationship between social change and religion in the late nineteenth century and how the narrowing of this space in the twentieth century contributed to the particularly violent form of religious fundamentalism.

Although we cannot mine the thought process of religious intellectual leaders, this chapter attempts to provide an interpretation of the historical record in order to lay the groundwork for a more effective and meaningful connection between the discourse of religious fundamentalism and the fundamentalist beliefs and attitudes that will be discussed in the later chapters of this book.

Controversy Over Islamic Fundamentalism

The term "fundamentalism" is controversial and readily acknowledged for its etymological variability and inherent ambiguity in current discourse about the nature of certain types of religious movements in the contemporary Muslim-majority countries that are dubbed fundamentalist. The religious origin of fundamentalism in the United States can be traced to the Presbyterian General Assembly of 1910 (Wills 1990; Smith 1998), the World's Christian Fundamentals Association founded in 1918, the Protestant movement in the 1920s, the Northern Baptist Convention of 1920, and especially the series of books called *The Fundamentals* published by evangelicals in that decade. The latter listed five defining characteristics of true Christian believers (Marsden 1980). These characteristics are beliefs that stem from the inspiration of the Bible and the inerrancy of Scripture with respect to:

- The virgin birth of Christ
- The belief that Christ's death was the atonement for sin
- The bodily resurrection of Christ
- The historical reality of Christ's miracles

In recent decades, the term has also been used to identify certain types of conservative movements in religious traditions other than Christianity, including Judaism and Islam. One prominent scholar of Islam, Aziz Ahmad (1964), has also used the term fundamentalism in passing to denote the religious views of Shah Waliallah (1703–1762) in India and Muhammad Ibn Abd al-Wahhab (1703–1787) in Najd, part of present-day Saudi Arabia. Historian Arnold Toynbee (1931, 117) applies the term to traditionalist Muslims: "If you looked in the right places, you could doubtless find some old fashioned Islamic fundamentalists still lingering on. You would also find that their influence was negligible." However, the emergence of the Society of the Muslim Brothers in Egypt in 1928 and its expansion into other Arab countries signified the emergence of an Islamic movement that was neither traditionalist nor modernist, but carried elements of both. Hence, many scholars decided to consider this and other such movements with broadly similar religious and political orientations as fundamentalist.

However, the application of "fundamentalism" to the contemporary Islamic movement has generated controversy among diverse scholars of Islam (Kramer 2003). Some reluctantly recommended its acceptance while others vehemently rejected it. Lewis (1988) conceded that the term is misleading, but suggested that it must be accepted. His detractor, Said (1977), did not object to the usage of the term but warned against its equation with Islam in general. Esposito (1992), on the other hand, recommends excising the term altogether because it is pejorative and portrays an image of the religious movement that is static, retrogressive and extremist. Instead, he suggests the term "Islamic revivalism." Nonetheless, this and such other alternative labels as Islamism, Integrism, neo-traditionalism, Islamic nativism, jihadism, militant Islam and so forth are not without problems either. For example, "Islamism," which is currently a preferred terminology over fundamentalism by a large group of scholars, may lead to confusion because it was used first by French scholars in the mid-eighteenth century as a synonym for Islam. Moreover, Islamism for Munson (1988, 4) is a "clumsy neologism." The term "jihadism" that became popular after the terrorist attack on the U.S. soil on September 11, 2001, is reserved for the most violent Muslim extremists.

As Moaddel and Talattof (2000) and Moaddel (2005) have argued, the central question is not whether Islamic and Christian fundamentalisms converge in their attitudes and orientation toward religion. Rather, the term "Islamic fundamentalism" is more effective than "Islamism" in distinguishing three general types of Islamic movements: orthodoxy,

modernism, and fundamentalism. Islamic orthodoxy consisted of the
schools of jurisprudence and the religious institutions that have been
dominant in historical Islam since the medieval period, particularly under
the three Muslim empires of the Mughals, Ottomans, and the Safavids.
Islamic orthodoxy became the object of criticisms by both the modernists
and fundamentalists. Islamic modernism was a religious reformist movement that emerged in different parts of Muslim-majority countries and
India in the second half of the nineteenth century and early twentieth.
Finally, Islamic fundamentalism is reserved for the type of religious and
political movement that was formed following the formation of the
Society of the Muslim Brothers in 1928 and then constituted the dominant
religious movement in many Muslim majority countries in the second
half of the twentieth century.

This taxonomy of Islamic movements is not intended to overlook the
vast substantive differences that may exist within each of the categories
of Islamic orthodoxy, modernism, and fundamentalism. Nonetheless, the
classification presumes that the principle factors that demarcate the variation between these movements are quite different from those underpinning the variation within each movement. We argued that the differences
between the orthodox, modernists, and fundamentalists revolve essentially on the manner in which the precursors of each movement have
resolved some of the basic issues facing Islam as a belief system and a
social institution. Significant among these issues are the status of rational reasoning in Quranic exegesis, the ideal form of government, the
relationship between religion and politics, the basis of identity, the
nature of the Western societies, the social status of women, and proper
methods of political action—revolutionary or radical versus reformist or
moderate.

What can be considered Islamic fundamentalism historically is thus
manifest in the sprawling scope of events and literature produced by the
leaders and activists of fundamentalist movements. The identifiable
marks of such movements were their specific positions on the set of sociopolitical issues that have been significant in Muslim-majority countries in
the contemporary period. Issues are important for understanding not
only such different Islamic movements as orthodoxy, fundamentalism,
and modernism, but also other diverse cultural movements that have
emerged in the contemporary Middle East. That is, territorial nationalism,
liberalism, anti-clerical secularism, and supra territorial nationalism
(e.g., pan-Arab nationalism) all are also identified in terms of their
positions on some or all of these issues. From this perspective, Islamic

modernism and fundamentalism were two distinctly different religious discourses produced by the intellectual leaders of these movements to address the same set of sociopolitical and cultural issues. The challenge for the social-scientific study of Islamic fundamentalism is thus to assess the linkages between the attitudinal measures of fundamentalism and the discourse of the religious fundamentalists as a set of positions on issues in concrete historical settings.

Whether or not one is justified to use the term fundamentalism to characterize a category of religious beliefs or movements, there are certain facts about the experience of religious-cum-political movements in the past decades that one cannot eschew. The fundamentalist clerics who came to power in Iran after the 1979 revolution have committed horrific crimes and often displayed disregard for human lives. Summary executions of political opponents, tortures and rapes of political prisoners, the imposition of a reign of terror in the country, and the perpetrations of terrorism abroad have all been the standard practices of the Islamic regime in Iran, which these clerics have justified in the name of religion and for the protection of their Islamic system. Likewise, such horrendous acts of terrorism as beheadings of civilians who worked for certain companies or governments, and the destruction of thousands of innocent lives as a result of suicide bombings by the Sunni extremists were also conducted for the sake of Islam. While those who displayed strong fundamentalist beliefs and attitudes may categorically reject these acts, the belief in the centrality of one's religion and its superiority over other religions still contradicts the liberal principle of the equality of all religious and cultural voices in a pluralistic society. It is thus not the term that may sound socially undesirable, it is rather the political behavior, beliefs, and attitudes associated with religious fundamentalism that are incongruent with an enlightened mind and with liberal values.

To be sure, despite the existence of value conflicts between fundamentalism and enlightened rational egalitarianism, one may still argue that individuals identified as fundamentalist may appreciate more often than non-fundamentalists the value of self-discipline, hard work, and independence—the individual attributes that are thought to have contributed to the rise of individualism, democracy, and capitalism. Moreover, the claim in the superiority of one's own religion over another's is not necessarily indicative of religious bigotry and support for inequality. What is important is the basis on which the claim to superiority is justified. A religion that provides theological justifications in defense of an egalitarian social order—one that is based on gender equality and democracy, for example—may be viewed as a religion better than one that supports social inequality.

What is more, historically, the issue of whose religion is closer to God or morally superior has often been a topic in legitimate religious disputations over which theologians of different faiths have debated one another, and the outcome of such disputations has not always been religiously motivated political violence. It has even led to the development of a more egalitarian and transcendental religious discourse. For example, the debate over miracles attributed to Prophet Muhammad, religious superstitions, and the Islamic roots of gender inequality, polygamy, and maltreatment of women between Christian missionaries and Muslim theologians in nineteenth-century Egypt and India contributed to the development of rational thinking, modernist thought, and Islamic feminism in these countries (see Lee 1924; *Calcutta Review* May–August 1844 and July–December 1845; Moaddel 2005).

By contrast, the rise of Islamic fundamentalism, most notably in Egypt and Iran in the twentieth century, benefited by the absence of such debates. In fact, when despotic regimes like the ones that came to power in Egypt, Iran, and other Middle Eastern countries in the second half of the twentieth century restricted public expressions, the outcome has been the development of extremist ideological movements in these societies. These restrictions had undermined the effectiveness of scholarly standards and methodological rules in governing debates on issues facing the faith and society. Under such conditions, extremist discourses acquired legitimacy for standing against authoritarian rulers. To be elaborated subsequently, this is perhaps one principal reason why such radical Islamism as that of a Sayyid Qutb or a Khomeini remained unchallenged.

ISLAMIC ORTHODOXY

The literal definition of orthodoxy is the right (*orthos*) belief (*doxa*). The concept of orthodoxy, however, has different meanings in different religious traditions. "Within Judaism," according to Hunter (1991, 44), "orthodoxy is defined mainly by commitment to Torah and the community that upholds it; within Catholicism, orthodoxy is defined largely by loyalty to church teaching—the Roman Magisterium; and within Protestantism, orthodoxy principally means devotion to the complete and final authority of Scripture." Although there is no such category in Islamic tradition as "orthodoxy," there has been a category of religious norms, beliefs, laws, and institutional practices in historical Islam that is similar to the Catholic understanding of the term. Orthodoxy in the context of Islam comes also very close to its literal meaning: obedience to the right path or the *sharia* law (or Islamic way of life). Generally, Islamic orthodoxy consists of those religious norms, beliefs, laws, and institutional practices that have been commonly accepted by the followers of the four major schools of jurisprudence in Sunni Islam and those who follow organized Shi'ism in Iran and Iraq. In the historical context of the Islamic tradition, the followers of the Islamic orthodoxy are those who consider a good government as one that implements only the *sharia* law.

In the modern period, Islamic orthodoxy came under sustained criticisms by Muslim intellectuals and theologians of various persuasions. In the eighteenth century, the harbingers of reformist fundamentalism rebelled against the orthodox ulama [theologians]. Chief among them were Shah Waliallah and Muhammad Ibn Abdul Wahhab. The principal concerns of these theologians revolved on the spiritual decline of Islam as a result of the contamination of the faith by what were deemed un-Islamic currents and the prevalence of disunity within Muslim communities. In their broadside on the dominant religious institutions and practices, they admonished Muslims for allowing their faith to be tainted by unlawful innovations and un-Islamic folkways. They criticized the ulama for their subservience to the authorities, questioned the Islamic credentials of the ruling monarch, rejected the belief in the mediation of the saint for individual salvation, and forcefully advocated the significance of direct worship of God and the view that the Quran is accessible to ordinary individuals. On the one hand, the criticisms of the established religion and religious practices implied their interests in religious reforms. On the other hand, the stress on the purification of the faith, a return to the fundamental principles of Islam as were practiced under the Rashidun caliphate, and intolerance of the outsiders, including other Islamic religious sects, were indicative of a fundamentalist orientation. The spiritual revivalist movements spearheaded by these two prominent thinkers, however, degenerated into violent religious movements, which were defeated by the mid-nineteenth century.

The nineteenth century, however, was a period of massive diffusions of modern ideologies into the Muslim world. Backed by new scientific discoveries and technological innovations, a new secular spirituality gained predominance in the work of indigenous intellectual leaders. This new spirituality rested on a differentiated conception of the universe; natural was separated from supernatural, mind or soul from matter, religious or sacred from secular learning, and human rational reasoning and sense experience were liberated from the totalitarian dictation of the religious institutions. With this new spirituality came a new sense of human empowerment to fully understand and control nature and create a more effective egalitarian social order. The rise of Islamic modernism in the late nineteenth and early twentieth century can be viewed as a religious outcome of secular spirituality that was dominant in this period. The Islamic modernists were preoccupied with the sociopolitical and cultural norms of Islam. They were critical of the orthodoxy for its obstructionism and inability to meet the challenges of modernity. Many of the Islamic modernist thinkers tried to formulate a natural theology that was in harmony with the principles and discoveries of the modern sciences. The twentieth century, on the other hand, ushered in a period of the decline of secularism and secular discourse and the rise of sacred spirituality, giving impetus to new religious fundamentalist movements. Once again, the orthodoxy came under attack for its non-political nature. Its main target of criticism, however, was the secular discourse in vogue in Muslim-majority countries as well as the policies implemented by the secular state. Although Islamic fundamentalism and modernism were influenced by the intellectual climate of the period, their religious discourse was also shaped in oppositional relations to religious orthodoxy. Thus, a fuller understanding of these religious movements requires an understanding of Islamic orthodoxy.

We know that the Islamic orthodoxy grew out of attempts to resolve the practical problems faced by Muslim communities. One thing is clear: it would be hard to identify a pattern of religious values, norms, and behaviors that are common to all Muslims, Islamic institutions, or Islamic states throughout history except for a set of general beliefs shared by most Muslims. These are the unity of God; the prophecy of Muhammad and the infallibility of his deeds; the completeness, finality, and inerrancy of the Quran; and such rituals of *ibadat* as praying, fasting, pilgrimage to Mecca, and *zakat*. Unless one is fully committed to an essentialist reading of historical Islam, the statement that Islamic values and their practical applications have changed according to changes in social conditions is hardly debatable. What made Islamic cultural tradition agreeable to change was the fact that, like other cultural traditions, it carried contradictory elements. On a most abstract level, these elements may be uncovered by deconstructing Islamic tradition in terms of a series of binary oppositions. Among them are *wahy* (revelation) versus *'aql* (reason), *towhid* (divine unity) versus *shirk* (idol worshipping), *shari'a* (Islamic law) versus *jahiliyya* (the state of ignorance), *dar ul-Islam* (the abode of Islam) versus *dar ul-harb* (the abode of war), *wilaya* (delegation by God) versus *mulk* (hereditary rule), *khilapha* (spiritual authority) versus *sultanate* (temporal authority), *umma* (universalistic Islamic community) versus *asabiyya* (particularistic tribal solidarity), and *Arabic* (as the sacred universal language of the umma) versus the *vernaculars* (particularistic ethnic languages). These oppositional binaries have informed debates about the nature of the true Islam and the Islamicity of the existing sociopolitical order.

We may argue that by providing the essential categories to stereotype different aspects of human social existence, these binaries have produced an Islamic cognitive framework, or an Islamic network of semantic elements, within which diverse sociopolitical thoughts emerged in historical Islam. That is, people are Islamic insofar as they use these binaries in order to stereotype and analyze the realities they encounter. At the same time, for the engineers of an Islamic society, these categories were indicative of serious practical problems that had to be resolved to ensure the stability of a social order deemed Islamic. For example, there have always been real conflicts between the theologians who favored literal interpretations of the Quran, or revealed laws of the faith, and practitioners of rational arguments or *aql* (Levy 1933; Hourani 1991); between those who would offer allegiance only to the true caliph and those who willingly obey royal power; between believers in the universality of the *umma* and the nationalists who did not want to forgo their distinctive way of life; and between believers in the sacredness of Arabic as the universal language of the faith and the non-Arab Muslims who desired their own local vernaculars and even those who preferred the decoupling of the Arabic and the sacred teachings of the faith.

The tension between literalists and rationalists was resolved by what appeared, broadly speaking, to be a middle way approach. The employment of reason became necessary because, as a result of the passage of time and the expansion of Islam into new territories, Muslim leaders and administrators faced problems for which there were no specific guidelines in the Quran or in the tradition of the prophet, *hadith*. Thus, prominent theologians constructed a series of rationally argued methodological principles to not only solve the existing practical problems and anomalies, but also establish a basis for the future rulings of the judges and control of the arbitrary conduct of Muslim generals and administrators. The principles of *qiyas*, juristic reasoning by analogy, and *ijma,'* or consensus among Muslim theologians, were formulated to apply to the cases where direct rulings were unavailable in the Quran or the tradition of the prophet. The orientations of Muslim theologians toward these principles created four different schools of jurisprudence—Hanafi, Shafi'i, Maliki, and Hanbali. For example, the Shafi'i school accepted all the four principles in the hierarchical order of the Quran, *hadith*, consensus, and *qiyas*. The Hanbali School, on the other hand, rejected consensus and *qiyas* and comes very close to the literalist position.

Likewise, in early Shi'ism, the dominant view was that all laws were implicit in the Quran and the *hadith*. These laws were to be discovered by the jurists, and therefore there was no need for *ra'y* (opinion) of the ulama, and its offshoots, the *qiyas* or *ijma*. With the passage of time, however, the Shi'i theologians began to experience problems similar to those encountered by their Sunni counterparts, which could not be resolved by reference to the Quran or the *hadith*. The Shi'i *fiqh* thus developed in a fashion similar to the Sunni and came to rest on the Quran, the *hadith*, *ijma*, and *'aql* (Momen 1985, 185; Levy 1933, 257–59).

In sum, these developments in the Islamic jurisprudence meant that the proofs of rational argument were to some extent acceptable, and that the ulama were thus instructed to follow one of these four schools in ruling on the practical matters posed before them. On the other hand, it blocked the further application of reason by forbidding the jurists to employ rationalist principles above and beyond the framework specified by these four schools, thereby closing the gate of *ijtihad* (independent reasoning).

Furthermore, to address the conflict between the Islamic theory of caliphate and the legitimacy of the Muslim rulers who had effective power but lacked the necessary Islamic credentials to be bestowed as the leaders of the Muslim community, the Islamic conception of politics underwent profound changes after its early formulation in the doctrine of the *khilafa* (caliphate). As the successor to Prophet Muhammad, the *khalifa* (caliph) was to assume the activities and privileges exercised by him save the prophetic functions. The question of who had the necessary qualifications to be the leader of the Muslim community, and how the Islamic conception of authority was to be reconciled with changing political reality after the death of the prophet, remained the arduous task of Muslim theologians cum political theorists. The Sunni theorists are unanimous about the legitimacy of the first four caliphs, given the honorific title of the *Rashidun*—exemplars of rightful Muslim rulers. Nevertheless, several significant shifts in political power in the post-Rashidun caliphate under the Umayyads (661–750), the Abbasids (750–1258) and thereafter, provided serious problems for Muslim jurists: How is one to reconcile the Islamic notion of sovereignty with the claims of a self-made caliph among the continuously emerging military leaders and tribal chiefs in different parts of the Islamic world?

In their sustained efforts to reconcile the theory of the caliphate and the changing political reality of their time in the post-Rashidun era, Muslim scholars steadily departed from the conception of politics as the unity of the political and religious leadership in the person of the caliph to take positions that progressively amounted to the admission of the reality of secular politics—the differentiation between religious and political leadership. That is, a strict adherence to the principles of the caliphate was relaxed in favor of recognizing the sultan's discretionary power, in different interpretations of these principles, by Abu al-Hasan Ali al-Mawardi (972–1058), Imam Muhammad al-Ghazali (1058–1111), Taqi al-Din Ahmad Ibn Taymiyya (1263–1328), and Abd al-Rahman Ibn Khaldun (1333–1406). This new political formula was predicated on the precept that the sultan was to protect the territorial integrity of the abode of Islam, maintain security, implement the *shari'a*, respect the ulama and seek their advice (Gibb 1937, 291–301; Rosenthal 1958, 28, 42, 239, note 34; Rizvi 1975, 283; Dina'nie 1991/1370, 47–48; Ibn Khaldun 1967, 385; *Encyclopedia of Islam* 4, 945).

In a parallel fashion a compromise was reached on the problem of nationalities, as the Ottomans devised the millet system in which religious minorities were allowed to enforce their own rules and customs in dealing with the educational, religious, security, and other issues within their communities that were not addressed by the Ottoman central government (Karpat 1982, 141–170; Shaw 1977). Finally, the tension between the Arabic and the vernaculars was resolved by a simple division of functions: Arabic became the exclusive language for understanding and interpreting religious texts, while such non-Arabic languages as Persian in Iran and in the state of Mughal India and Turkish in Turkey remained the language of the state and civic culture.

To be sure, there have been other forms of legal and political developments in historical Islam, including Sufism, which adhered to the inner, mystical, somewhat exclusively spiritual dimension of the religion, and several heterodox movements such as the one that developed into the Druze sect (see Chapter two). Nonetheless, it was the Islamic orthodoxy that appeared to have provided the guiding principles of the prevailing sociopolitical order in Muslim countries in the pre-modern period. They governed the relationship between the state and religion as well as the relationship between religious institutions and society under the three Muslim empires—the Mughals (1526–1858) in the Indian subcontinent, the Safavids (1502–1736) in Iran, and the Ottomans (1299–1923) in Asia Minor, which for several centuries sheltered almost the entire abode of Islam.

Although the principles of the Islamic orthodoxy summarized above displayed an aura of permanency, they were in effect provisional. Shaped by the nature of the social forces of the time and the dictation of political expediency, these principles, however, were vulnerable to attack as these forces declined or political conditions changed. After all, the closing of the gate of independent reasoning (*ijtihad*) was neither fully accepted nor totally followed by theologians (Hallaq 1984). Nor did all Muslim theologians seriously or entirely accept the legitimacy of the royal power. While more often than not agreeing that the caliphate ceased to exist after the death of the fourth caliph, they almost always did not wish Muslims to rebel against the sultan who had usurped power. Such a rebellion, they thought, would have led to chaos (*fitneh*), which is a condition worse than having an illegitimate Muslim ruler in power (Rosenthal 1958; Hourani 1983).

The presence of different schools of jurisprudence constituted a favorable context for intellectual debates and religious disputations among the ulama (Muslim theologians). Moreover, because the acceptance of the sultan's discretionary power was predicated on his commitment to implement the *shari'a* and protect the Muslim community, it provided a framework for assessing the ruler's performance. These features of the Islamic orthodoxy, we may argue, have provided the necessary *discursive space* for the recognition, discussion, and resolutions of normative inconsistencies in the structure of the sociopolitical thought in historical Islam. And when favorable social conditions became available, as they did in the late nineteenth and early twentieth century, Islam made a relatively smooth transition to democratic politics.

Eighteenth-Century Reformist Fundamentalism

By the medieval period, the Islamic orthodoxy had resolved many of the serious issues facing Muslim communities. Despite the challenges it faced, it remained a powerful institution particularly under the three Muslim empires. In the modern period, however, it was first challenged by the reformist fundamentalism of the eighteenth century. This movement emerged against the backdrop of the decline of the three empires, which started to accelerate in the 1700s. The manifestations of this decline were defeats in wars, primarily against non-Muslim powers, the impotence of Muslim rulers to resist European interventions into their affairs, and these rulers' failure to maintain political stability. Economic transformation further exacerbated this political weakness, including the development of capitalism, commercialization, the rise of the merchant class, and the integration of the indigenous economies into the world capitalist market.

In India, a multitude of factors provided ample opportunities for the British East India Company to begin a phase of rapid imperial expansion in 1757 with large-scale acquisitions of Indian territory. These included: the growing disparity between the authority and the power of the Mughal emperor; the slow accumulation of wealth resulting from the expanding commercial economy of the seventeenth century; the rise of literate Muslim gentry and of Hindu landholders and merchants; the emergence of semiautonomous kingdoms within the ambit of the imperial domain; the rapid disintegration of the Mughal empire after 1707; and the ensuing half century of predatory civil strife. By the early nineteenth century, the country had become the East India Company's state. And the Mughal emperor was reduced in European eyes to the status of a pathetic "tinsel sovereign," surrounded by the emaciated ladies of his harem and chamberlains who maintained the shadow of his authority through the reiteration of court rituals (Bayly 1988; Gopal 1972). The decline of the Mughals and the growing power of the East India Company also facilitated a shift in the balance of power between the Muslim and Hindu communities, as Muslim political power declined and Hindu ascended in economic power.

The decline of the Ottoman Empire was not as dramatic, although it also steadily weakened from the eighteenth century on and eventually disintegrated after World War I. Successive defeats of the Turkish army by European powers after the Ottoman retreat from Vienna in 1683 underscored the reality of Ottoman weakness vis-à-vis European military superiority (Ma'oz 1968, 1, 4). The increasing inequality of power between a decaying empire and thriving imperialisms changed the framework for economic transaction in favor of Europe. The treaty of capitulation limited the Ottomans' customs duties on imports from European states and accorded various extraterritorial privileges to them. The European goods paid very low customs duties on entry into the empire, while Ottoman goods seeking to enter Europe were subject to prohibitive duties or barred outright (Petran 1972, 42–43).

Furthermore, the Tanzimat (a series of Ottoman reforms instituted between 1837 and 1876) expanded the religious and cultural freedoms of the religious minorities living under its dominions and changed the traditional Islamic principle of the empire (Lapidus 1988, 598–600; Ma'oz 1968, 21–27). By the time Sultan Abdülhamid (1876–1909) decided to halt the process of change under the banner of pan-Islamism, after initially promoting the first Ottoman constitution, the sociopolitical forces for change were too strong to be contained by a ruling despot. One consequence of the Ottoman decline was the increase in the autonomy of the Arab countries under its dominion. The Mamluk rulers of Egypt, for example, were so powerful that by the 1700s the Turkish viceroy was a mere pawn in their hands (Vatikiotis 1980, 30). The Safavid Empire in Iran also followed a similar course of decline. Its disintegration in 1736 was followed by a period of intense conflict between various tribal groups, large landowners, and kingmakers for political supremacy, until the Qajars managed to defeat all their rivals and Aqa Muhammad Khan was formally crowned as the new king and founder of the Qajar dynasty in 1796.

Such were the macro sociopolitical contexts in which Shah Waliallah and Muhammad Ibn Abd al-Wahhab reflected about Islam and the Islamicity of their community, the status of the ulama and the Islamic orthodoxy, and the nature of the ruling authority. We surmise that these theologians were aware of the glaring contrast between the past Muslim glories and the current conditions of decline. We have little knowledge of their thought that might help explain why the outcome of their reflections was a project that sought a distinctly religious solution to the problem of decline and why this religious orientation was both reformist and fundamentalist. Nonetheless, insofar as their attention span fixated on the past and this past was believed to be both truly Islamic and glorious, they might have associated the current sociopolitical decline with the deviation of Muslim rulers and the orthodox ulama from the normative and spiritual principles of early Islam.

Our speculation of the thought process of these religious luminaries may become tenable, considering intellectual reflections in a broader comparative context. We suggest that fixation on a glorious past that is not Islamic may bring about a secular ideological resolution. Here, we cite the concerns of nineteenth century Iranian intellectual leaders who were also reflecting about the decline of their country, the role of the ulama, and the efficacy of the Qajar ruling elite. They also fixated on the past Iranian grandeurs and glories. This past, by contrast, was not Islamic. What is more, this past ended as a result of the Arab invasion in the seventh century and the imposition of an Islamic rule on the country. The outcome of this reflective process, as a result, was a nationalist secular project, which was also anti-Arab. The ulama also came under attack not because of their lack of religious zeal to defend the faith, but because their obstructionism had stifled rationalist thought and undermined the country's development.

However, for Shah Waliallah and Muhammad Ibn Abd al-Wahhab, the decline of Muslim communities was a result of the contamination of the faith with un-Islamic beliefs and traditions. This contamination promoted unlawful innovations (i.e., *bid'a*), the deviation of the ulama from the true path, political corruption in high places, and the rise of religious sects and sectarianism. They thus attacked the religious perspective of the Islamic orthodoxy and the official ulama as well as the prerogative of the sultan. For Muhammad Ibn Abd al-Wahhab, the Islamic faith rests on the rejection of all gods except God. Assigning partners to God (*shirk*), he said, "is evil, no matter what the object, whether it be 'king or prophet, or saint or tree or tomb'; to worship pious men is as bad as to worship idols" (Hourani 1983, 37). He argued that the true Islam was that of the first generation and protested against all those later innovations that had in fact brought other gods into Islam. Furthermore, the Islam the Ottoman sultan protected, claimed Muhammad Ibn Abd al-Wahhab, was not the true Islam, and thus he was not considered the true leader of the Muslim community (Hourani 1983, 38). Muhammad Ibn Abd-al-Wahhab was a follower of the Hanbali school of jurisprudence, but he rejected *taqlid* (emulation) and "was opposed to any of the schools (*madh'hab*) being taken as an absolute and unquestioned authority" (Mortimer 1982, 61). He also rejected Shi'ism as a heretical sect.

In a similar fashion, Shah Waliallah concluded that the development of monarchy, as opposed to the early republican tradition of Islam, and the closing of the gate of *ijtihad* (independent reasoning by theologians), were the causes of the prevailing deterioration of Muslim societies. Shah Waliallah declared that Muslim jurisprudence must be totally subordinated to the Quran and the tradition of the Prophet. He insisted that the meanings of the Quran were accessible to the ordinary audience, and that its message was as applicable today as it had been in the days of the Prophet. In his endeavor to make the Quran understood, he considered it proper to accept or reject the approved wisdom on Quranic exegesis (*tafsir*) that was inherited from the past (Nickel 1987, 3; Jalbani 1967, 9; Ahmad 1966, 13–14). "His object was primarily to convey the word of God in translation to the average educated Muslim and secondarily to break the monopoly of the theologians, who had become petty minded and far too preoccupied with externalities of ritual, converting himself into the Muslim counterpart of the Hindu Brahmin" (Ahmad 1964, 205).

Shah Waliallah believed that Islam consists of only the tradition of Islam (*sunna*) and the Islamic law, whereas other views and practices were un-Islamic and part of unlawful innovation in the faith. In the Indian environment, innovation or *bid'a* became a synonym for the Hindu folk-ways and mores that were retained by the converts to Islam and thus diffused into Muslim society. The fundamentalism of Shah Waliallah rested on his belief that social reform meant a greater Islamization of the society to keep Islam free from *shirk*—from associationism of all kinds with Divine Unity, Divine Will, and Divine Power (Malik 1981, 256; Ahmad 1964, 209). His reformism, on the other hand, meant bringing the religious law of Islam into the open, fully dressed in reason and argument (Ahmad 1964, 205). Shah Waliallah initiated a renewed emphasis on independent reasoning as "an exhaustive endeavor to understand the derivative principles of canon law" (Ahmad 1964, 204).

The immediate outcomes of these teachings were militant Islamic movements for the rehabilitation of the faith and the imposition of a monolithic Islamic rule on society. This was perhaps a result of the social and political conditions in the period between the late eighteenth and early nineteenth century. This period marked the rise of Hindu and Sikh that successfully challenged Muslim power on the one hand, and the imposition of Europe-centered uniformitarian rationalist cultural policies by the East India Company on Indian society (Moaddel 2005) on the other. By 1784, the Mughal emperor appeared so weakened as to have submitted to the protection of the greatest of the Maratha warlords, Mahadji Scindia (Bayly 1988; Moaddel 2005). At about the same time, Maharaja Ranjit Singh, known as *sheer-i Punjab* (the lion of the Punjab) and belonging to a Sikh clan of Northern India, occupied the Punjab territories and founded the Sikh Empire. Likewise, within the context of the declining Ottoman Empire, the eighteenth century saw the emergence of modern states as distinctive political entities in different localities among Arab populations in the Persian Gulf region. Between Yemen and Oman, a cluster of small princedoms and city-states led by people who were considered saints came to the limelight (Voll 1994, 65–67). These changes might have warned the followers of Ibn Abd al-Wahhab of the impending decline and disunity of their religious communities—hence, the popularity of the Wahhabis' reintroduced emphasis on God's unity as a unifying force to create a new Islamic order that transcended the existing sectarian divisions.

Branding themselves the spirit of the true Islam, but labeled as Wahhabis by their detractors, the militant followers of Muhammad Ibn Abd al-Wahhab first gained control of central Arabia and the Persian Gulf, then sacked Karbala on the fringes of Iraq. Next, they occupied the Hijaz until, at the request of the Ottoman sultan, the ruler of Egypt Muhammad Ali destroyed their power in Arabia in the nineteenth century (Hourani 1983, 38, 53). Likewise labeled as "Wahhabis" by the British and "mujahidin" by its followers, the Indian movement was led by Sayyid Ahmad Barelvi (1786–1831), a disciple of the divine's (Shah Waliallah's) son and successor Abdul Aziz, whose circle he joined in 1807. Two learned scions of the family of Shah Waliallah, Shah Isma'il and Abdul Hayy, joined him as his disciples, marking the progress of Shah Waliallah's program "from theory to practice, from life contemplative to life active, from instruction of the elite to the emancipation of the masses, and from individual salvation to social organization" (Ahmad 1964, 210; Lapidus 1988, 566). Barelvi declared the abode of war (*dar ul-harb*) the territories of India occupied by the British and other non-Muslim forces and called upon the regional Muslims to join him in a holy war against the infidels. The movement was crushed by the British in 1858, suffered another defeat in 1863, and was persecuted all over India (Barelvi, n.d.; Ahmad 1964; Ahmad 1966; Hardy 1972).

Despite the defeats of the Mujahidin, Shah Waliallah's emphasis on *ijtihad* remained his main contribution to modernist thinking among Indian Muslims. If he was indeed discerning a "sign of the times," perhaps he perceived that in the midst of a failing Mughal Empire political fortunes might not guarantee the survival of Islam (Nickel 1987, 38). His efforts inspired the neo-Mu'tazilite modernism of Sayyid Ahmad Khan, Shibli's scholasticism, and religious reconstruction in the thought of Muhammad Iqbal (Ahmad 1964, 205; Baljon 1970, 2; Nickel 1987, 1,38; Iqbal 1934, 136). In fact, by attacking the spiritual claim of the sultan, the dogmatism of the ulama, unlawful innovations in Islam, reverence for the saints and the worship of their shrines, and various forms of superstition that had crept into Islamic theology and rituals since the first generation of leaders in Islamic history, Shah Waliallah and Ibn Abd al-Wahhab opened the Pandora's box of rational criticism that expanded the range of permissible expressions in Islamic theology (Rahman 1968, 237–43; Troll 1978, 24–25). They weakened the ideological rigidity of Islamic orthodoxy and gave a religious authenticity to the worldviews of Islamic modernists, enabling the latter to more effectively respond to the biting criticisms of their conservative colleagues. On various occasions, for example, the harbinger of Islamic modernism in India, Sir Sayyid Ahmad Khan, claimed that he was a Wahhabi. Similarly, the prominent leader of the Islamic modernist movement in Egypt, Muhammad Abduh, often expressed sympathy for Abd al-Wahhab's religious views (Troll 1978, 57).

SECULAR SPIRITUALITY AND ISLAMIC MODERNISM

Between the decline of these movements and the rise of religious fundamentalism in the second half of the twentieth century, Muslim-majority countries experienced more than a century of social transformation. This transformation involved the decline of the traditional economic system, the development of capitalism, the integration of national economies into international trade relations, the decline of the old and the rise of new social classes, the expansion of modern education and the rise of an educated elite, and the formation of the modern state in massive bureaucratic and military organizations. This transformation was also associated with a change in culture and the diffusion of modern ideologies into Muslim societies—all creating a new context for a group of Muslim intellectual leaders to reflect on the causes of the decline of Muslim countries. Like the reformist fundamentalism of the earlier period, the latter's point of departure was the inability of the Islamic orthodoxy to respond effectively to the problems faced by Muslim communities and prompted a return to the Quran and the fundamentals of the faith.

These intellectual leaders, however, were situated in a political and cultural context that was quite different from that of their predecessors. Progress and civilizational change, being the seminal ideas of the time, had gained considerable currency in the Muslim world in the nineteenth century. News about impressive discoveries by the European sciences was widely disseminated via various journals and newspapers in the Middle East. Articles were published on a variety of subjects ranging from breakthroughs in medicine, technological inventions, literature, and the causes of Western progress and Eastern backwardness to the role of women in society. The inventions of electricity, telephone, phonography and photography had astonished people the world over. These momentous contributions to human progress enhanced the prestige of Western sciences among the educated elite in the Muslim world, stimulating the desire to uncover the secret of Western advancement (Moaddel 2005).

On a more general and abstract level, the idea that the regularities of the temporal world—both social and physical—were governed by causal laws, which could be discovered via human intellectual exertion, contributed to the worldviews of indigenous intellectual leaders. So did also the firm belief in the use of human faculty, in rationalist thinking and experience to attain a comprehensive understanding of the social and natural world, in the employment of modern technology to control nature once and for all, and in effective social engineering to construct more democratic, transparent, and responsive governments as well as egalitarian social relationships. Such epoch-changing, mind-broadening new vistas not only eclipsed religious knowledge, which for many in comparison to science appeared increasingly as nothing short of a set of superstitious beliefs, but was also empowering. Events were no longer manifestations of the will of God to be passively accepted, but were rule-governed happenings that can be explained, predicted, controlled, or manipulated. The comprehensive understandings brought about or anticipated by the modern sciences and the firm belief in humans' ability to control their destiny through progress toward a civilized order constituted the fundamental ingredients of secular spirituality.

While such ideas permeated virtually all Muslim societies, countries that displayed stronger cultural pluralism such as Egypt and India in the second half of the nineteenth century provided a more favorable context for the rise of Islamic modernism. The pluralistic context was characterized by the active presence of such diverse groups as Westernizers connected to different colonial administrations, the followers of the eighteenth-century Enlightenment, and Christian missionaries who were all vying for the intellectual control of Muslim societies. In different manners, these groups were challenging various teachings of the religion of Islam, particularly its view of the role of rational reasoning in religion and science, politics, gender relations and status of women, other religions, and the status of non-Islamic subjects living under its dominions.

These were serious challenges, and the simple assertions that the existing Islamic institutions and practices had deviated from its true path, and that one must return to the fundamentals of the faith, were not adequate; Muslim intellectual leaders needed to detail the sociopolitical and cultural parameters of the true Islam that had also taken into consideration the points raised by its non-Muslim critics. The intellectual dynamism of nineteenth-century Egypt and India was conducive to critical thinking and prompted these thinkers to recognize and resolve shortcomings in the sociopolitical norms of Islam on issues that included the status of rational reasoning in Quranic exegesis, forms of government, the role of religion in politics, the status of non-Muslim subjects, and the status of women. They did so by offering a modernist reading of the Quran and the *hadith*. They resolved that the best way to defend the faith against its detractors and make the *shari'a* once again the guiding principle of the nation was to reconcile Islamic political theory and constitutionalism, acknowledge favorably Western culture and its impressive technological progress and political democracy, advance a feminist exegesis of the Quran in order to defend women's rights, and proscribe a revolutionary method of change in favor of a reformist approach.

In India, Sir Sayyid Ahmad Khan was preoccupied to demonstrate the congruity of Islam with natural theology, Chiragh Ali with legal reforms, Shibli Nu'mani's and Amir Ali with rationalist approach toward historical Islam and hagiographical studies, and Mumtaz Ali with feminist interpretations of the Quran and the norms governing gender relations. Led by Sir Sayyid Ahmad Khan, the Aligarh intellectual movement initiated a new educational program, founded the Aligarh College, and started new publications and periodicals—all to bridge Islam and modern sociopolitical thought. Likewise, in Egypt, Islamic modernism started with Rifa'a al-Tahtawi but gained considerable momentum decades later when al-Afghani organized a circle of Muslim scholars to address the sociopolitical and theological issues facing the faith. It further flourished in Abduh's theological works and Quranic exegesis, in Qasim Amin's reexamination of the status of women in Islam, in Muhammad Farid Wajdi's equation of Islam with civilization, and in Ali Abd al-Raziq's reconsideration of the Islamic conception of authority. Islamic modernism in Iran was not as strong as it was in India or Egypt. The major modernist attempt occurred during the Constitutional Revolution (1905–11), when the ulama were divided between the royalist camp, supporting monarchical absolutism, and those supporting the struggle for constitutional change.

Cultural pluralism was an important factor in the development of Islamic modernism in Egypt and India. Equally important was the presence of a discursive space in the Islamic sociopolitical thought that made it possible for Muslim intellectual leaders to detect and recognize inconsistencies and anomalies in this thought. The recognition of the utility of a constitutional government by a group of the Shi'i ulama, which led them to defend the Constitutional Revolution of 1906, provides a case in point. It demonstrates the significance of this discursive space for the development of a transcendental alternative conception of politics. Given that the country had a relatively low level of economic development compared to that of Egypt, India, and Turkey, and given that its cultural environment was under the control of the Shi'i ulama (hence, a relatively weak cultural pluralism), then how do we explain the religious support for constitutional change? What did prompt a significant section of the ulama to see and appreciate the benefits of constitutionalism over monarchical absolutism for their faith and nation?

While we cannot know the thought processes of the Constitutionalist ulama, we may reasonably speculate that it consisted of a series of logically consistent and interrelated propositions that directed these ulama toward realizing the utility of substituting a constitutional government for monarchical absolutism. For these leaders, the point of departure was recognizing a lack of goodness-of-fit between the dominant Islamic theories of government and the existing political reality in the country. These propositions may be formulated as resolutions:

WHEREAS the ruler's discretionary power has been incorporated in Islamic theory of government (i.e., the reality of secular politics is recognized);

WHEREAS this recognition rested on a differentiated conception of religious and political leadership;

WHEREAS religious authority has been under the control of the ulama and political leadership under the control of the ruler (the sultan or the shah);

WHEREAS this recognition has been contingent on the ruler's willingness to consult with the ulama, protect the faith, and establish security for all Muslims living under his rule;

WHEREAS the secular politics that was represented by the ruling monarch is not only arbitrary and despotic but also ineffective in defending the economic interests of Muslims and the territorial integrity of the country;

THEREFORE, BE IT RESOLVED that it is beneficial for Islam and Muslims to substitute a despotic government for a constitutional one.

Fixing their gaze not on Western intervention in their country but on the imposing presence of an ineffectual monarch, the Constitutionalist ulama brought an Islamic rationale to bear in support of establishing a constitutional government. Furthermore, it should be noted that nineteenth-century Iran experienced a much lower level of economic development and a much smaller impact of globalization or colonialism than such other Muslim-majority countries as Algeria, Egypt, Lebanon, or Turkey. Therefore, it would be inadequate to attribute the outbreak of the

Constitutional Revolution to such oft-cited sociological factors as commercialization, development of social classes and class conflict, international rivalries or defeats in wars, and economic crisis. Against the
background of the relative absence or weakness of these factors, the rise
of Shi'i modernism in the early twentieth century may be attributed, in
part, to the presence of a favorable discursive space in Shi'i political
thought. This discursive opening had prompted the ulama to recognize a
tension in Shi'i political theory and to resolve this tension in constitutional terms. That is, it is proposed that the receptivity of the ulama for
constitutionalism was an outcome of the presence of a discursive space in
their cognitive structure that enabled them to articulate a distinctly
Islamic argument for the utility of a parliamentary system. More specifically, they could easily remove the element of the Shah's discretionary
power in their political thinking and insert in its stead a constitutional
principle, while at the same time arguing that the political alternative
they were proposing was closer to the true Islam than the current despotic
system. As a prominent leader of the 1906 Constitutional Revolution,
Sayyid Muhammad Tabataba'ie stated:

> I have not seen constitutionalism, but according to what I have heard, and
> been told by those who had visited the constitutional countries, constitu-
> tionalism will bring security and prosperity to the country (cited in Adamiyat
> 1976, 193).

A much more effective defense of constitutionalism was advanced by
Ayatollah Na'ini. A despotic regime, according to Na'ini, displayed three
negative aspects from a religious viewpoint. It had usurped the authority
of God and hence had committed an injustice against Him. It had
oppressed the imam by usurping His authority. Finally, it was based on the
oppression of the people. A constitutional government, on the other
hand, was free of the first and third kinds of oppression. It had usurped
only the authority of the imam. Thus, there was no doubt that a constitutional government was far superior to a despotic one. His political exposé
was also to refute the anti-constitutionalist discourse developed by prominent Shaikh Fazulallah Nuri, who had mobilized his followers in support
of monarchical absolutism (Hairi 1977).

It is important to note that insofar as the problem was the establishment of modern political order, the modernist ulama, and Muslim intellectual leaders in general, were willing to consider liberal politics to be far
superior to a despotic system of government that had dominated the
Islamic world hitherto. To be sure, they wanted the political order to be

Islamic. Their Islamicity, nonetheless, was rather civilizational and cultural, not strictly religious. For example, to make Islam adaptable to the conditions of modern life, Indian modernist Chiragh Ali (1988, xxvii) made a distinction between Muhammadan revealed law of the Quran and the Muhammadan common law that had been developed in the course of Muslim history. He argued that "The several chapters of the Common Law, as those on political Institutes, Slavery, Concubinage, Marriage, Divorce, and the Disabilities of non-Moslem fellow-subjects are to be remodeled and re-written in accordance with the strict interpretations of the Koran." He thus removed these laws from the level of religion (i.e., sacred laws to be discovered via exegesis) and placed them within the category of the secular (laws that were manmade). Similarly, Abduh made a distinction between acts directed toward the worship of God (*ibadat*) and those directed toward other men and life in the world (*mu'amalat*). He maintained that there was a systematic difference between the teaching of revelation in regard to the one and the other. While Islam laid down specific rules about worship, it contained only general principles about relations with other men, leaving it to men to apply them to all the circumstances of life (Hourani 1983, 148–149).

Islamic modernism was not confined to Egypt, India, and Iran. In fact, it constituted a dominant religious and intellectual force in the Muslim world that attracted large followings in many other Muslim-majority countries, including Algeria and Indonesia.

SACRED SPIRITUALITY AND ISLAMIC FUNDAMENTALISM

The rise of such secular revolutionary ideologies as liberalism, different forms of nationalism, and socialism among the publics in the twentieth-century Middle East that shaped different modalities of politics was predicated on the premise of technological development, prosperity, a responsive government, and human empowerment. It was first territorial nationalism and liberalism that shaped political action. Then perceived as wanting, these ideologies gave way through military coups to pan-Arab nationalism in several major Arab countries and to monarchy-centered nationalism in Iran in the fifties through the sixties. *Pari passu* with the rise of pan-Arab nationalism in Egypt was the emergence and growth of the Society of Muslim Brothers in the 1930s and 1940s. In many other Arab countries, radical Islamism emerged following the decline of pan-Arab nationalism. And in Iran, it developed in reaction to the Shah's land reform program and cultural policies in the 1960s and 1970s.

It would be difficult to identify one set of factors that commonly explains the decline of liberal nationalism in the Middle East. In Algeria, for example, it was the French failure to make peace with the moderate leaders of the liberation movement that contributed to the decline of liberalism and to the radicalization of anti-colonial struggle, leading to the Algerian war of independence in 1954–1962 (Ruedy 1992). In Egypt and Syria, the inability of the politicians coming from landowning-merchant or industrialist families to promote economic development and control the military, as well as the identification of the national government and the parliament with the particularistic interests of these classes, eroded the universalistic appeal of parliamentary politics (Gershoni and Jankowski 1995; Khoury 1987; Moaddel 2005). In Iran, the U.S.-British engineered coup in 1953 overthrew the democratically-elected premiership of Mohammad Mosaddiq and abruptly ended the national-liberal episode. The continued and steady support of the dictatorial monarch by Western governments delegitimized pro-Western liberal politics, contributing to the decline of liberalism and the rise of anti-Western cultural movements in the sixties and the seventies (Moaddel 1993). The Arab nationalist regimes failed to create a unified Arab state. T heir performance was far removed from the political ideals projected by this nationalist ideology since the ruling military junta failed to create a prosperous and empowering society. Moreover, instead of realizing Arab unity, Arab nationalism in power progressively degenerated into despotism. The property of politics under these regimes faded to such an extent that their identities became synonymous with the personal whims of their ruthless dictators, who had in effect created what Saad Eddin Ibrahim aptly described as al-Jumlikiyya (Republican Monarchy). And indeed, in regimes existing in places like Egypt, Iraq, Libya, Syria, and Yemen, the dictator's son was groomed for or successfully installed as the president of the "republic".

Why should the decline of territorial nationalism, liberalism, and pan-Arab nationalism as well as the different modalities of politics that were shaped by these ideologies contribute to the rise of religious fundamentalism and political Islam? While it has been argued that the discourse of twentieth-century fundamentalism in the Middle East was shaped, as it were, in oppositional relations to the secularist ideology of the authoritarian regimes (Moaddel 2005), we may also interpret the shift from secular to religious ideologies as a reflection of a broader change in the sources people sought for spiritual fulfillment. We may recall that the social conditions in the second half of the nineteenth-century Middle Eastern societies had given rise to a new vista that optimistically forecasted the future of these societies as scientifically organized, technologically accomplished, and socio-politically democratic. Nonetheless, political development in the region in the twentieth century portrayed a picture that appeared hopelessly disappointing to indigenous intellectual leaders.

The liberal-nationalist governments that came to power in different Middle Eastern countries between the 1920s and 1940s were dominated by the selfish members of dominant classes, a factor that contributed to their downfall. The rulers who came to power via military coups in the second half of the century were not only as self-serving but also much more brutal in dealing with their own people, political dissidents in particular, and bolder in social-engineering. For intellectual leaders, the political scene was thus a duality between the powerless and destitute masses on the one hand and the all-powerful dictator on the other; Gamal Abdul Nasser in Egypt, Houari Boumedienne in Algeria, Hafiz al-Assad in Syria, Saddam Hossein in Iraq, and Muhammad Reza Shah in Iran. For seekers of spirituality, these rulers had bestowed upon themselves Godly power. Only the wrath of God could empower and mobilize the faithful against them and their international allies.

Here we focus on Egypt and Iran in order to illuminate our point that the rise of religious activism was not just a reaction to secularism but rather a reflection of the decline of secular spirituality and the rise of the sacred. The shift was not indicative of the revival of cultural traditionalism or the reassertion of Islamic orthodoxy. In fact, religious fundamentalism was shaped by discourses and an organizational style of modernity. The orthodox ulama and traditionalists had difficulties going beyond the discursive framework of their educational upbringings in order to more effectively challenge modernity. The case of the ill-fated royalist Shaikh Fazlulah Nuri who attempted to defend monarchical absolutism by resorting to the discredited Islamic theory of government during the Iranian Constitutional Revolution is a prime example. The fundamentalists, on the other hand, displayed an impressive skill in "discursive literacy—that is, the ability to read and write non-formulaic text" to use Mann's (1992, 141) famous phrase. Even though there were considerable cross-national variations in such skills among religious fundamentalists, this literacy provided the possibility to engage in debates over the issues that were also the concerns of other and opposing cultural movements in society. On a religious-cum-intellectual level, the fundamentalists were thus subject to and in fact influenced by the moderating influences of the forces of intellectual markets.

However, these movements were affected, we shall argue, by factors that were quite different from, if not the opposite of, the ones that gave rise to

Islamic modernism. In the second half of the twentieth century, the seekers of sacred spirituality faced a *monolithic* cultural context imposed from
above by the secular authoritarian interventionist state. State authoritarianism narrowed down the discursive space that was necessary for critical
reflection, while state secularist policies heightened the perception that
the faith was under attack, giving rise to the condition of *besieged spirituality*. Under uncompromising state power, the outcome was an increasing
radicalization of the Islamic movements. This radicalization eventually
produced a degenerate militant Islam and suicide terrorism in the form of
al-Qaeda or state-sponsored violence by the Islamic regime in Iran.

Egypt

Islamic fundamentalism in the twentieth century first emerged in Egypt
in the late 1920s in the form of the Society of the Muslim Brothers. The
radicalization of a section of this movement occurred in the second half
of the twentieth century. A host of sociological factors contributed to the
impressive expansion of the Muslim Brothers in the 1930s and 1940s.
Among these factors were the economic bust of the 1930s following
the boom of the 1920s, the decline of the Wafd nationalist ruling party, and
a deepening crisis of legitimacy of Egyptian parliament given its domination by wealthy landowners, merchants, and industrialists. Hasan al-Banna's skillful leadership might have also enhanced the Brothers' success. He
borrowed from modern ideologies, including Fascism and Communism—
even though he was staunchly anti-Communist—and dexterously repli-
cated the organizational model and proselytizing style of the missionaries,
who had been active in Egypt since the first quarter of the nineteenth century, while at the same time expressing concerns to the king about their
activities in Egypt (Mitchell 1969; Banna 1978; Lia 1998; Moaddel 2005).

These factors, nonetheless, are not adequate to explain the distinctly
religious nature of the Muslim Brothers. Furthermore, because its leadership and the educated Egyptians who later joined the movement were not
part of the organized religious institutions in the country, the emergence
of the movement cannot be considered a conservative reaction to liberalism and secular politics. The Brothers even displayed critical attitudes
toward the ulama and al-Azhar. The latter, they believed, had failed in its
role as the guardians of a living and dynamic Islam, and had not been
vigorous enough in resisting encroachment on the Islamic preserve by
foreign ideas and values (Mitchell 1969, 212).

To be sure, the Brothers' Islamic project did not go far beyond generalities: "the insistence on: (1) Islam as a total system, complete unto itself, and the final arbiter of life in all its categories; (2) an Islam formulated from and based on its two primary sources, the revelation in the Qur'an and the wisdom of the Prophet in the Sunna; and (3) and Islam applicable to all times and to all places" (Mitchell 1969, 14). Notwithstanding that these hardly constituted new religious ideas, the novel aspect of the Brothers' religious movement was the adoption of modern organizational style. This style reflected a combination of such diverse elements as "a Salafiyya message, a Sunni way, a Sufi truth, a political organization, an athletic group, a cultural-educational union, an economic company, and a social idea" (ibid). This is not a minor development in the country's religious movement. These features in fact fit very well with the profile of the seekers of spirituality described subsequently, as the organizational style of the Muslim Brothers appears to have provided a comforting, reassuring, and empowering environment for its members in a modern context.

Far from reflecting traditionalism, the religiosity of the movement was provoked by the secularism of the nationalist parties and intellectual leaders as well as the secularist policies implemented by the state. The objective of this type of secularism was not simply limited to the formation of a modern and ideologically-neutral state in order to reflect the universal interests of the public (Moaddel 2002). On the contrary, Egyptian (and Iranian) secularism appeared as a totalizing discourse—a master narrative and an all-encompassing set of ideas about society and history. Its key feature was an overly critical orientation toward religion. Subscribing to a Europe-centered secularist project, nationalist policy makers narrowed the cultural and social spheres of religious institutions: they rewrote history to fit their nationalist conception of the past and to overlook the Islamic period, glorified pre-Islamic kingship and ancient history, reformed educational institutions to undermine the influence of religion, imposed feminism from above, and attacked religion and religious rituals in terms of Western standards (Moaddel 1993, 2002, 2005). Vatikiotis (1980, 306–307) has aptly summarized the attitudes Egyptian liberal nationalists had toward religion and religious institutions:

> This brand of liberal, secular rationalism constituted a far more dangerous attack upon Islam and its tradition. Salama Musa, Ismail Mazhar and Husayn [Hussein] Fawzi did not equivocate over the proclamation of Man as the hero of modern civilization; over the assertion that law must be manmade if it is to be dynamic and creative. Nor did they hesitate in introducing a socio-economic interpretation of history, culture and politics. Above all,

they proclaimed Western civilization as the highest stage of man's spiritual and material development; declared Islamic civilization and culture dead and useless; and advocated the adoption of Western civilization and culture without reservations as the only way for the advancement of their country. ... Moreover, unlike the *literati,* their secular humanism and commitment to the application of science to the study of society were so strong as to lead them to an attack on Islamic reformers. Thus to them al-Afghani was an "ignorant reactionary." Evolution, science and a positivist philosophy constituted the formula which they advocated for the advancement of Egypt.

Therefore, the objective of the secularist intellectual leaders and policy makers was not simply to form a national state to organize the mundane affairs of Egyptians. For them, it was also to create a new system of meaning to expand Egypt's historical horizon beyond the Islamic period, on the one hand, and establish an affinity with the Western culture on the other. One of Egypt's most prominent intellectual leaders of this period, Taha Hussein (1954 [1938]), claimed that Egypt and Europe had shared a common intellectual heritage since the time of the Pharaohs and that Egypt was a Western, not an Eastern, nation.

In opposition to these policies, Hasan al-Banna blamed Egypt's problems squarely on secular nationalist parties like the Wafd and Liberal Constitutionalists as well as the state's educational and cultural policies. In his commentaries on the state of the country and the problems that Egypt was facing, he repeatedly attacked secular policies, including:

> the disputed control of Egypt between the Wafd and Liberal Constitutionalist parties, and the vociferous political debating, with the consequence of 'disunity', which followed in the wake of the revolution of 1919; the post-war 'orientations to apostasy and nihilism' which were engulfing the Muslim world; the attacks on tradition and orthodoxy—emboldened by the 'Kemalist revolt' in Turkey—which were organized into a movement for the 'intellectual and social emancipation' of Egypt; the 'non-Islamic' currents in the newly reorganized Egyptian University, whose inspiration seemed to be the notion that 'the University could not be a lay university unless it revolted against religion and fought the social tradition which derived from it'; the secularist and libertarian 'literary and social salons', societies, and parties; and 'the books, newspapers, and magazines' which propagated those ideas whose sole goal was 'the weakening of the influence of religion (cited in Mitchell 1969, 4).

In fighting back against the secularist onslaught on religion, al-Banna attempted to reassert the significance of the social and spiritual function of Islam for Egypt. In a 1943 message, al-Banna displayed alarmist attitudes, warning his followers that Egyptians may not able to appreciate the ideas of their movement, because they are "unknown to many people," that "the official ulama will consider [them]... strange," and that "the government will obstruct you" and "retrain you." Then he assured his followers that "God has promised that he will assist you," because "you are a new soul in the heart of the nation" and "a new light... to destroy the darkness of materialism." The following passage, reported at some length, best reflects the alarmist attitudes and besieged mentality that al-Banna conveyed to his followers:

> I would like to avow to you frankly that your message is yet unknown to many people, and that when they know it and recognize its purposes, they will meet it with the severest opposition and the cruelest enmity. You will then be obliged to face numerous hardships and obstructions. Only then will you have begun to march on the road of the bearers of missions.... The common people's ignorance of the reality of Islam will stand in your way. You will discover that the people of religion and the official 'ulama' will consider your understanding of Islam a strange thing and deny your struggle on its behalf. Your chiefs and leaders, as well as people of rank and title, will envy you. One government after another will obstruct you, and each of them will attempt to hinder your activity and block your progress.
>
> All the oppressors will exert ever effort to restrain you and to extinguish the light of your message. They will win the help of weak governments and weak morals....
>
> This will lead you to the stage of trial, wherein you will be imprisoned, detained, and banished; your property will be confiscated, your special activities stopped, and your homes searched. Indeed, your period of trial may last long.... But God has promised that he will assist those who struggle and do good.... Are you resolved, my brothers, to be the defenders of God?
>
> Ye Muslim Brothers, listen: I have tried with these words to place your message before you. Perhaps we may have a critical period of time during which we will be separated from one another. In this case, I will not be able to talk or write to you. Therefore, I advise you to study them when you can, and gather around them, for each word carries several meanings.
>
> My Brothers: you are not a benevolent society, nor a political party, nor a local organization having limited purposes. Rather, you are a new soul in the heart of this nation to give it life by means of the Qur'an; you are a new light which shines to destroy the darkness of materialism through knowing God; and you are the strong voice which rises to recall the message of the Prophet.... You should feel yourselves the bearers of the burden which all others have refused (cited in Mitchell 1969, 29–30).

At the outset, the Society of Muslim Brothers was a moderate group and expressed little interest to realize their ideal Islamic order through engaging in revolutionary activities against the constitutional monarchy. In fact, it enjoyed a good relationship with the monarch. Further, the Muslim Brothers attempted to promote their religious objectives through participation in parliamentary politics. Their participatory approach, however, faced considerable obstacles. They were first blocked by the nationalist government, and when later allowed to take part in the elections, the sure success of some of their candidates in the June 1945 elections was denied as a result of electoral fraud. Finally, the Society was dissolved by the government in 1948, and al-Banna was assassinated in 1949. Such undemocratic action undermined the legitimacy of the parliamentary system in Egypt. As one prominent member of the Muslim Brothers claimed, the upper class monopolized the government, and the people were compelled to choose the parliament from among their oppressors: the landlord commanded the votes of his tenants; and the lord of finance those of his debtors. All the elections since 1923 were spurious (Mitchell 1969, 219).

The 1952 military coup, while ending the era of constitutional monarchy in Egypt, did not produce a friendlier environment for the Muslim Brothers. The radicalization of a section of the movement that clashed with the new military regime, and a failed assassination attempt on Jamal Abdul Nassir, the country's new dictator, resulted in a new and more severe crackdown on them in 1954 than they had ever experienced since their founding in 1928. However, the totalitarianism of the post-coup pan-Arab nationalist regime contributed to the radicalization of the Islamic movement in the country. One of the most effective spokespeople of the new radical Islamic trend was Sayyid Qutb (1906–66)—a secular intellectual-turned Islamic activist. Qutb did not simply criticize the secularism of the state; he questioned the very Islamic nature of the existing order. For him, Egypt was a throwback to the pre-Islamic conditions in Arabia where people lived under the state of ignorance (*jahiliyya*). By implication, it was thus incumbent on the faithful to rebel against it.

A literature major from Cairo University, Sayyid Qutb became a modernist literary critic. Until the late thirties he was associated with Abbas Mahmud al-Aqqad. At that time, he "distinguished himself as an outspoken partisan of the new school of poetry, especially the views advanced by al-Aqqad, a leader of the Diwan group whose writings and theories appear to have been greatly influenced by English writers, such as Hazlitt, Coleridge, Macaulay, Mill and Darwin" (Musallam 1983, 78–79). During the formative years of his intellectual career, he was influenced by liberal nationalism, believing in such secular ideas as the separation of religion and literature, which he expressed forcefully in his writings in the 1930s (Musallam 1983, 251–252). He was also a member of the Wafd party until the mid-forties. Disenchanted, he resigned from the party and started writing against the British and the monarchy. He joined the Muslim

Brothers in 1950 and rose quickly in the Brothers' organizational hierarchy in 1952 (Al-Ghazali 2006, xx–xxi).

The state's exclusionary policies and the imposition of a monolithic pan-Arab national-socialist discourse on Egyptian society further amplified Sayyid Qutb's extremism. The assassination of al-Banna during the critical pre-coup period, the victims of the 1954 hangings, the appalling conditions of Tura Prison in Cairo's southern suburbs (where most of the leaders of the Muslim Brothers were held), the extensive use of physical and psychological torture—all made a deep impression on the thinking of Muslim activists. Such inhumane treatment prompted Sayyid Qutb to question the Islamic credentials of the regime, characterizing the existing order as a state of *jahiliyya* (ignorance of divine guidance), a throwback to the state of ignorance that characterized pre-Islamic order in Arabia. In all likelihood, Qutb had little knowledge of the state of affairs in the pre-Islamic era to demonstrate its identity with the conditions in Egypt in the fifties. As the passage below shows, his religious argumentation was rather rested on a trick of definition—*jahiliyya* as a state of affairs. Since the existing affairs are un-Islamic, then it must be similar to pre-Islamic Arabia:

> Jahiliaya signifies the domination (*hakimiyya*) of man over man, or rather the subservience to man rather than to Allah. It denotes rejection of the divinity of God and the adulation of mortals. In this sense, jahiliyya is not just a specific historical period (referring to the era preceding the advent of Islam), but a state of affairs. Such a state of human affairs existed in the past, exists today, and may exist in the future, taking the form of jahiliyya, that mirror-image and sworn enemy of Islam. In any time and place human beings face that clear-cut choice: either to observe the Law of Allah in its entirety, or to apply laws laid down by man of one sort or another. In the latter case, they are in a state of jahiliyya. Man is at the crossroads and that is the choice: Islam or jahiliyya. Modern-style jahiliyya in the industrialized societies of Europe and America is essentially similar to the old-time jahiliyya in pagan and nomadic Arabia. For in both systems, man is under the domination of man rather than of Allah (Sivan 1985, 23–24).

A more extremist and militant version of Islamic fundamentalism was offered by Muhammad Abd al-Salam Faraj (1954–1982). In his view, the current rulers of Muslim countries were all apostates and should be overthrown in order to establish a truly Islamic state (Akhavi 1992, 94–95). Faraj was the head of the Cairo branch of the *Tanzim al-Jihad* (Jihad Organization) that assassinated President Anwar al-Sadat. Building on Sayyid Qutb's argument, Faraj proclaimed that "the establishment of an Islamic State is an obligation for the Muslims.... The laws by which the

Muslims are ruled today are the laws of Unbelief; they are actually codes of law that were made by infidels who then subjected the Muslims to these (codes)..." (cited in Sageman 2004, 15). These ideas formed the foundations of such radical organizations as *Jamaat Islamiyyat*, Islamic Jihad, and al-Qaeda, justifying the use of terror for the realization of their ostensibly Islamic objectives.

Iran

As was mentioned in the previous chapter, despite economically being much less developed than Egypt or Turkey, Iran was the first to experience a revolutionary movement for constitutional change in 1905–1911. However, like their Egyptian counterparts in the late nineteenth century, the Iranian clerics who supported the Constitutional Revolution were favorably predisposed toward liberalism and parliamentary politics. Like Egypt also, religious fundamentalism was a response to the secular ideology and policies of the authoritarian state. The two countries, however, differ in terms of the relationship between religious fundamentalism and other secular oppositional forces. In Egypt, the opposition to parliamentary politics and secularism emerged in the liberal period and was clearly branched out in organization and discourse into pan-Arab nationalism and the religious fundamentalism of the Muslim Brothers. Pan-Arab nationalists sought the empowerment, security, and prosperity of Egyptians in Arab unity and the formation of a unified Arab state. The Muslim Brothers, on the other hand, stressed that such objectives are achievable only if Egyptians returned to their Islamic roots and form pan-Islamic unity. In Iran, by contrast, the people who were spearheading the sixties' intellectual shift toward religion and the new leaders of the secular opposition to the Shah's cultural and economic policies were not organizationally and discursively as separate. Some of the key figures in these trends—e.g., Samad Behrangi, Jalal Ale Ahmad, and Ali Shari'ati—did not belong to any political organization. The major trends within the opposition movement were united by their common hostilities to the state's cultural policies that were perceived as an attempt at complete Westernization.

The remarkable overlap between the secular and religious oppositional trends was partly an unintended consequence of the state's effective repression of its pre-coup (1953) nemeses. It managed to practically destroy the Tudeh [Communist] party and effectively disrupt the political organizations of the liberal National Front after its leader, Premier Mosaddiq, was overthrown in 1953 and was put under house arrest for life.

What is more, the Shah's implementation of a land-reform program, feminism from above, and other reform initiatives put the left on the defensive. At the same time, he succeeded in portraying the religious oppositions (who instigated the 1963 riots in Tehran and other major cities, where hundreds of demonstrators were killed by the security forces) to his policies as reactionary supporters of feudal landowners (Abrahamian 1982; Moaddel 1993). Thus, if the Shah could not be readily attacked as someone impervious to the needs of the impoverished masses, he was vulnerable on the cultural ground: his uniformitarian Westernization policies, which were only supported by a small section of the population. In this process, the "orthodox" left that attacked the Shah's economic policies lost grounds and the cultural left instead gained the upper hand. The more the Shah tried to further secularize and create uniformity within the very monolithic culture he had imposed on the society, the stronger the credibility of the cultural criticisms of these policies. The most noteworthy examples of such policies were the dissolution of the existing official political parties and the establishment of a single-party political system, the celebration of the 2,500 years of monarchy, and the changing of the Islamic calendar to a vaguely-defined monarchical calendar. He insisted that all Iranians to submit to the principles of the Shah-people revolution, the single party system, and official royal history. As a result, both religious and secular opposition groups united in displaying alarmist attitudes that were driven not just by the notion that the religion was under siege but that the country's entire culture was besieged as well. The cultural critique of the Shah commonly advanced by the religious and secular opposition, and the alarmist attitudes it generated, blurred the line demarking these two groups. The extremism of such religious fundamentalists as Ayatollah Khomeini was well hidden under the cover of anti-Western cultural opposition or somewhat "protected" by the Shah's authoritarianism that would not allow free and objective assessments of the ayatollah's anti-authoritarian pretensions, fanatical understanding of religion, and archaic theory of government.

To be sure, a vehemently anti-secular religious extremism was founded in 1946 by young cleric Navvab Safavi (1924–1955) and the *Fedaiyan-i Islam* (Devotees of Islam). The group rested on the belief that Iranian society had strayed from the right path and needed to be purified. It called for the strict applications of Islamic law and demanded prohibitions of alcohol, tobacco, opium, films, gambling, wearing of foreign clothing, the enforcement of amputation of hands of thieves, the veiling of women, and an elimination from school curricula of all non-Muslim subjects such as

music (Abrahamian 1982, 259). To this end, the Fedaiyan launched a campaign of terror against the politicians and intellectuals it considered
responsible for corrupting the individuals in society. One of its most
heinous acts was the assassination of Ahmad Kasravi, Iran's prominent
historian and noted social critic, in 1946. The group was suppressed and
Safavi executed in 1955. The organization, however, survived, and its members became staunched supporters of Ayatollah Khomeini and his religious government. It was reorganized by Sadiqh Khalkhali, the infamous
ruthless judge who after the 1979 revolution executed thousands of the
supporters of the former regime and political dissidents.

Nonetheless, the Fedaiyan was a minor trend in the religious movement. Although the group's religious agitation might have been in
response to the secular trend that was expanding since the Constitutional
Revolution was reinforced by the state's secular policies and onslaught on
the religious establishment, during the liberal national episode (1941–
1953) the ulama enjoyed considerable political and cultural influence and
thus showed little interest in supporting religious extremism. The religious establishment turned against the Shah when he definitively broke
with the clerics and launched a series of reforms at the center of which
was a land reform program in the early 1960s. The shift in the intellectual
climate in the sixties brought new oppositional force to the fore.

Reflecting this shift were the ideas of three lay intellectuals. One was
Samad Behrangi (1939–1968), a secular Marxist popular revolutionary
writer and teacher, who attacked not simply the state's economic policies
but was also critical of the Shah's educational policies for being titled
toward emulating the American educational model. These policies, which
he called Americatoxication (*Amrikazadegi*), were at variance with the
reality of Iran's educational needs (Hanson 1983). The other was Jalal Al-e
Ahmad (1923–1969), a secular social activist and member of the Tudeh
Party, who initially discounted religion as a force in the opposition.
Disenchanted, he left the party, departed from Marxism, and turned to
religion. Ale-Ahmad used the term Westoxication (*Ghabzadegi*), although
not originally his (Hanson 1983, 8), as the corner stone of his critique of
the state cultural policies. According to him,

> The West, in its dealing with us, not only struggled against this Islamic total-
> ity (in the case of the bloody instigation of Shi'ism of Safavid times, in the
> creation of friction between us and the Ottomans, in promoting the Baha'i
> activities in the middle of the Qajar period, in crushing of the Ottomans
> after the first World War, and finally in the opposition to the Shi'ite clergy
> during the Constitutional Revolution and afterward...), but it also tried to as

quickly as possible [to] tear part that unity which was fragmented from within and which only appeared whole on the surface.... The stopping of Ottoman artillery outside the gates of Vienna in the nineteenth [sic] century was the end of a prolonged event that had begun in 732 in Spain... [Andalusia]. How can we view these twelve centuries of struggle and competition between East and West [as] anything but a struggle between Islam and Christianity? (Cited in Moaddel 1993, 148–149)

Finally, the third is Ali Shari'ati (1933–1977), a lay religious activist who rejected both liberalism and Marxism as Western fallacies. Among the three, Shari'ati, a devote Shi'i, more clearly addresses broader spiritual issues, the failure of other ideologies in empowering humans, and hence the significance of his Islamic alternative.

> Humanity arrived at liberalism, and took democracy in place of theocracy as its key to liberation. It was snared by crude capitalism, in which democracy proved as much a delusion as theocracy....
>   The desire for equality, for liberation from this dizzying whirl of personal avarice, so horrifying accelerated by the machine, led humanity into a revolt that resulted in communism. This communism, however, simply represents the same fanatical and frightening power as the Medieval Church, only without God. It has its popes, but they rule not in the name of the Lord but in the name of the proletariat (Shari'ati 1980, 92).

Much of Ale-Ahmad's and Shari'ati's statements were factually incorrect, permeated with the spirit of intolerance, and thus outright irresponsible. In the authoritarian political environment of the period, however, there was little opportunity for a free exchange of ideas and intellectual debates over issues. As a result, the truth or falsity of their ideas remained unchecked. Nonetheless, the works of these intellectuals were much more acceptable to educated Iranians than those suggested by the Fedaiyan or Ayatollah Khomeini. These individuals probably provided an effective cover for the much more extremist and intolerant religious views espoused by Ayatollah Khomeini. In fact, there was substantial overlap between the views of *Fedaiyan-i Islam* and Khomeini. Like the Fedaiyan, the Ayatollah was not tolerant of the people who were critical of the faith. Kasravi, who was assassinated by the Fedaiyan, was the subject of Khomeini's criticism in his first book, *Kashf al Asrar* (Key to the Secrets). He proclaimed that "all those who criticized Islam" are *mahdur ad-damm* (their blood must be shed), an assertion that amounted to a death sentence for Kasravi (Taheri 1986, 98, 101). Over four decades later, as the absolutist ruler of Iran's religious regime, Khomeini exhibited the same intolerant attitudes toward the dissenting views, as he ordered the mass execution of several thousand political prisoners in 1988 (Wikipedia 2012) and issued a fatwa to kill

Salmon Rushdie for writing *The Satanic Verses* a year later. Furthermore,
almost all of the policies—forced veiling, gender segregation, banning
Western music, the Islamization of the judiciary and the imposition of
Islamic penal code, Islamic economic, and educational policies—were
remarkably consistent with the religious views of the Fedaiyan. In addition, Khomeini devised a system of Islamic government in which the
jurisprudent enjoys absolute power. This absolutism was to ensure that
the state would remain firmly under clerical control (Taheri 1986; Moaddel
1993; 2005; Moin 2000).

The rise of Islamic fundamentalism was not confined to Egypt and Iran.
Broadly similar movements also emerged with varied strength in almost
all Muslim-majority countries in the 1980s and 1990s, including Algeria,
Afghanistan, Indonesia, Morocco, Pakistan, Tunisia, and Turkey. Posed
within a broader historical context of the rise and demise of a sequence of
religious and secular movements, this fact may reflect a significant shift in
the spiritual sources people consider desirable in satisfying their needs for
meaning, security, and empowerment. This shift appears to entail a departure from the secular sources and toward the sacred.

Conclusions: Common Fundamentalist Themes

In this chapter, we used the concept of the cycle of spirituality and attempted
to show the historical trajectory of a sacred-secular-sacred cyclical pattern
of spirituality in the Muslim world between the eighteenth and twentieth
centuries. We followed Weber by arguing that human spiritual needs are
not reducible to economic or political interests. We suggested that a more
comprehensive understanding of religious movements is provided by considering such movements within this cycle. Then, we illustrated how various intellectual, sociological, and psychological factors strengthened or
weakened the movements of religious response to secularism.

Using this framework, we began by suggesting that the reformist fundamentalist religious movements that were spearheaded by the religious
thought of Shah Waliallah in India and Muhammad Ibn Abdul Wahhab in
the Arabian peninsula reflected the rise of a new spirituality in Islam. We
speculated that these thinkers' mindsets were shaped by the sociopolitical
conditions of the process of the decline of the Muslim empires in the eighteenth century. The militant religious fundamentalist movements that followed the views of Shah Waliallah or Muhammad Ibn Abdul Wahhab were
defeated by the mid-nineteenth century. By attacking the orthodoxy of the

ulama and the prerogatives of the sultan, these movements, however, provided a favorable discursive context for the rise of Islamic modernism decades later. The second part of the nineteenth century also signified the rise of secular spirituality supported by new scientific discoveries, impressive technological innovation, and worldwide economic expansion. Various secular ideologies resting on such seminal ideas as progress and civilization attracted a large following in Muslim-majority countries. Secular spirituality, however, started to decline in the second half of the twentieth century, and once again the Muslim-majority countries began to experience the rise of sacred spirituality and religious fundamentalism.

Within this broader historical context, we pointed to a series of intellectual, sociological, and psychological factors that had strengthened or weakened these diverse religious movements. On the intellectual level, we used the concept of discursive space, which was introduced in the previous chapter as the interstitial capacity or opening in the structure of thought that enables intellectual leaders to recognize, discuss, and in some cases reconcile inconsistencies in their thought. By the structure of thought, we meant the currently existing discursive framework employed by intellectual leaders to address the issues and obstacles they faced. In pointing to a discursive space in Shi'i political thought during the Constitutional Revolution, we meant the presence of such a space in the specific Shi'i political theory that was en vogue in that period, not in the theory of political sovereignty suggested in the early Islamic conception of caliphate. The discursive space in the nineteenth-century Shi'i (as well as Sunni) political thought was provided, we argued, by (1) the recognition of the reality of secular politics (i.e., acceptance of the sultan's or ruler's discretionary power), and (2) the ineffectiveness of the ruler to provide for the security and economic prosperity of the nation.

This space functioned as a mechanism that connected the Shi'i theory of government to the utility of setting up a constitutional system in the country. Other examples of favorable discursive space would be the freedom to criticize the principles of Islamic jurisprudence, including the notion that the gate of independent reasoning (*ijtihad*) was closed or the freedom to rethink the status of non-Muslims living under Muslim rules. As a result, Muslim intellectual leaders were cognitively prepared to revise Islamic sociopolitical thought in light of the standards of modernity—hence, the development of such moderate and transcendental religious movements as Islamic modernism. Other key concepts shaping religious movements were the nature of the intellectual environment—whether pluralistic or monolithic—and the extent of the state's intervention in this environment. We argued that the pluralistic intellectual environment in the last quarter of the nineteenth century and the limited state's intervention in the cultural affairs further expanded the discursive space. We then discussed the rise of sacred spirituality in the twentieth century. This change coincided with the decline in social support for parliamentary politics on, the one hand, and the rise of a secular authoritarian interventionist state, on the other. The monolithic cultural environment imposed by the state on society contracted the discourse space and contributed to the rise of religious fundamentalism. Among the psychological factors that rein forced this process was the perception of besieged spirituality that promoted alarmist attitudes toward the outsiders and the presumed enemy of the faith.

Finally, as discussed elsewhere (e.g., Moaddel 2005), Islamic fundamentalism constitutes a discourse—a set of distinctive positions on historically significant issues. This discourse is produced or invoked by Muslim intellectual leaders as they attempted to resolve the sociopolitical and cultural issues they faced. To elaborate, the differences between Islamic modernist and fundamentalist thinkers are based on whether they advance an individualistic or collectivist conception of the role of religion in society and politics, believe in laissez-faire capitalism or support extensive state interventions in the economy, reconcile Islamic political theory and liberal democracy or reject the latter in favor of the unity between religion and politics in an absolutist Islamic government, acknowledge the progress of Western culture in science and social organization or discard this culture as decadent, question gender inequality and display a more egalitarian attitude toward women or support patriarchal values and gender hierarchization, and whether they tend to engage in moderate or militant political activities, respectively.

Islamic fundamentalist movements, in both the Shi'i and Sunni variants, have exhibited characteristics that are consistent with the attitudinal features of religious fundamentalism advanced in this book. That is, they rest on the principles that: (a) the society has strayed from the true path, (b) extant religious institutions are ill-equipped to restore social order on the fundamentals of the religion, (c) the faith must be purified from un-Islamic elements and folkways, (d) the movement is the carrier of the true religion (religious exclusivism), and (e) other cultural currents have deviated from the faith and must therefore be suppressed (intolerance). These movements have also disregarded the historical developments in the faith and stressed returning to the teachings and practices of the founders of the faith.

CHAPTER TWO

STATE STRUCTURE, RELIGION, SECT, AND ETHNICITY

As discussed in chapter one, fundamentalist beliefs and attitudes are thought to vary both at the macro social context and the micro individual levels. Pertinent features of the social context for the analysis of cross-national variation in religious fundamentalism are a country's history, state structure, and culture as well as its religious and ethnic profile. Relevant characteristics that are proposed to correlate with fundamentalism include individual respondents' perceptions of besieged spirituality, sources of epistemic authority, religiosity, and the bases of identity, social-psychological factors, and demographics.

This chapter describes cross-national differences in the social context between Egypt, Iran, Lebanon, and Saudi Arabia. We focus first on these countries' attributes of state structures, religious profiles, and historical experiences. Second, these four countries are compared in terms of religions, which include Christianity and Islam, and religious sects, including the Druze, Sunni, and Shi'i Muslims; and Maronite, Catholic, and Orthodox Christians. Finally, in terms of language-based ethnicity, Egyptians, Saudis, and Lebanese are Arabs. Among Iranians, the major ethnic or language groups being considered are Persians, Azeri-Turks, Gilakis, Lurs, and Kurds.

As discussed in the introductory chapter, we assess how religious fundamentalism is enhanced by such features of the national context as the state authoritarianism, elite homogeneity, state religiosity, lack of historical experience of secular nationalism, and having a unified religion. Regarding the influence of religion and ethnicity, we do not suggest that there are *a priori* reasons that are inherent to a particular religion, either Islam or Christianity, or to a particular ethnic group that would cause it to be more or less fundamentalist prone. Nonetheless, within the context of lived religion, we consider religious diversity, in-group solidarity, the degree of centralization of religious authority, and the extent to which a religious sect is allied with a co-religious state (i.e., a Shi'i sect with Iran's Islamic regime or a Sunni sect with Saudi Arabia) beyond its border, or whether a religious sect lives under a religious regime, may shape the fundamentalist orientations of its followers. We thus propose that, for example, given their historical secular experience and international ties, Lebanese Christians, the Maronites in particular, would have a weaker fundamentalist orientation than would Muslims. On the other hand, religious fundamentalism among the Lebanese Shi'is and Sunnis may be tied to the strength of their favorable attitudes toward Iran and Saudi Arabia, respectively. We also suggest that religious fundamentalism among ethnic groups depends on whether they have used religious or secular oppositional framing in dealing with or demanding autonomy from their national governments.

THE STATE, HISTORICAL EXPERIENCE AND RELIGIOUS PROFILE

Egypt

The Egyptian state under former President Hosni Mubarak was secular and authoritarian, with a massive bureaucratic structure. These attributes of the state, an outcome of post 1952 coup and subsequent political development, set the stage for the radicalization of the Islamic movement and reproduction of religious extremism in the country. To underscore the significance of political conditioning of radical Islamism, we should note that it took well over one hundred years, between the Napoleon invasion (1798–1801) and the nationalist revolution of 1919, for liberal nationalism to constitute the dominant (hegemonic) discourse in Egypt's sociopolitical and cultural landscape. The invasion ended the rule of the Mamluks and set the stage for the rise of a new dynastic power (1805–1953). Muhammad Ali (r. 1805–1848), the founder of the new dynasty, was an ambitious young officer who had come to Egypt in 1801 with the Albanian detachment in the Turkish expeditionary force against the French. Under his rule, a modern state emerged with massive bureaucratic and military organizations. Muhammad Ali first brought under this firm control the guilds, village administration, and religious institutions. He established a system of state monopolies and a modern industry, dispossessed the Mamluks, changed the system of land ownership and taxation, and encouraged foreign merchants to settle in Egypt. His principle interest being the creation of a strong military, he sent students to Europe to learn about military technology and translate technical works.

These students, however, gained knowledge of things other than the military; they also learned about Western culture and modern principles of social organization. Under his successors, major ground works were laid down for the development of culture: the School of Languages and

Administration and Dar al-Ulum teachers college were founded, the press was expanded, and Syrian and Lebanese émigrés to Egypt formed a critical mass that played a prominent role in modern cultural activities (Vatikiotis 1980, 101–107, 183–188). These changes contributed to the rise of Egyptian identity, territorial nationalism, liberal values, and a new set of claim-makers who demanded liberation from foreign domination and a constitutional government. All these culminated in revolutionary movements against the British, first in the Urabi rebellion (1879–1882) and then successfully in the 1919 nationalist revolution (Heworth-Dune 1968; Marsot 1977; Vatikiotis 1980; Hourani 1983).

As noted in chapter one, the nineteenth century marked the rise of secular spirituality. Indigenous intellectual leaders predominantly accepted the century's seminal ideas of progress and civilization, which were thought to be possible through human intellectual exertions and the reorganization of social life based on the principles of national sovereignty and political equality. Even though the country came under the British colonial rule in 1882, which was obviously both foreign and non-Islamic, the dominant oppositional trends were framed by secular ideologies, not Islam. Muslim intellectual leaders were also impressed by secular ideas and made persistent efforts to reconcile Islamic sociopolitical teachings with the ideology of the eighteenth-century Enlightenment. Islamic modernists, however, warned against transplanting European laws and customs to Egypt because such laws had no roots in the country's culture or relevance to the daily lives of Egyptians. Instead, they believed that modern Islam was capable of adapting to the conditions of modernity. For them, modern Islam was in fact the only appropriate basis for legislation that would transcend the existing social divisions between those Egyptians who favored change toward modernity and the traditionalists who resisted it.

The significance of the national secular state in shaping the production of religious oppositional discourse must be underscored because neither Egypt nor such other countries as Algeria, Iraq, Lebanon, and Syria experienced religious fundamentalist movements while they were directly ruled by either the British or French in the nineteenth and the first half of the twentieth century. Religious fundamentalism in the Middle East emerged within the context of the post-independence nationalist government and in opposition to its cultural policies (Moaddel 2005). In Egypt, in particular, the secular policies of the nationalist government shaped the religious discourse of the Muslim Brothers. The overthrow of the parliamentary system and the dissolution of secular political parties by the pan-Arab nationalist military officers right after the 1952 coup did not expand political freedom for the Muslim Brothers, despite their cooperation with the military leaders of the coup. On the contrary, the period of cooperation was short-lived, and sporadic armed conflicts between the military and the Brothers' secret apparatus resulted in the army launching a severe crackdown on the movement in 1954.

With the suppression of the Muslim Brothers, political power was not only monopolized by the military, but this power was also personalized. The period of collective leadership under the first president, Muhammad Naguib (1953–1954) ended and by 1954 Nassir emerged as "a native *sultan*" (Vatikiotis 1980, 417). The 1964 constitution declared Egypt as the Arab Socialist Republic, a part of the Arab nation, and Islamic (ibid., p. 401). The elections of Nassir as the president of the republic were all based on plebiscite, rather than electoral competition. Nassir was glorified as the hero and spokesperson of Arab nationalism, a true defender of the Arab people against all forms of imperialistic aggression. The military regime also expanded its popular basis by mobilizing the middle and lower classes against landowners, merchants, and industrialists as well as foreign interests. It launched a land reform program and nationalized foreign concerns, private industries, and the banking system. As a result, the state bureaucracy swelled from 350,000 employees in 1952 to approximately 1.2 million by 1970. The number of ministries increased from fifteen to twenty-eight during the same period. Public corporations, an artifact of the nationalization of foreign firms and socialist law, jumped from one in 1957, the first year of the expropriations, to 38 in 1963. By 1970, their number had reached 46 (Ayubi 1980, 241, 243).

The military regime's populist policies and nationalization of private enterprises were intended to empower the working people and enhance their security and economic prosperity under the banner of the pan-Arab nationalist ideology. These policies to some extent were successful in mobilizing the public against both the liberals and the Muslim Brothers. However, the regime's shocking defeat in the 1967 six-day war with Israel that undermined the credibility of the pan-Arab ideology, the open-door economic policies of Muhammad Anwar al-Sadat (1918–1981) who succeeded Nassir after his death in 1970, and the restoration of a multi-party system benefited religious extremist groups for whom the state appeared an all-powerful body that acted against the religion and the Islamic public with impunity.

By the early 1970s, they had developed alarmist attitudes not only toward the policies of the secular state but secular intellectuals as well.

They felt the need to mobilize the forces of God against the "Godless" ruler, whom they labeled the Pharaoh. As a result, the country fell into a cycle of violence by extremist groups against the government and the government against its enemies. In 1974, a group calling itself the Islamic Liberation Organization plotted to launch a coup by trying to kill President Sadat and his top officials. In 1976, a puritan group was formed that ran afoul of the law and, in 1977, kidnapped and killed a former minister. In 1981, a religious extremist army officer assassinated President Sadat. In the 1980s, religious extremists launched a campaign of terror against Egyptian officials, secular writers, and the Copts. In 1995, there was an attempt on Mubarak's life in Addis Ababa, Ethiopia, and in 1997, more than sixty tourists were massacred in Luxor. While state authoritarianism contributed to the radicalization of political Islam, religious extremism reinforced state repression, in particular after the assassination of President Sadat (Hinnebusch 1981; Bellin 2004). Political violence by religious extremist groups provided the necessary justification for the state's repressive policies and a considerable expansion in the security apparatus (Magnarella 1999).

As noted previously, although we cannot determine the extent to which public beliefs and attitudes were linked to such historical movements, we report here the extent of support for religious fundamentalism among Egyptian youth. In particular, we assess how fundamentalist beliefs and attitudes are linked to the perception of besieged spirituality and other sociological factors that have shaped the religious fundamentalist movement, as we suggested, historically.

Iran

Iran represents an intriguing case regarding the relationship between religion and broader social conditions. The puzzle was posed by the contrasting cases of the Constitutional Revolution of 1905–1911 and the 1979 revolution. Iran remained a backward country throughout the nineteenth century. Its subsistence economy, rudimentary conditions of commerce and industry improved little. To be sure, after about a century of tumultuous conditions—between the disintegration of the Safavid Empire in the eighteenth century and the suppression of the Babi religious movement in the middle of the nineteenth centuries—a stable political order was formed in the second half of the nineteenth century. This process, coupled with the increasing contact with the Western and neighboring countries that was facilitated by the introduction of new means of communication and transportation, contributed to improvements in the economic conditions, on the one hand, and to changes in cultural relations, on the other.

Yet the modernity of the Constitutional Revolution cannot be derived from the dynamic of Iran's domestic economic production, which remained imposingly subsistent, or from changes in class and group relations. Certainly, sociological factors are important in providing a partial explanation of the revolution and the aftermath: an ailing monarch and generally the state's weakness, division among the ulama, the rise of modern intellectuals, the mobilization of the merchants, and economic difficulties. Nonetheless, the fact that a large number of Muslim activists and theologians found that parliamentary democracy, which was outside the Islamic modality of politics, was beneficial to Islam and the country's prosperity may in fact be attributed to the significance secularism and secular spirituality had gained in their perception.

Despite being its ideal motivating force, parliamentary democracy was the first casualty of the revolution. Post-revolutionary political development favored political consolidation, power centralization, and national integration in a secularist direction, but not democracy. Chief among these factors was a lack of consensus between the religious and secular intellectuals on the limits to ulama formal political power and the freedom of people's representatives in the parliament to legislate as they saw fit. Among the royalist ulama, Sheikh Fazlullah Nuri was one of the most prominent critics of the Constitutional Revolution, which he characterized as a great sedition (*fitneh*). He conspired with anti-Constitutionalist Crown Prince Muhammad Ali Shah of Qajar who, aided by Russian troops, staged a coup against the parliament in 1907. While the Constitutionalists defeated them and Nuri was captured, tried, and executed, dissention and conflict among different political forces continued.

In addition, other factors hampered the country's political stability under a constitutional regime, including the rise of movements for autonomy by ethnic minorities and the restiveness of the dominated classes, the peasantry in particular, during the decades following the Constitutional Revolution. To make matters worse, in August 1907, where struggles for constitutional change intensely raged, an Anglo-Russian agreement divided the country into a Russian zone in the North and a British zone in the South. Out of the need to defeat these movements and ensure political stability, the modern state was formed. The chief state builder of modern Iran was Reza Khan, a Russian-trained Cossack brigade commander, who staged a coup in 1921, got control of the dysfunctional government, stabilized the country, ended the Qajar era, and founded the Pahlavi dynasty (Abrahamian 1982; Afary 1996).

Reza Shah was an efficient secular dictator. He reformed the judiciary, undermined the power and influence of the religious institutions, and expanded modern education. In 1941, however, he was overthrown by the Allies out of their concern with the increasing German influence in the country and the Shah's sympathy for Nazi Germany. Reza Shah's son, Muhammad Reza, was installed as the new king. However, the breakdown of the state's authoritarianism resulted in the inauguration of a liberal-nationalist episode that lasted more than a decade, but was abruptly ended by a U.S.-British engineered military coup in 1953 that restored the Shah's absolutist power. The post-coup marked the rise of a secular ideological interventionist state in the country, where the state was actively involved in transforming the economy and culture. It implemented a series of reforms, the most important of which was a land reform in the early 1960s. In its economic program, the regime opted to promote large industrial firms in alliance with international capital, a policy that antagonized the bazaar merchants. On the cultural front, it promoted secular education and culture, glorified pre-Islamic culture and ancient history, and changed the Islamic calendar to a monarchical one (Abrahamian 1982; Moaddel 1993).

It has been argued that the authoritarian state, by disorganizing and disrupting collectivities within the civil society, channeled oppositional politics among Iranians through religion (Moaddel 1993). This argument is, however, inadequate on two grounds. First, the state also successfully disrupted and destroyed religious collectivities in the 1920s through the 1970s. Furthermore, it is not clear how the state's destruction of secular opposition directed people to depart from secularism and orient their mental and emotional energy toward the religious subject. One thing may be clear: Life under an authoritarian regime is stressful for those seeking security, happiness, and empowerment. A secular authoritarian regime may undermine secularism insofar as it manages to make the secular forms of resistance ineffective. Thus, it appears that the National Front and the Tudeh Party declined not because the ideal of political democracy or economic equality became less attractive to their followers and potential recruits. It was because their style of politics, organizational form, and discourses became ill equipped to deal with an authoritarian monarch. The Western support for the Shah undermined pro-Western liberalism of the National Front. The pro-Moscow orientation of the Tudeh party, in addition to its political failure to predict and resist the 1953 coup, questioned the credibility of the party as an independent champion of the downtrodden. The alternative leftist groups, like the Fedayeen guerillas, while recognizing the overwhelming power of the state repressive apparatus, stopped at simply conceptualizing state-masses power relations in terms of an oppositional binary of the state's absolute power, on one extreme, and the masses' absolute powerlessness, on the other. They came short of formulating a new mobilizing discourse and organizational style that would project a revolutionary future where these masses are empowered, prosperous, and secure. To make matters worse, their tactics of resorting to armed violence and terrorism were too extreme to attract very many followers beyond the circles of university students.

Besides, under the declining influence of secular ideology, the "martyrdom" operations of a group of godless Communists were no match for the increasing power of Muslim activists who were mobilizing the forces of God against the Shah, whom they labeled *taghout* (the Quranic term for false god). This process was further reinforced by the fact that the Shah had broken ties with the religious establishment, and thus a section of the ulama had turned against him beginning in the early 1960s. To be sure, there were many other sociological and psychological factors that contributed to the making of the Iranian Revolution of 1979. Nonetheless, our contention is that the rise of a new cycle of spirituality constituted an important element of change. It thus introduces an additional factor into the explanation of the revolution, which also accounts for the contrast between the Constitutional Revolution (1905–1911) and the 1979 Revolution.

At any rate, the Iranian Revolution of 1979 brought the clerics to power, but failed to empower Iranians and create a secure and prosperous country. Instead, the pro-Western monarchical absolutism was replaced with a religious absolutism of the Shi'i cleric that proved to be much more brutal than the prior regime in repressing the dissidents and the treatment of political prisoners. Nonetheless, unlike the previous regime as well as the authoritarian regimes in Egypt and Saudi Arabia, where the power block appeared homogeneous and was under the control of a single individual, the structure of power relations was heterogeneous and the members of political elite diverse. This heterogeneity was in fact an outcome of the post-revolutionary contention for power, which resulted in the creation of contradictory structures.

There were, for example, the offices of the leader of the Islamic revolution (the so-called supreme leader) and the Constitutional Guardians, on the one hand, and the office of the president and the parliament, on the other. Likewise, there were somewhat heterogeneous armed forces of the revolutionary guards that were created by the ruling clerics, and the army that was the legacy of the old regime. Finally, there were religious over-seers in various governmental offices who were directly controlled by the clerical leader of the revolution and the secular members of the civil ser-vice who were attached to the office of the president. The Islamic Republic, despite being an ideological regime, was thus an amalgam of religion and secularism. While the office of the religious leader claimed that it derived its sovereignty from the *sharia*, the presidency and the parliament derived theirs from the electorate. Further, from the perspective of historical Shi'ism, the monolithic religious structure imposed from above after the revolution has been at variance with the pluralistic historical tradition of the Shi'i ulama.

Saudi Arabia

Saudi Arabia is a religious authoritarian state. In fact, the kingdom owes its foundation to a solid alliance between tribal warriors and the Wahhabi religious movement. In a span of thirty years (1902–32), this alliance brought Abd al-Aziz Ibn Abd al-Rahman al-Saudi, the founder of the king-dom, to power and enabled him to incorporate the disparate regions of the Hijaz, Asir, Hasa, and Najd into the unified Kingdom of Saudi Arabia in 1932. Al-Saudi succeeded because the two key ingredients of state-building—military prowess and ideology—were present and worked in his favor. On the one hand, the *ikhwan* tribal warriors who supported him were effective in defeating al-Saudi's rivals. On the other hand, Wahhabis provided zealous *mutawwa'a* volunteers who played a crucial role in legiti-mizing his rule, domesticating the population in the name of Islam and enforcing Saudi authority under the guise of a vigorous program to con-vert the people of Arabia to "true" Islam (al-Rasheed 2002, 23; Okruhlik 2002, 23).

The kingdom, however, experienced considerable changes since its for-mation. These included the state's bureaucratic expansion, occupational differentiation, settlement of tribes, urbanization, demographic growth, and impressive rate of economic development, which was made possible by the availability of vast petrodollars. Despite these changes, and given the imposing presence of religious authoritarianism, the rise of militant religious fundamentalism in the kingdom since the late 1970s is enigmatic for both theoretical and historical reasons. Considering Stark and col-leagues' (Stark and Bainbridge 1985; Stark and Finke 2000) premises that religious pluralism is the natural state of religion and that religious monopolies would lower the quality of religious services, one would expect that religion in the kingdom to play only a weak oppositional role in politics. Further, from a historical perspective, given that liberalism and anti-clerical secularism emerged in late nineteenth-century Iran and Syria in oppositional relations to the existing monarch-ulama alliance, one would expect the rise of liberal oppositional movements in the kingdom rather than religious fundamentalism.

For sure, there have been liberal and reformist groups in the country that called for a substantial restructuring of the social and political life, the establishment of a constitutional monarchy, elected institutions, separation of powers, freedom of expression, egalitarian gender relations, and recognition of the rights of the Shi'i minority (Dekmejian 1994, 8; 2003, 400–413; al-Rasheed 1998, 121–138; ICG 2004,10; Okruhlik 2002, 26). Gender inequality is particularly marked in Saudi society. Women were discouraged or barred from participation in the labor force. Although they constitute 58% of the university graduates in Saudi Arabia, women make up only 5% of the labor force (Cordesman 2003, 178–179–). Nonetheless, the Islamic awakening (al-Sahwa al-Islamiyya) movements appear to be much more powerful than the liberal and reformists movements. The religious fundamentalism of these movements is reflected in their call for the reorganization of the kingdom based on the virtuous state of the early Islamic period.

Nonetheless, we argue that there may not be a need to either amend the theory or rethink past historical cases without assessing the significance of two major events in 1979 that energized radical Islamism and shifted considerable resources to its favor. One was the outbreak of the Iranian Revolution in February 1979 and the formation of the Islamic regime in Iran. This event demonstrated to Islamic activists across the globe the possibility of successfully overthrowing a powerful secular authoritarian regime and establishing an Islamic government. At the same time, the revolution marked the rise in Shi'i political fortunes, which was not quite a welcome development for the Saudi Sunni perspective. The ruling clerics in Iran scarcely veiled their disapproval, if not categorical rejection, of what they called "Wahhabis" in Saudi Arabia. The other was the Soviet invasion of Afghanistan in 1979 that provided an opportunity for the U.S. and its ally Saudi Arabia to mobilize Muslims against the infidel Communists who invaded a Muslim nation. The arrangement of political forces favoring the rise of religious fundamentalism was further reinforced in Pakistan, where the country was under the rule of General

Zial-ul-Haqq since 1977, who had already launched his Islamization campaign.

Thus, facing Shi'i extremism from Iran, on the one hand, and home-grown Islamic militants led by a certain Juhaiman al-Utaibi, who tried forcibly to take over the sacred mosque in Mecca in 1979 (Okruhlik 2002: 23), on the other hand, the Saudi authorities opted to appease the religious establishment, a policy that inadvertently contributed to the rise of both religious fundamentalism and Islamic extremism. They allocated large sums of money to the religious institutions, increased mosque construction, reinforced the Islamic content of the schools' curricula, and further empowered the religious police. By 1986, more than 16,000 of the kingdom's 100,000 students were enrolled in Islamic studies, and by the early 1990s, one-quarter of all university students were studying in religious institutions (Okruhlik 2003; Prokop 2003: 78). One unintended consequence of these policies was the rise of a new generation of sheikhs and religious instructors who were sympathetic to al-Sahwa, were incensed by the subservience of the official clerics, and denounced the state's failure to live up to Islamic values (ICG 2004: 7; Dekmejian 1994: 638).

The regime also initiated some reform measures, which after 9/11 were expanded as a result of pressure from abroad. These included the setting up or reconstituting the Shura Council in 1993 (an unelected body appointed by the king to advise the government); the expansion of its membership from sixty to ninety members in 1997; the crown prince's decision to meet with reformers and sponsor three rounds of national dialogue on religion, extremism and women in 2003; and the Council of Ministers' issuance of a decree allowing women to obtain commercial licenses in their own names (Fandy 1999: 140; ICG 2004: 16, 25; Dekmejian 1998; Layish 1987). These reforms, however, do not seem to have thus far considerably expanded the resources for, or transformed the opportunity structure in favor of, the liberal and reformist groups.

It is not clear, however, whether or not the degree to which the revival of religious fundamentalism in Saudi Arabia is supported by the rise in the fundamentalist outlook among the Saudi public. Nor is it clear how minority Islamic sects are affected by these developments. A crucial part of the problem is that Islamic sects are not counted in the kingdom, and 96% of the estimated 24 million people residing in the kingdom are categorized simply as Muslims. In 2006, the Saudi National Security Assessment Project (SNAP), a Riyadth-based think tank, estimated that the Shi'is constituted 7% of the Saudi population.

These estimates, however, contradict the figures given by the Shi'is themselves, who often insisted that they represented as high as 20% of the population (Obaid 2006: 6; Louër 2008: 7). Although some live in the cities of Mecca, Medina, and Riyadh, the majority of the Shi'is are concentrated in the two oases of Qatif and al-Hasa in the kingdom's Eastern Province, which includes Dammam and Al-Khobar, a region that is also home to most of Saudi Arabia's massive oil reserves. Most of these Shi'is are from the "Twelver" branch. A smaller community of around 100,000 Isma'ilis makes its home in Najran near the southern border with Yemen.[1] For theoretical reasons, the present study assesses the differences in religious fundamentalism between the residents of Jeddah and Riyadh, who are almost all Sunnis, and those living in Dammam and Al-Khobar, who have a sizable Shi'i population.

Lebanon

Lebanon provides a remarkable contrast with Egypt, Iran, and Saudi Arabia. This contrast is not simply reflected in the fact that Lebanon is a democratic and pluralistic state, and that the other three countries are not. Its democratic pluralism is also rather unique. The country is certainly unlike Western secular democracies, where religion and politics are separated. It is also far from the religious regimes of the Islamic Republic of Iran or the Kingdom of Saudi Arabia in which religious monopolies purportedly shape the behaviors of the state and orientations of the ruling elite. Rather, it represents an intermeshing of secularism and religion. While religious affiliation is the constitutive feature of political life, national politics is decidedly secular. Claims are made on the national level, demands for change in the inter-confessional relations are rigorously, and occasionally violently, pushed forward, and political alliances are formed in terms of either practical political expediency or the ideal principle of political equality of all Lebanese citizens.

Lebanon's distinctive political synthesis, as will be discussed and empirically assessed in the following chapters, has both attenuated and reinforced religious fundamentalism. This political synthesis, however, is an outcome of the history of different confessions' struggle for empowerment and attainment of political equality. To elaborate, in twentieth-century Egypt and Iran, despite the ulama's endorsements of the

---

[1] See http://www.merip.org/mer/mer237/jones.html, retrieved, October 8, 2010; Jones (2009: 8).

construction of the modern democratic state in the early part of the century, there have been persistent conflicts between religion and secularism that were provocatively started by secular politicians encroaching on the privileges and prerogatives of the religious institutions. In Lebanon, by contrast, there have been little instances of such intense conflicts. Religion constituted the key element of confessional-cum-communal politics for political empowerment within the broader secular framework.

Secularism appears to have played a significant role in providing a discursive vehicle for diverse confessional groups to empower their communities and enhance their national political standing. This process started in the nineteenth century when Lebanon, like the rest of the Arab world, was part of the Ottoman Empire. The formation of Lebanon as a separate political unit was a consequence of the struggle primarily of Lebanese Christian Maronites for independence. Although this was a confession-based movement, the call for the formation of an independent Lebanon was coached in a distinctly secular framework. This call rested on the principle of the equality of all the political voices, which transcended ethnic and religious boundaries in Lebanon (and Syria) and unified diverse sections of the Lebanese population against the Ottoman rule in the nineteenth century.

Contributing to the rise in the political power of Lebanese Christians was the large-scale historical processes that also created modern Lebanon. Chief among these processes were the incorporation of the Middle East into the world capitalist economy, the development of capitalism, the changes in class relations, the decline of the Ottoman Empire, the heightening interventions of the European powers into the affairs of the Middle Eastern societies, the diffusion of modern culture including the ideas of the eighteenth-century Enlightenment into the region, the expansion of modern education, and the rise of an educated elite who were the primary producers and consumers of modern culture in the country (Ma'oz 1968: 1, 4; Petran, 1972: 42–43; Chevallier 1968; Issawi 1966).

One historically significant consequence of these changes was the accumulation of wealth by members of the Christian community (Lapidus, 2002: 598–600; Ma'oz, 1968). In addition, Christians had a numerical majority in the autonomous district of Mount Lebanon under the Ottomans. In 1914, Christians were four-fifths of its estimated population of 400,000 while the rest were Muslims. Among Christians, 60% belonged to the Maronite sect (Yapp 1991: 104–115). Wealth and demography naturally brought resources and power to the Christian community. Nonetheless, these conditions by themselves do not generate the political discourse that would give credence to the claim of political supremacy in an independent Lebanon. A favorable discursive space had to become available for Christian claim-makers to accord themselves this right.

The contour of this discursive space was provided by a broader vision for the formation of an independent Lebanon. The principles underpinning this vision were both universal and secular, and thus provided a unified framework for Christians and Muslims to fight for independence. Included among these principles were the rejection of the Ottoman's religious authoritarian rule, the admission of the principle of the equality of all religious faiths, the recognition of the right of different people to a political community, the organization of such a community in terms of principles other than religion (i.e., language), and a conception of history that went far beyond the Islamic period.

The Ottomans themselves contributed to the rise of this alternative secular vision by relaxing the norms of religious inequality under their dominion. The Tanzimat or reforms instituted between 1837 and 1876 expanded the religious and cultural freedoms of the minorities living under the Ottomans' dominion. In particular, such reforms as the *Hatt-i Sherif* (Noble Rescript) of Gülhane in 1839, which recognized the right to life, property, honor, and the equality of all religious groups before the law, the *Hatt-i Humayun* (Imperial Rescript) in 1856, which guaranteed the right of non-Muslims to serve in the army, and a new civil code, the *Mejelle*, issued in 1870, changed the very concept of Ottoman society and challenged the notion of Muslim supremacy (Lapidus 2002; Maoz 1968: 21–22, 27). The establishment of modern educational institutions in Lebanon reinforced the process of change and institutionalized the emerging cultural movements. In Beirut province (*wilayat*), the number of state schools alone rose from 153 in 1886 to 359 in 1914, a growth rate faster than that of the population. Beirut's influential Ottoman Islamic College became the training ground for a whole generation of pre-war Beirut Arabists (Khalidi 1991). Prominent Christian intellectuals—including Butrus al-Bustani, Adib Ishaq, Ibrahim al-Yaziji, Ahmad Faris al-Shidya, Faris Nimr, Ya'qub Sarruf, and Shahin Makarius—all promoted Arabist and secular political egalitarian ideas.

Thus, the demand for independence from the Ottomans that was first voiced by young educated Christian Arabs was in fact in harmony with the liberal trend that existed in other parts of the empire and beyond (Antonius, 1946: 79–80; Zeine, 1981: 55). Given that Christians continued to play a leading role in the independence movement, they naturally developed a stronger sense of the ownership of modern Lebanon in the making. The rise in Christian political fortune continued in the first part of the twentieth century and was institutionalized in the First Republic, when under the French Mandate the Lebanese Republic was formed in 1926 and then gained independence in 1943. The 1926 unwritten pact guaranteed that executive power was entrusted to the President of the Republic who exercises this full power with the assistance of Ministers.

The French, as well as members of economically dominant classes who had vested interests beyond Mount Lebanon, supported the formation of Greater Lebanon. The geographic expansion of the new country increased the proportion of its Muslim (both Shi'i and Sunni) population. This change complicated the politics of Lebanon by setting the stage for conflict between the country's three major religious confessions, the Christians, Shi'is, and Sunnis. Considering that there have already been political and cultural rivalries between the Sunnis and Christians (even while they were united in their demand for reform under the Ottoman and later for the independence of their country), this expansion gained an added significance.

First, the nationalism of Christian intellectuals was not to the liking of Muslim Arabs. They were in fact outraged "at the spectacle of Christians assuming the air of masters of Arab learning. Attacks on the pretensions of Yaziji and other Christian literary men were popular" (Dawn, 1994: 132). There were also political differences between the two groups. After the independence, Christians, Maronites in particular, promoted Lebanese nationalism and closer relationships with Western countries. A radical nationalist trend among Christians represented by the Phalange (formed by Maronite Pierre Gemayel in 1936) defended this view. The Sunni Muslims, on the other hand, promoted the idea of pan-Arabism and closer alliance with the rest of the Arab world. In general, Beirut had been a cauldron of liberal thinking and pluralism as other groups, including Greek Orthodox, Catholics, and Sunni individuals from Sidon and Tripoli served to buffer the tensions between extreme Maronites and Sunni activists (Salibi 1988).

The same secular principles of political equality and the right of a people to form their own sovereign political community that shaped the Christians' struggle for independence and enabled them to acquire substantial political capital were also used by the Sunnis to demand a greater share of political power. The Maronites managed to dominate Lebanon because they were at the forefront of the liberation struggle against the Ottomans. Christians' political supremacy and the country's independence went hand in hand, but when these Christians were perceived by other confession-based power contenders as being too cozy with the Western power and Israel, they lost considerable political capital. In fact, during the 15-year civil war, it is likely that those fighting the Christians did not view Christians as fellow Lebanese so much as collaborators with "imperialism" and the "Zionist enemy"—attitudes that were also promoted by Palestinians and the former Soviet Union. These attitudes might have also been supported by the Sunnis, who felt that they were being marginalized as a result of the 1982 Israeli invasion of Lebanon (Traboulsi 2007).

The civil war weakened the Christians, and its conclusion in 1990 resulted in a shift in power relation in favor of the Sunnis and the inauguration of the Second Republic. This change was institutionalized after in Taif, Saudi Arabia, an agreement was reached to end the civil war. The Taif Agreement, also known as the "National Reconciliation Accord," ratified on November 4, 1989, significantly reduced the power of the Maronite-controlled presidency, which lost the prerogative to appoint the prime minister or the refusal to promulgate laws in favor of the power of the Sunni-controlled premiership. The Accord also declared Lebanon as an Arab country (Mühlbacher 2009).

Likewise, the rise in Shi'i power in recent decades conforms to this same dynamic of political capital accumulation, which appeared to have worked hitherto so well for the Christians and Sunnis. Predominantly residing in southern Lebanon, the Shi'is were the most populous religious confession in the country, but their political power was far below this numerical superiority. By the mid-1970s, that is, more than a quarter century since independence, they were still denied access to leadership positions in the political system. Sunni representation among the ruling elite was heavy; even the much smaller Druze sect held more than its share of influence. The Shi'is were naturally not content with the Taif agreement, which had institutionalized Maronite-Sunni partnership in controlling political power without highlighting any remarkable role for the Shi'is (Saseen 1990: 69).

To be effective in the political arena, the Shi'is needed to overcome political fragmentation, as they tended to follow such groups as the Baathists, the Communists, and the Nasserites. However, political unity, while important, by itself would be no guarantee of success in effectuating a shift in political power in favor of one's group. Equally important is how this unity is used to defend and protect such a shared common good as the integrity and national sovereignty of the country as a whole. To this end, the Shi'is first experimented with a peaceful approach, when in 1974 prominent Shi'i cleric Musa Sadr founded the Movement of the Dispossessed (*Harakat al-Mahroumeen*). As the 1975–1990 civil war approached, it spawned a militia called the Lebanese Resistance Movement (*Afwaj al-Moqawama al-Lubnanieh*), popularly known by the acronym AMAL. Sadr was a man of peace. He established a political forum designed to communicate his community's concerns to the state. He worked hard to build dialogue between Muslims and Christians and promote a unity government (Ajami 1986).

The peace dividend under the condition of uncompromising Israeli force that had occupied part of the country in its war with Palestinian guerrilla fighters was too small to provide much political capital for Sadr and his followers. Furthermore, backed by the Islamic regime in Tehran, another Shi'i political group, the Hezbollah, was formed whose approach was dramatically different from that of Sadr and AMAL (Ranstrop 1977; Saseen 1990). Either by political calculation or genuine desire to defend the country against the Israeli intrusion, the Hezbollah had discovered the route to an impeccable political success. It managed to accomplish something that the neighboring Arab regimes had failed to achieve; fighting the Israeli forces so consistently that the invader was exasperated and decided to leave the country.

The rise of the Hezbollah follows a pattern similar to that of other militant group formation and nationalist claim-makers. Christians advanced their own conception of nationalist ownership of Lebanon as an independent country within the context of struggle against the Ottomans, aided by European power. This struggle rested on the principles that were also shared by non-Christian members of Lebanese political community. The Sunnis also reasserted their power within the context of struggle against foreign rule and against Christian approach toward the West and Israel, which were perceived as the enemy by the Lebanese Sunnis and Shi'is. In a parallel fashion, the Hezbollah-led Shi'i political ascendency and later claim for a larger share of political power transpired within the context of struggle against Israeli occupation of southern Lebanon. Hezbollah's impressive success in forcing Israelis out of Lebanon underpinned their popularity in the region, their accumulation of substantial political capital, and their attempt to use that capital for more direct influence in the country's politics.

Although the national politics has been governed by secular discourse and although confessional groups have advanced their interests in making reference to political equality and patriotism, the dynamics of inter-confessional competitions and political rivalries contributed to in-group solidarity and the weakening of inter-confessional trust. We propose that in-group solidarity, by promoting confessional centralism and intolerance of outsiders, is in turn linked to religious fundamentalism. Further, inter-group rivalries have also provided opportunities for regional and international powers to interfere in Lebanon's internal politics by supporting and patronizing one religious confession against another. Insofar as the foreign interfering power appeared to have a religious agenda, it may tend to reinforce religious fundamentalism among the confession group with which it has historical affinity. We thus propose that religious fundamentalism among the Shi'is is positively linked to their favorable attitudes toward the Islamic Republic of Iran and among the Sunnis to their favorable attitudes toward the Kingdom of Saudi Arabia.

NATIONAL STATE AND COMPARATIVE INFLUENCES ON FUNDAMENTALISM

We now turn to examining how the five factors that reflect these countries' state structures, cultural orientations and religious profiles may be expected to strengthen (+) or weaken (–) the countries' overall levels of religious fundamentalism:

a. Authoritarianism: Lebanon is democratic (–), while Egypt, Iran, and Kingdom of Saudi Arabia (KSA) have authoritarian regimes (+)
b. Homogeneity of the ruling elite: Lebanon and Iran have heterogeneous ruling elites (–), while the ruling elites in Egypt and Saudi Arabia are homogeneous (+)
c. State culture and religiosity: Egypt and Lebanon have secular regimes (–), while Iran and Saudi Arabia have religious regimes (+)
d. Religious structure: Egypt, Iran, and Saudi Arabia are religiously unified (+), while Lebanon is religiously non-unified and pluralistic (–)
e. Lack of historical experiences of secularism and nationalism: Egypt, Iran, and Lebanon have had experienced secularism and nationalism in the past (–), while Saudi Arabia has not (+)

These characteristics of the state and religious profile of the four countries are summarized in Table 2.1. As this table shows, the factors promoting aggregate fundamentalism on this level are all absent in Lebanon and present in Saudi Arabia, while Egypt and Iran fall between these two extremes. That is, in terms of variation in state authoritarianism, elite structure, state religiosity, secular experience, and the country's religious

Table 2.1. Predicted levels of fundamentalism.

Country	Authoritarianism	Elite Homogeneity	State Religiosity	No Secular Experience	Unified Religion	Total Influence
Lebanon	−	−	−	−	−	− 5
Egypt	+	+	−	−	+	+ 1
Iran	+	−	+	−	+	+ 1
KSA	+	+	+	+	+	+ 5

profile, Egypt and Iran have the same number of positive and negative scores. Lebanon and Saudi Arabia, on the other hand, are on the opposite poles. All the factors that are said to contribute to religious fundamentalism are weak in Lebanon, while they are strong in Saudi Arabia. Based on this analysis we thus propose that on the aggregated level, the fundamentalist orientation would be the lowest among the Lebanese, highest among the Saudis, and intermediate and at approximately the same level among Egyptians and Iranians.

Contrasting Religions and Religious Sects

It is often cited that the key difference between Christianity and Islam is that Islam does not recognize the separation of religion and politics and that these two functions are united in the Islamic conception of authority. The presumed unity between religious and political leadership in Islam is then considered the reason for the rise and persistence of political Islam and religious fundamentalism in contemporary Muslim-majority countries. This interpretation, however, is debatable. In fact, there have been Islamic thinkers who questioned whether there has ever been an Islamic theory of government. For example, Ali Abd al-Raziq (1888–1966) in his *al-Islam wa Usul al-Hukm* (*Islam and the Fundamentals of Authority*, 1925) argued that "if we were to collect all his [Muhammed's] direct teachings on the question of government, we would get little more than a fraction of the principle of law and organization needed for maintaining a state" (Ahmed 1960: 118).

Even if one considers al-Raziq's conclusion controversial and accepts that under the prophet and the four Rashidun caliphs there was in fact a unity of religious and political authority, political developments in post-Rashidun Islam, as was discussed in Chapter One, resulted in the admission of the reality of secular politics by prominent Muslim political theorists-cum-theologians. Furthermore, by instructing Muslim theologians to abide by the methodological principles set by organized religion in both Shi'i and Sunni Islam, the Islamic orthodoxy, despite its conservatism and oft-cited obstructionism, have nonetheless resisted in different historical instances religious fundamentalism. Finally, the rise of Islamic modernist movements also signifies the problematic nature of an explanatory model of fundamentalism in terms of what amounts to be an essentialist reading of Islam's conception of politics.

We start with the premise that there is nothing inherent in the belief system of Islam that prompts its followers to favor fundamentalist beliefs and attitudes more strongly than do Christians, and vice versa. However, we argue that the presence of religious diversity within a religion, the extent of in-group solidarity among the members of a religious confession, and ties with religious or secular entities beyond its national borders may be linked to fundamentalist tendencies among its followers. Using these factors, we assess religious fundamentalism across the two religions, Christianity and Islam, and six religious confessions. These are the Maronites, Orthodox, and Catholics among the Lebanese Christians and the Druze, Shi'is, and Sunnis among Muslims.

Diversity among Lebanese Christians: The Maronites, Orthodox, and Catholics

Despite its small size, religion in Lebanon is diverse in terms of both between faith and within faith variation in religious affiliations. Eighteen religious groups are formally recognized by the Lebanese government: Alawite, Armenian Catholic, Armenian Orthodox, Assyrian Church of the East, Chaldean Catholic, Copts, Druze, Greek Catholic, Greek Orthodox, Isma'ili, Jewish, Maronite, Protestant, Roman Catholic, Sunni, Shi'i, Syriac Catholic, and Syriac Orthodox. These groups have the right to handle family law according to their own courts and traditions. Each of these religious confessions has considerable formal and informal influences on their members. The members of each sect also share extensive historical memory. It thus appears that there is almost a total overlap between ethnicity and religious sect; people who belonged to the same religious confession also form a distinctive ethnic group in the Lebanese context. These confessions are certainly very important in Lebanese politics. It is nonetheless incorrect to assume that they are internally homogeneous groups.

Lebanon is a small country, with an area of 4,035 square miles and a population of four million. About 91% of the Lebanese population lives in urban areas. Exact data on the distribution of the population into different religious confessions are not available. The last national census was taken in 1932, which was almost a decade before Lebanon became an independent country in 1943. Any attempt at taking a new census is considered a potential disturber of the intricate balance of power among different confession-based political groups. Available estimates, however, indicate that 60% of the country's population are Muslims, consisting of Shi'i, Sunni, Druze, Ismaili, Alawite; 39% are Christians, which include Maronite Catholic, Greek Orthodox, Melkite Catholic, Armenian Orthodox, Syrian Catholic, Armenian Catholic, Syrian Orthodox, Roman Catholic, Chaldean, Assyrian, Copt, Protestant; and 1.3% other. They are 95% Arabs, 4% Armenians, and 1% other (CIA 2005: 316). The most recent demographic study conducted by Beirut-based research firm Statistics Lebanon showed that of the total population, there were 28% Sunni, 28% Shi'i, 21.5% Maronite, 8% Greek Orthodox, 5% Druze, and 4% Greek Catholic (http://www.state.gov/g/drl/rls/irf/2009/127352.htm, retrieved March 8, 2010).

Diversity among Christians is higher than it is among Muslims. There are more than twelve Christian sects in Lebanon. As was mentioned earlier, here we focus on the three largest sects because their share in the sample is large enough for statistical analysis: Maronites, Orthodox, and Catholics. The Maronites are the largest Uniate[2] or Syriac[3] Eastern Catholic Churches, with a heritage reaching back to Maron, the Syriac Monk in the early fifth century. The first Maronite Patriarch, John Maron, was elected in the late seventh century. The Maronites established communion with the Roman Catholic Church in 1182. The communion broke thereafter and was formally reestablished in the sixteenth century. In accordance with the terms of the union, the Maronites retained their own rites and canon law and use Arabic and Aramaic[4] in their liturgy as well

---

[2] A Uniate is a Christian of a church adhering to an Eastern rite and discipline but submitting to papal authority (http://www.merriam-webster.com/dictionary/uniate, retrieved March 8, 2010).

[3] Syriac is a literary language based on an eastern Aramaic dialect and used as the literary and liturgical language by several Eastern Christian churches (http://www.merriam-webster.com/dictionary/syriac, retrieved March 12, 2010).

[4] Aramaic is one of the Semitic languages, an important group of languages known almost from the beginning of human history and including also Arabic, Hebrew, Ethiopic, and Akkadian (ancient Babylonian and Assyrian). It is particularly closely related to Hebrew, and was written in a variety of alphabetic scripts. (What is usually called "Hebrew" script is actually an Aramaic script.) (http://cal.huc.edu/aramaic_language.html, retrieved March 12, 2010).

the Karshuni[5] script with old Syriac letters. Being persecuted by other Christians in the late seventh century, they withdrew from the coastal regions and moved into the mountainous areas of Lebanon and Syria. During the Ottoman era (1516–1914) they remained isolated and relatively independent in these areas (Crawford 1955; http://www.country-data .com/cgi-bin/query/r-7970.html, retrieved on March 7, 2010).

Most Maronites have been rural people and are scattered around the country, with a heavy concentration in Mount Lebanon. The urbanized Maronites reside in East Beirut and its suburbs. They have traditionally occupied the highest stratum of the social hierarchy in Lebanon. Leaders of the sect have considered Maronite Christianity as the "foundation of the Lebanese nation." The Maronites have been the leaders of the independence movements from the Ottomans in the nineteenth century and then under the French Mandate (1918–1943). They were also closely associated with the political system of the country after independent in 1943. In pre-Civil War Lebanon, it is estimated that members of this sect held 20% of the leading posts (http://www.country-data.com/cgi-bin/ query/r-7970.html, retrieved on March 7, 2010). Historically, they have had good relationships with the Western world, France and the Vatican in particular. The outbreak of the civil war in 1975 resulted in the formation of closer ties between Israel and the Lebanese Maronite community (Zisser 1995).

The second Christian denomination is the Orthodox, which includes Greek Orthodox, Armenian Orthodox, and Syrian Orthodox. The Orthodox is the second largest Christian group. The followers of this church are present in many parts of Arab countries, and Greek Orthodox Christians have been noted for pan-Arab or pan-Syrian orientations. This religious group has had less affiliation with Western countries than has the Maronites.

Finally, the category of "Catholics" includes Greek Catholics (Melkites), Roman Catholics, Syrian Catholics, Chaldeans, Assyrian Catholics and Copts. The Melkite Greek Catholic Church is an Eastern Catholic *sui juris* particular Church in full union with the Roman Catholic Church. The church's origins lie in the Near East, but currently Melkite Catholics are

---

[5] When Arabic began to be the dominant spoken language in the Fertile Crescent, texts were often written in Arabic with the Syriac script. These writings are usually called *Karshuni* or *Garshuni*. Garshuni is often used today by Neo-Aramaic speakers in written communication such as letters and fliers (http://www.britannica.com/EBchecked/ topic/578972/Syriac-alphabet, retrieved June 23, 2012). See also Hatch (1946).

dispersed, with a worldwide membership of approximately 1.3 million. The Melkite Church has a high degree of ethnic homogeneity, but its patriarch,[6] episcopate, and clergy as well as many of its followers are Arabic, French, English, Portuguese, and Spanish speaking. The church is a product of a schism within the Antiochian Orthodox Church in 1724 triggered when the pro-Western Seraphim Tanas was elected patriarch as Cyril VI in a move, which was seen by the patriarch of Constantinople as a pro-Catholic coup. The Melkite Catholic Church retains its Byzantine roots and liturgical practices similar to those of the Eastern Orthodoxy while maintaining communion with the Catholic Church in Rome (Perry and Melling 1999; Dick 2004; Faulk 2007).

On the macro level, we suggest that religious diversity among Lebanese Christians may weaken in-group solidarity among the members of various Christian confessions. Diversity and lower in-group solidarity coupled with the historical ties of major Christian groups to the secular West have functioned to attenuate religious fundamentalism among Christians.

Islam and Muslim Sects: Druze, Shi'is, and Sunnis

The major Islamic confessions being considered in this book are the Druze, Shi'i, and Sunni. In this study, our focus is on the Druze in Lebanon; the Shi'i in Iran, Lebanon, and Saudi Arabia; and the Sunni in Egypt, Iran, Lebanon, and Saudi Arabia. We depart from any notion that relates religious fundamentalism to doctrinal differences among these religious confessions. Nonetheless, we consider the differences in the structure of religious market, in-group solidarity, the structure of organized religion, and the religious confession's ties with the states beyond the national borders as factors explaining group differences in religious fundamentalism.

The Shi'is versus Sunnis

Between the two major Islamic religious confessions, the Shi'i population is much smaller than the Sunni population. Approximately 10% to 15% of the World's total Muslim population are Shi'is. They are also predominantly concentrated in two countries. The great majority of the followers

---

[6] Patriarch is: (a) any of the bishops of the ancient or Eastern Orthodox sees of Constantinople, Alexandria, Antioch, and Jerusalem or the ancient and Western see of Rome with authority over other bishops; (b) the head of any of various Eastern churches; and (c) a Roman Catholic bishop next in rank to the pope with purely titular or with metropolitan jurisdiction (http://www.merriam-webster.com/dictionary/patriarch, retrieved March 8, 2010).

of Twelver Shi'ism is in Iran and Iraq, where 89% and more than 60% of
their total populations, respectively, are Shi'is. Other countries with a significant percentage of Shi'is are Bahrain (70%), Lebanon (30%); Kuwait
(25%); Pakistan (20%); and Afghanistan (19%). In addition, between 10%
and 15% of the Muslim population of Turkey and of Saudi Arabia is Shi'i,
and approximately 2% of the population of India (CIA 2005; Pew Research
Center 2009: 10).

Given their concentration in Iran and Iraq, we argue, it may be easier to
identify and assess the set of sociological factors that shape Shi'i fundamentalism. The Sunnis, on the other hand, are much larger in terms of
population, comprising at least 85% of the world's 1.5 billion Muslims.
They are also scattered in more countries and occupy a wider geographic
span, from North Africa to East Asia. They are thus exposed to the influences of a broader set of sociopolitical and cultural forces, which may
have varying effects in shaping fundamentalist attitudes and beliefs in different national contexts. While we depart from the notion that one religious confession is more fundamentalist-prone than the other, it has been
argued that the Wahhabi dominated Hanbali School of Islamic jurisprudence in Saudi Arabia has a stronger tendency to support fundamentalism than other schools (e.g., Schwartz 2002). For our present discussion,
however, a key difference between the two sects pertains to the structure
of religious authority. In Shi'ism, this structure has been decentralized,
but in Sunni Islam it has been centralized. Consistent with the theoretical
framework discussed in the introductory chapter, we argue that decentralized structure is less conducive to religious fundamentalism than the
one that is centralized.

The Druze

The literature on the Shi'i and Sunni Islam is extensive. However, there is
not much discussion about the Druze in the literature. For a better understanding of the Druze and their differences with the other Islamic confessions, the narrative below intends to provide some historical background
on the Druze's emergence and belief system. Although a significant group
in Lebanon's politics, the population of the Druze within and outside
Lebanon is much smaller than the other two, the Shi'is or Sunnis.

The Druze originated from Sevener Shi'ism or the Ismaili sect, a small
branch in Shi'ism. They are called Ismailis, after Ismail ibn Jafar, who died
circa 760, the elder brother of the seventh Shi'i imam. His father had
denied him the title of imam because of his intemperance. A group of
Shi'is, however, refused to accept this decision as a sufficient reason for his

being passed over. For them, drinking wine does not prejudice Ismail of infallibility and divine gift of impeccability. For these Shi'is, he thus became the "hidden" Mahdi (Hitti 1967: 442). They continued following his son Muhammad Ibn Isma'il, on through Muhammad's adopted son Abd Allah Ibn Maymun al-Qaddah and a series of imams and hidden imams directly to the Fatimid dynasty (909–1171). The Fatimid formed a heretical caliphate in North Africa, an area including present-day Algeria, Tunisia, Sicily, Egypt, and Syria. The Fatimid rulers traced descent from Muhammad's daughter Fatima (hence Fatimid) via Ismail and thus presented a threat to the political and religious authority of the orthodox Sunni Abbasid caliph. This threat became more significant following the Fatimid conquest of Egypt in 969. The Fatimids founded the city of Cairo (al-Qahira, "the triumphant") and established it as their new capital in 973 (Betts 1988: 6; Makarem 1974; p.11; www.metmuseum.org/toah/hd/fati/hd_fati.htm, retrieved March 3, 2010).

Under the sixth Fatimid caliph and sixteenth Ismaili imam, Abu Ali Mansur Tāriqal-Hakim (called al-Hakim bi Amr Allah, literally "ruler by Allah's command"), the Druze religion was born and flourished (Betts 1988: 7). The new faith was founded by Hamza Ibn Ali Ibn Ahmad, a Persian Ismaili mystic and scholar, who came to Egypt in 1016 and assembled a group of scholars from across the Islamic world to form a new Unitarian movement. The outgrowth of a deity cult was encouraged (at least in its early stages) by Caliph al-Hakim, when a number of Ismaili religious leaders in Cairo began publically to discuss al-Hakim's divinity. Thus, following the caliph's proclamation (sijill) in which he revealed himself to be the manifestation of the deity, Hamza, aided by two disciples—Baha al-Din al-Samuqi and Muhammad al-Darazi—started on the first day of 1017 to pursue missionary work of the new faith throughout the Fatimid empire. Some sources credit al-Darazi with having planted the new religion in the region of southern Lebanon that is regarded as its cradle today, and with having given these converts the name by which they became commonly known (Betts 1988: 10; Momen 1985: 55).

As a result, Druzism spread throughout the empire. It must be recognized that even in its earliest stages Druzism was not merely a sect of Islam but a new religion, which aimed at establishing a new world order. Caliph al-Hakim, however, disappeared in 1021 at the age of 36, and Hamza went into hiding. It is generally accepted that the caliph was murdered with the collusion of his sister, Sitt al-Mulk, whom he had accused of immoral behavior. Al-Hakim's successor, al-Zahir (1021–1035) denied any claim by his ancestors to divinity and ruthlessly persecuted the followers

of Druzism. He succeeded in wiping them out in nearly all their strong-
holds, from Cairo as far north as Aleppo. Those who survived were found
principally in southern Lebanon and Syria (Betts 1988: 11–12).

The religious views and the teaching of the Druze were organized and
codified by Baha' al-Din in 1027–1043, during which he pursued active missionary work. He collected the various epistles, 111 in total, composed by
al-Hakim, Hamza, and Baha' al-Din himself, and arranged in six books as
Druze Canon, or *al-Hikmat al-Sharifa* (the Noble Knowledge). The last of
these epistles is dated 434/1042, and in the following year the proselytizing was formally ended, twenty-six years after its proclamation by Hamza
in Cairo. After this date no new adherents were to be accepted into the
faith (Betts 1988:13).

According to the Druze tradition, Hamza, who was still in hiding in
Cairo, left Egypt and journeyed to "the land of the Chinese oases," where
he joined up with the caliph al-Hakim, who continued to send mystic
meditations to Baha' al-Din as late as 439/1047. From this date until the
appearance fifty years later of the Crusaders on Syrian soil in 1097, the
Druze all but disappeared from the stage of history, to reappear only
briefly from time to time. They, however, rose as a major political force in
the Levant following the Ottoman conquest in 1516. Having survived the
initial wave of persecution launched immediately after al-Hakim's disap-
pearance, under Baha' al-Din's leadership the Druze were bound together
in a tightly knit society by the *tawhid* (Betts 1988: 13).

The Druze believe in the transmigration of souls (*tanasukh* in Arabic, a
non-Muslim belief) and that the number of all souls of believers and non-
believers was fixed and limited at the Creation. Thus, when a Druze dies,
another Druze is born. The soul of the former enters the body of the latter
instantly by a system of metempsychosis. The stern Islamic message of
the Day of Judgment does not exist in the Druze faith in this form.
Judgment Day, for the Druze, is the end of a long journey in repeated rein-
carnations for the full development of the soul. Unlike the teaching of
Islam, the Druze faith promises not a paradise full of earthly delights but
rather a beatific vision of the Holy One, with hell being the failure to
achieve this ultimate goal of the just man (Betts 1988: 17; see also Najjar
1973).

Marriage is monogamous; polygamy, temporary marriage, and concubinage are forbidden. The Druze women have always had the right to own
property and dispose of it freely. Women are, however, legally and morally
entitled to be supported by the nearest male relative (Abu-Izzeddin 1984:
230). The Druze do not observe the Muslim commandment of ritual

prayer five times daily toward Mecca as the prophet Muhammad commanded. They regard prayer in the allegorical sense of "association of one's soul with the unity of God... developed into prayer as a constant state of being" (Makaren 1974: 96). They, however, conduct simple services of worship on Thursday evenings at a place for seclusions called a place of retreat, *khalwa*, or for a meeting place or conference, *majlis* (Betts 1988: 21).

And instead of five pillars, Hamza substituted the seven duties (*al-shurut al-sab'a*), which all Druze are required to observe (Betts 1988: 19; Makarem 1974):

- Recognition of al-Hakim and strict adherence to monotheism,
- Negation of all non-Druze tenets,
- Rejection of Satan and unbelief,
- Acceptance of God's acts,
- Submission to God for good or ill,
- Truthfulness, and
- Mutual help and solidarity between fellow Druze.

The Druze religion separates itself from Islam by declaring that the revelations of al-Hakim contain the ultimate truth, not those of Prophet Muhammad. According to Druze belief, as is described by Assad (1974: 162–63):

> God manifested himself in physical forms only at times when a new revelation was necessary and a new deliverer commanded to reveal it, prepared its members to accept the new revelation, *Din al-Tawhid* and the new prophet, Hamza. And, since every prophet superseded previous prophets and exalted his *Shari'a* over the previous ones, Hamza superseded Muhammad and *Din al-Tawhid* was exalted over Islam.

The Seveners and Druze are much smaller sects in Islam than the Twelver Shi'is. In the Arab world, the Seveners today only are only found in Syria. They are fewer than a hundred thousand. The total population of Druze throughout the world probably approaches one million. According to the Estimate of the American Druze Public Affairs Committee, there are about 300,000 Druze in Lebanon, 420,000 in Syria, 75,000 in Israel (exclusive of nearly 15,000 Syrian Druze in the Golan Heights), 15,000 in Jordan, and a maximum of 80,000 elsewhere—mostly the Americas, Australia, and West Arica (Betts 1988: 55–56).

The focus of this study, however, is on the Druze in Lebanon. It assesses the extent to which in-group solidarity among the Druze is linked to religious fundamentalism.

RELIGION AND COMPARATIVE INFLUENCES ON FUNDAMENTALISM

In assessing the relationship between people's religious affiliation and religious fundamentalism, we consider several variable organizational features of these religions that may either weaken (–) or strengthen (+) fundamentalist attitudes and beliefs among its followers. These are diversity, in-group solidarity, the structure of organized religion, and international ties. Our focus is on lived religion in its national context. As a result, the Sunni in Lebanon, for example, may be influenced by different organizational factors from the Sunni in Egypt and Saudi Arabia.

Religious Diversity

This feature refers to the extent to which there is more than one organized religion that is active in the community. Based on this criterion, religion in Lebanon is highly diverse (–). In relative terms, Christianity is even more diverse than Islam because there are more than twelve Christian sects in the country, while there are about five Islamic sects. Religion in Egypt, Iran, and Saudi Arabia is much less diverse (+). To be sure, there are certain areas in Egypt where Christian Copts live in a close proximity to Muslims, and Iran, in which there are sizable religious minorities. Our data, however, does not allow for a systematic comparison between those areas and the rest of the countries in order to assess the relationship between diversity and fundamentalism. Our data from Saudi Arabia covers the Dammam-Khobar region that has a sizable Shi'i community, living side-by-side with the Sunni. We have thus considered this region as religiously diversified (–).

In-Group Solidarity

Insofar as a religious community is turned into an ethnic group distinct from other groups in a society, this feature may enhance in-group solidarity, and this solidarity may strengthen religious fundamentalism. Lebanon provides prime examples of religion-turned ethnicity, where almost all religious confessions have their own distinctive civic laws and custom as well as political parties. Rivalries between these confession-based political parties provide a key mechanism for the reproduction of ethnic solidarity (+). Religion in Egypt, Iran, and Saudi Arabia does not constitute an ethnic group, or at least not in the same sense that it does in Lebanon (–). In the Dammam-Khobar region of Saudi Arabia, on the other hand, where the Shi'is define themselves as a community distinct from the Sunni dominated country, we propose that there is a higher degree of in-group solidarity among the Shi'is in this region (+).

The Structure of Organized Religion

The hierarchical structure of organized religion may be centralized or decentralized. A decentralized structure may promote more competitions and debates among different members of the religious organization than when the organized religion has a centralized structure. Such competitions and debates may in turn weaken religious fundamentalism. The organized religions in Egypt and Saudi Arabia are centralized (+). In Iran, it is decentralized (–). This is so despite the efforts of the religious regime to impose a centralized structure on the Shi'i establishment. There is a considerable number of grand ayatollahs in the country who do not recognize the authority of the supreme leader. In the Dammam-Khobar region, it is also considered decentralized as different Shi'i religious activists take their cue from different leading ayatollahs in Iraqi and Iran (–). In Lebanon, we also consider this structure to be decentralized (–). Even though Lebanese Shi'is are dominated by the centralized religious and political organization of the Hezbollah, the organization of the Shi'i establishment in the country is still decentralized.

International Ties or Relationship with National Regime

The nature of the relationship a religious group has with organizations or states beyond the national borders may also reinforce or weakened fundamentalist beliefs and attitudes among its members. This is particularly the case in Lebanon. We propose that Christians, the Maronites in particular, having ties to the West will weaken religious fundamentalism (–), while the Sunnis having ties with the Kingdom of Saudi Arabia and the Shi'is with the Islamic Republic of Iran will strengthen religious fundamentalism (+). We also propose that fundamentalism is strengthened among the Iranian Shi'is, who live under the religious fundamentalist regime, and Saudi Sunnis, who are dominated by the Wahhabi cleric (+). Such, however, is not the case among Egyptian Sunnis (–) or Lebanese Druze (–). Finally, Shi'i fundamentalism in Saudi Arabia is undermined by the Sunni influence but strengthened by their ties to the Islamic regime in Iran (–/+).

These relationships are summarized in Table 2.2. According to this table, Christians are the least fundamentalist, followed by the Druze, and the Sunnis in Saudi Arabia are the most fundamentalist. Other religious groups would fall in between the Druze and Saudi Sunnis.

Table 2.2. Predictors of levels of fundamentalism in the dominant religious sects in each country.

Country	Religious sect	Diversity	Centralized structure of organized religion	In-group solidarity	International ties		Total influence
					West	Iran/KSA	
Lebanon	Christian	−	−	+	−	−	− 3
	Druze	−	−	+	+	−	− 1
	Shi'i	−	−	+	+	+	+ 1
	Sunni	−	−	+	+	+	+ 1
Egypt	Sunni	+	+	−	+	−	+ 1
Iran	Shi'i	+	−	−	+	+	+ 1
KSA	Shi'i area	−	−	+	+	+	+ 1
KSA	Sunni	+	+	−	+	+	+ 3

Ethnicity in Iran: The Azeri Turks, Gilakis,
Kurds, Lurs, and Persians

To assess the variation in fundamentalism by ethnicity, we focus on several ethnic groups in Iran. While Iran is unified in terms of religious affiliation—89% of the population are Shi'is, 9% Sunnis, and 2% are Baha'is, Zoroastrians, Jews, and Christians. In terms of ethnicity, the country is diverse. It consists of Persians (51%), who constitute the dominant group, Azeris (24%), Gilakis and Mazandaranis (8%), Kurds (7%), Arabs (3%), Lurs (2%), Baluchs (2%), Turkmans (2%), and others (1%). Key identifiers of ethnicity are language and the geographic area of residence. Of the total population of more than 68 million in 2005, 58% speak Persian and Persian dialects, 26% Turkic and Turkic dialects, 9% Kurdish, 2% Luri, 1% Baluchi, 1% Arabic, 1% Turkish, and 2% other (CIA 2005: 265).

The percentage of the population that does not understand Persian varies by provinces. According to a 1986 estimate, in eight provinces (Yazd, Semnan, Fars, Kerman, Esfahan, Chahar Mehalva Bakhtiyari, Boushehr, and Tehran), less than 1% of the population did not understand Persian. In ten provinces (Hormozgan, Khorasan, Markazi, Mazandaran, Gilan, Khuzestan, Kohkiloyehva Boyerahmad, Hamadan, Lurestan Bakhtaran), between 1% and 25% did not understand Persian. In six Provinces (Sistanva Baluchestan, Ilam, Zanjan, East Azerbaijan, Kurdistan, and West Azerbaijan), more than a quarter of the population did not understand Persian. In East and West Azerbaijan and Kurdistan, more than one-half of the population did not understand Persian. Together, more than seven million (84%) of those individuals who did not understand Persian reside in these three provinces (Nomani and Behdad 2006: 71–72).

Azeri Turk

The Azeri-Turks (known also as Azerbaijanis) live in northwestern Iran and the Republic of Azerbaijan. The Azeris have a mixed heritage of Iranic, Caucasian, and Turkic elements. They have historically played a significant role in Iran's politics and culture. The Safavids (1501–1722), who made Shi'ism Iran's state religion, rose from Azeri background. Iran's wars with Russia, which were concluded in the two humiliating treaties of Gulistan in 1813 and Turkmenchay in 1828, resulted in the loss of its northern territories to Russia, and the Azeri population was divided between the two countries. The Iranian Azeris, however, have played a prominent role in the country's intellectual movement, constitutional revolution, and political development in the nineteenth and twentieth centuries (Adamiyat 1970, 1976, 1978; Abrahamian 1982; Moaddel 2005). Many of them have been cognizant of their Iranian identity. For example, one of the precursors of liberal thought in Iran, Mirza Fath Ali Akhundzadah (1812–78), famously proclaimed that "even though I am a Turk, I belong to the Persian ancestry" (cited in Adamiyat 1970: 118).

Following the breakdown of the former Soviet Union, the independence of the Republic of Azerbaijan was restored in 1991 (The Azerbaijan Democratic Republic was first declared in 1918). Currently, there are an estimated 24 to 33 million Azerbaijanis in the world, but the census figures are difficult to verify. The vast majority of these people live in Azerbaijan and Iranian Azerbaijan. Between 16 and 23 million Azeris live in Iran. Approximately 7.6 million Azeris are found in the Republic of Azerbaijan. A diaspora, possibly numbering in the millions, is found in neighboring countries and around the world. There are also sizable Azeri communities in Turkey, Georgia, Russia, UK, USA, Canada, and Germany. Azerbaijanis in Iran are mainly found in the northwest provinces: East Azerbaijan, Ardabil, Zanjan, Hamedan, Qazvin, West Azerbaijan and Markazi. Many others live in Tehran, Fars province, and other regions. Generally, Azeris in Iran are regarded as "a well-integrated linguistic minority" by academics prior to the 1979 Iranian Revolution. Despite friction, Azerbaijanis in Iran came to be well represented at all levels of political, military, intellectual, and religious hierarchies. The majority of Azerbaijanis are Twelver Shi'i Muslims. Religious minorities among them include Sunni Muslims (mainly Hanafi), Zoroastrians, Christians and Bahá'ís (Lewis 2009).

Gilaki

The Gilakis inhabit northern Iran along the Caspian Sea. They are primarily located in the Gilan province. They are also found in the neighboring province of Mazandaran. Along with the Mazandarani people, the Gilakis form one of the Caspian Sea peoples. They speak the Gilaki language, closely related to Mazandarani. As of 2000 there were about 2.4 million Gilakis, having risen from the population of 1.9 million in 1990. The Gilaki language has not yet been given a written form. Most Gilakis are Shi'i Muslims.

The Kurds

The majority of the Kurds are Sunni Muslims, belonging to the Shafi'i school of jurisprudence. Mystical practices and participation in Sufi orders are also widespread among the Kurds. There is also a minority among the Kurds who are Shi'is, primarily living in the Ilam and Kermanshah provinces of Iran and central and southeastern Iraq (Fayli Kurds). The Alavi [Alawi] Kurds mostly live in Turkey. The Alavis are a sect originating from Ismaili Shi'ism (Mackenzie 1961; Leonard 2006).

The Kurds have their own language (Kurdish) and live in the generally contiguous areas of Turkey, Iraq, Iran, Armenia, and Syria – a mountainous region of southwest Asia known as Kurdistan ("Land of the Kurds"). Following the breakup of the Ottoman Empire after World War I, the 1920 Treaty of Sevres, which created the modern states of Iraq, Syria and Kuwait, was to have included the possibility of a Kurdish state in the region. However, it was never implemented. After the overthrow of the Turkish monarchy by Kemal Ataturk, Turkey, Iran and Iraq each agreed not to recognize an independent Kurdish state. Mustafa Kemal Ataturk, Turkish leader, rejected the treaty, and Turkish forces put down Kurdish uprisings in the 1920s and 1930s. With backing of the former Soviet Union, the Iranian Kurds succeeded in establishing the republic of Mahabad in 1946. A year later, however, the Iranian monarch crushed the embryonic state. The Kurds in northern Iraq, under the British mandate, revolted in 1919, 1923 and 1932, but were crushed. After the Persian Gulf War in 1991, northern Iraq's Kurdish area came under international protection, and following the American-led invasion of the country, the Iraqi Kurds gained substantial autonomy (http://www.washingtonpost.com/wp-srv/inatl/daily/feb99/kurdprofile.htm, retrieved March 8, 2010; Hassanpour 2005).

With an estimated population of between 25 and 35 million, the Kurds are the fourth largest ethnic group in the Middle East after Arabs, Persians and Turks. They comprise 20% of the population in Turkey, 15–20% in Iraq, perhaps 8% in Syria 7% in Iran and more than 1% in Armenia. In all of these countries except Iran, the Kurds form the second largest ethnic group. Roughly 55% of the world's Kurds live in Turkey, about 18% each in Iran and Iraq, and a slightly over 5% Syria (CIA 2005; Hassanpour 2005).

Lurs

The Lurs are an ethnic group who speak Luri and who predominantly inhabit the Southwestern part of Iran. They primarily live in Lurestan, Chaharmahal and Bakhtiari and Kohgiluyeh and Boyer-Ahmad provinces, parts of Khuzestan and Hamadan of Iran. The Lurs are closely related to the Bakhtiaris, a politically influential ethnic group in pre-revolutionary Iran who also speak Luri. There were about 500,000 Lurs in Iran in mid-1980s. The Lurs are divided into two main groups, the Posht-e Kuhi and the Pish-e Kuhi. These two groups are subdivided into more than sixty tribes, the most important of which include the Boir Ahmadi, the Kuhgiluyeh, and the Mamasani. Historically, the Lurs have included an urban segment based in the town of Khorramabad, the provincial capital of Lurestan. Prior to 1900, however, the majority of the Lurs were pastoral nomads. Traditionally, they were considered among the fiercest of Iranian tribes and had acquired an unsavory reputation due to their habit of preying on both Luri and non-Luri villages. During the 1920s and 1930s, the government of Reza Shah undertook several coercive campaigns to settle the nomadic Lurs. Following the abdication of Reza Shah in 1941, many of the recently settled tribes reverted to nomadic life. Mohammad Reza Shah Pahlavi's government attempted with some success through various economic development programs to encourage the remaining nomadic Lurs to settle. By 1986 the majority of all the Lurs were settled in villages and small towns in the traditional Luri areas or had migrated to cities (http://countrystudies.us/iran/38.htm, retrieved March 11, 2010).

SUMMARY

This chapter presented a description of the national and historical context of Egypt, Iran, Lebanon, and Saudi Arabia. It also discussed different religions, religious sects and ethnicities about which sample data are available for a comparative analysis of fundamentalism. Table 2.3

Table 2.3. Religion, sect, and ethnicity in Egypt, Iran, Lebanon, and Saudi Arabia.

Country	Ethnicity	Religion	Sects	Further divisions
Egypt	Arab	Muslim	Sunni	
Saudi Arabia	Arab	Muslim	Sunni	
Iran	Persian	Muslim	Shi'i	Twelver
	Kurd	Muslim	Majority Sunni	
	Azeri	Muslim	Shi'i	Twelver
	Gilaki	Muslim	Shi'i	Twelver
	Lur	Muslim	Shi'i	Twelver
Lebanon	Arab	Muslim	Shi'i	Twelver
	Arab	Muslim	Sunni	
	Arab	Muslim	Druze	Offshoot of Sevener
	Arab	Christian	Maronite	
	Arab	Christian	Catholic	Greek Catholic (Melkites), Roman Catholic, Syrian Catholic, Copts Chaldean, Assyrian Catholic
	Arab	Christian	Orthodox	Greek Orthodox, Armenian Orthodox, Syrian Orthodox

summarizes the countries, ethnic groups, religions, and sects that are included in the study for a comparative analysis. The following chapter will compare religious fundamentalism across nation, religion, sect, and ethnicity. It assesses the extent to which religious fundamentalism is connected to cross-national variation in the state's culture—religious (Iran and Saudi Arabia) versus secular (Egypt and Lebanon)—and state structure—democratic (Lebanon) versus authoritarian and interventionist (Egypt, Iran, and Saudi Arabia), religiously unified (Egypt, Iran, and Saudi Arabia) or pluralistic (Lebanon). It will also evaluate variation in fundamentalism among Christians, Muslims, and different religious sects— Maronite, Orthodox, Catholic Christians, and Sunni, Shi'i, and Druze Muslims. Moreover, it will examine the degree to which fundamentalism is linked to ethnic solidarity as is measured by the level of intra-ethnic trust. Next, it will examine the extent to which fundamentalist beliefs and attitudes among Lebanese Islamic sects are linked to the attitudes of the members of these groups toward the countries with which they had historic ties—the attitudes of the Shi'is toward the Islamic Republic of Iran, and of the Sunnis toward Saudi Arabia. Finally, this chapter will analyze fundamentalism in terms of ethnicity among Iranians, including Azeri Turks, Gilakis, Lurs, Kurds, and Persians.

CHAPTER THREE

METHODOLOGY AND MACRO COMPARISONS

The previous chapter provided the background and parameters of the social context for macro comparisons of fundamentalism across nation-states (Egypt, Iran, Lebanon, and Saudi Arabia), religions (Christianity and Islam), religious sects (Catholics, Maronites, Orthodox among Lebanese Christians; Shi'is, Sunnis, and Druze among Muslims), and ethnicities (Azeri-Turks, Gilakis, Lurs, Kurds, and Persians among Iranians). These parameters included, first, features of the nation-state that vary across the four countries: democratic (Lebanon) versus authoritarianism (Egypt, Iran, and Saudi Arabia); the ideology of the ruling regime: religious (Iran and Saudi Arabia) versus secular (Egypt and Lebanon); whether the ruling elite is homogeneous (Egypt and Saudi Arabia) or heterogeneous (Iran and Lebanon); and whether the country had past secular experiences (Egypt, Iran, and Lebanon) or had no such experiences (Saudi Arabia). These features of the social context cannot be dissected in order to assess their individual effects on fundamentalism separately. Plausibly, however, what can be said of the relationship between social context and religious fundamentalism across the four countries is that Lebanon and Saudi Arabia represent two opposite poles; Lebanon displays all the features that attenuate and Saudi Arabia those that intensify fundamentalist beliefs and attitudes, with Egypt and Iran falling somewhere in between.

Furthermore, with respect to the effects of religion, religious sect, or ethnicity, we have not developed an *a priori* set of hypotheses from either of these variables to predict fundamentalism. We have presumed that there was nothing specific in the basic beliefs of the religious sects or the ethnic groups being discussed here that could be linked to religious fundamentalism at the aggregate level. However, in assessing the connection of fundamentalism with religion and religious sect, we consider, as was proposed in Chapter Two, the effect of religious diversity, the centralized or de-centralized structure of the dominant organized religion in the country, the extent of in-group solidarity among the members of a religious sect, and the sect's international ties either as attenuating or strengthening factors. Since our analysis of the variation of fundamentalism by ethnicity is limited to Iran, we propose that one key factor that may shape fundamentalist attitudes among the members of an ethnic group is the nature of the group's relationship with the ruling regime in the country.

In this chapter, we first discuss and conceptualize the components of religious fundamentalism and measure these components. The survey data from the four countries is then examined to describe religious fundamentalism and its variation across nation, religion, religious sect, and ethnicity. We also discuss variation in fundamentalism in terms of urban-rural differences, education (university versus below university), and gender. Since only youth (age 18–25) are sampled in Egypt and Saudi Arabia, only that age group is included in Iran and Lebanon to establish a uniform basis for comparative analyses when comparing all countries. Analyses in Chapter 5, which involves comparisons only between Iran and Lebanon, however, will use data from all age groups.

COMPONENTS OF RELIGIOUS FUNDAMENTALISM

Based on the discussion thus far, we have proposed that fundamentalism from the experience of Muslim-majority countries constituted a series of historically-specific religious movements that are unique but that also share common characteristics. These common features consisted of, first, specific positions on a set of historically significant issues and, second, a set of beliefs about and attitudes toward the religion of Islam. In Chapter Six, we assess the relationship between these two features of fundamentalism. In this chapter, we capitalize on the second set of common features to adopt a generalizable perspective that permits comparisons across a variety of Muslim and Christian populations. As will be argued below, both Islamic and Christian fundamentalists share this generalizable perspective. This perspective consists of a set of general beliefs and attitudes concerning attributes of deity, the teachings of the scriptures, the conditions for redemption, and eternal salvation. These beliefs are not necessarily contrary to the core principles of the religious tradition of which fundamentalism is a part, but are rather particularistic conceptions of these principles.

To reiterate, we maintain that religious fundamentalism is not confined to a single dimension, such as inerrancy (see also e.g., Antoun 2008), but is rather a multifaceted concept that is comprised of several interrelated and logically consistent belief and attitudinal components.

These components by and large cover the principle aspects of religion. Specifically, these aspects include views on the nature of the deity, humanity, and punishment; the inerrancy of the scriptures and their historical accuracy in explaining the past events and predicting the future; exclusivity and religious centrism; and intolerance of other religions. We now describe these components in greater detail and how they collectively provide the conceptual rationale for measuring the degree of people's beliefs and attitudes that constitute religious fundamentalism (Altemeyer 2003).

Nature of the Deity

The basic tenets of this component of fundamentalism derive from beliefs regarding the omnipotence, omniscience, and omnipresence of God in the three Abrahamic faiths of Judaism, Christianity, and Islam. God is seen as the creator of life and the universe, who has sent his prophets to guide mankind through the true path of redemption and eternal salvation, although this is a matter of some complexity for Judaism.[1] Muslim and Christian religious fundamentalists certainly follow these principles. They, however, embrace a form of Manichaeism by bringing the God versus Satan duality to the center of their etiology of the good and evil in real life. Satan is the source of all evils in this world; he causes humans to deviate from the right path. Satanic temptations must be overcome through the persistent awareness that God will punish severely those who violate his law. The faithful are repeatedly reminded to fear the wrath of God on Judgment Day and the horrific conditions of Hell, where humans are punished according to the severity of their sins (Meyer 1995, La Fontaine 1998; Hendryx 2009). They also stress the other- rather than this-worldly benefit promised by religion (Quinney 1964; Stark and Bainbridge 1985; Macedo 1995, Darnell and Sherkat 1997).

Under stable social conditions, this image of God may be in harmony with the everyday functioning of social life, where the faithful feel relatively calm, secure, healthy, and happy, and such feelings are attributed to

---

[1] In contrast to Islam and Christianity, the afterlife is almost entirely irrelevant in Judaism, which focuses on living a meritorious and moral earthly life. There is no explicit reference to heaven in the Torah, for example, and only vague references to a Jewish afterlife. The Talmud—the Jewish oral tradition interpreting the Torah—does contain nonspecific references to a Jewish afterlife. There are such references during the Rabbinic period beginning in the second millennium, but one very different, a non-physical space, or even that heaven is actually on earth. All are in stark contrast to the fully elaborated versions of heaven in Islam and Christianity. (e.g., see: http://www.worldofjudaica.com/judaism/beliefs/does-judaism-believe-in-an-afterlife/ retrieved 1/12/2012)

their obedience to God and His rule. This image, however, is often difficult to sustain when the faithful are challenged by long periods of immeasurable suffering, the result of which can be an alternative image of God as the one who is hidden, growing, or absent and thus less relevant to their daily lives.

Under other conditions, particularly when the seekers of spirituality believe that the faith is under siege or people have abandoned religion, religious adherents may become preoccupied with the necessity for the strict observance of God's law. This situation may give rise to a perception of God not as a human enabler but rather as a strict parent who uses the threat of punishment to enforce obedience to Him and the observance of His law. The faithful see themselves under God's constant surveillance, as all his powerful attributes—the omnipotence, omniscience, and omnipresence—are summoned to monitor humans, detect sins, and punish severely those who violate His instructions.

With regard to sexual norms in Christianity, for example, the story of Susannah and the elders had been widely interpreted as a lesson for married women in particular of the importance of cultivating the fear of God as a means of internalizing a salutary sense of shame. Augustine argued that Susannah resists the advances of the elders not because of her inherent virtue but "because she was afraid of him whom she did not see, but whose divine eyes were nonetheless fixed on her; because she did not see God, does not mean that she is not seen by God" (cited in Rice 2010: 131–132; Clark 1991: 236). This rule applies to men as well: "whereas women are protected from sexual error by so many societal devices as well as their own sense of modesty, Augustine claims, men have nothing to rely on but the surveillance of God" (Clark 1991: 235). God's surveillance is thus unceasing and inescapable.

Religious fundamentalists thus adopt a disciplinarian conception of God. His swift and certain discipline is considered an effective way to ensure the observance of His laws and to keep the faithful on the path of righteousness. They stress that God will severely punish those who do not follow the principles of religion as laid out in the scriptures. The omnipresence of God is balanced by the omnipresence of Satan. While God is seen as the source of everything good, Satan is the cause of injustices and is constantly scheming to undermine God's law. God is kind and forgiving insofar as the faithful are willing to recant their pagan beliefs and practices and confess their sins. Nevertheless, there is the sense that those with more fundamentalist beliefs are less inclined to emphasize the loving, tolerant, and forgiving attributes of God, and instead are keenly aware

of Satan, stress the fear of God and the horror of Hell, and encourage the
faithful to repent.

Inerrancy and Literalism

From the fundamentalist perspective, religion is an inerrant, comprehensive system of universal truth. The scriptures are deemed infallible, literally true, and historically accurate (Ford 1960; DeJong and Ford 1965;
Chicago Statement 1997; Marsden 1980; Miller and Wattenberg 1984;
Kellstedt and Smidt 1991). There is no inconsistency in the word of God. Its
narrations of past historical events are accurate. The believer need only follow the literal word as handed down from God. Since they are the word of
God, to amend or question the scriptures is sinful. There is also no need for
man-made laws. Nor is there a need for a secondary interpretation of the
scriptures. As such, it tends to disregard the interpretive functions of the
clergy to uncover the true meanings of the sacred texts not directly accessible to ordinary individuals, hence rejecting institutional mediation
between the Supreme Being and the faithful. The view of Hood, Hill and
Williamson (2005) on the structural similarities between sacred texts in different religious traditions and their notion of intratextuality are consistent
with the inerrancy component of fundamentalism advanced in this book.

Since the scriptures are always correct, it follows that religious beliefs
take precedence over scientific laws and discoveries. From a fundamentalist perspective, the scriptures have even correctly predicted major scientific discoveries and technological innovations.[2] While the relationship
between religion and science in people's perception is complex, it may be
confined to specific issues and is often mediated by a host of moral and
non-epistemological factors (Evens 2010, 2011). Generally in the fundamentalist perception, if a conflict arises between religion and science,
religion is always right. That is, people with a stronger religious fundamentalist orientation tend to favor religion rather than science.

Exclusivity and Religious Centrism

The belief in the absolute moral, literal, and historical inerrancy of the
scriptures also tends to promote religious centrism and exclusivity, where
one's religion is portrayed as closer to God than the religions of others.
Fundamentalists are thus exclusivists in that one's faith is considered
decidedly superior over other faiths. For religious fundamentalists, only

---

[2] http://www.bibleandscience.com/science/bibleandscience.htm. Retrieved January
21, 2011.

those who believe in their scriptures are members of the true religious community. Those who adopt other interpretations of the Bible or the Quran are seen as deviating from the true path and have lost the meaning of the faith. For the fundamentalists, religious beliefs take precedence over ethics and sincerity. There is no universal human right above and beyond that which is dictated by their true religion. In this sense, only the followers of the true faith will be redeemed, attain salvation, and go to heaven; others will not, no matter how nice and sincere they are.

Religious Intolerance

Finally, to maintain the purity of the faith, there should be little contact or interaction with the followers of other faiths. In the fundamentalists' perception, the weird beliefs and pagan ways of other faiths may contaminate one's beliefs and undermine the role of the true religion within their community. As a result, the followers of other faiths should not be given the same rights as those given to the followers of one's faith. Nor should they be allowed to freely practice their religion or build their places of worship. Religious intolerance entails the rejection of inter-faith interaction and inter-faith religious instructions. Furthermore, because it is premised on the purity and the inerrancy of the faith, the fundamentalists do not accept the criticism of their religion or religious leaders.

SAMPLING AND SURVEY METHODOLOGY

These dimensions of religious fundamentalism were operationalized using a series of Likert-scale items to be described subsequently. The items were embedded in large-scale national values surveys carried out in Iran in 2005 and Lebanon in 2008, and youth surveys carried out in Egypt and Saudi Arabia in 2005. Surveys, samples, and procedures in each country are described separately. The combined questionnaire used for the youth survey in Egypt and Saudi Arabia is in Appendix A and the questionnaires used in the surveys in Iran and Lebanon are in Appendix B and Appendix C, respectively.

Iran

The Iran survey involved a nationally representative sample of 2,903 adults conducted in summer, 2005. It used multi-stage random sampling procedures in different provinces, stratified according to urban and rural areas of the country in proportion to their size, with roughly equal proportions of male and female respondents. The Kurdish population was oversampled to allow comparisons with the rest of the population. The size of the portion of the sample covering such other ethnic minorities as the Azeri Turks, Gilakis, and Lurs is large enough for inter-ethnic comparisons. Statistical tests used weighting procedures when appropriate to take oversampling into consideration. The interviews required approximately one hour to complete, and the response rate was about 90% of the people contacted.

The sample included 2,429 (83.7%) Shi'is, 429 (14.8%) Sunnis, and 24 (0.8%) members of other religious denominations. In terms of ethnicity, 563 (19.4%) were Azeri Turks, 69 (2.4%) Arabs, 120 (4.1%) Gilakis, 422 (14.5%) Kurds, 133 (4.6%) Lurs, and 1,533 (52.8%) Persians. About 68.2% of the sample was from the urban areas and the rest from the rural areas of the country. The respondents averaged 33.29 years of age, 1,442 (49.7%) were male, and 524 (18.1%) had a college degree. In terms of class, 37 (1.3%) of the respondents described themselves as members of the upper class, 1,091 (37.6%) upper middle class, 1,360 (46.8%) lower middle class, and 379 (13.1%) lower class. Only 1,182 or 40.7% of the respondents indicated that they had jobs.

Lebanon

The Lebanon survey consisted of a nationally representative sample of 3,039 adults drawn from all religious confessions of Lebanese society in proportion to their estimated sizes. The sample included 954 (31%) Shi'is, 753 (25%) Sunnis, 198 (7%) Druze, 599 (20%) Maronites, 338 (11%) Orthodox, 149 (5%) Catholics, and 48 (2%) respondents belonging to other religions. It covered all six governorates in proportion to size—960 (32%) from Beirut, 578 (19%) from Mount Lebanon, 621 (20%) from the North, 339 (11%) from Biqqa, and 539 (18%) from the South and Nabatieth.

The interviews took approximately 50 minutes to complete and were conducted face-to-face by Lebanese personnel in the respondents' residences. The total number of completed interviews represented 86% of attempted observations (86% response rate). Data collection started in April 2008 and was completed at the end of September 2008. Turbulent political and security situations in Lebanon in the spring and summer prolonged the survey period. The respondents averaged 33 years of age, 1,694 (55.7%) were male, and 998 (32.8%) had a college degree. In terms of class, 55 (1.8%) of the respondents described themselves as members of the upper class, 847 (27.9%) upper middle class, 788 (25.9%) lower middle class, 683 (22.5%) working class, and 522 (17.2%) lower class. Only 1,597 (52.6%) indicated they were employed.

Egypt and Saudi Arabia

Comparable surveys of late adolescents and young adults (ages 18–25) were conducted in Egypt and Saudi Arabia in the spring and summer of 2005. Survey interviews required approximately 45 minutes on average to complete and were conducted in face-to-face interviews in respondents' residences. Importantly, they were conducted by indigenous personnel with considerable experience in their respective countries: the Saudi survey by a branch of the Pan Arab Research Center in Jeddah, Saudi Arabia, and the Egyptian survey by the Egyptian Research and Training Center in Cairo, Egypt.

The Egyptian sample included three cities and rural surroundings: Alexandria, population 3.8 million; El-Minya, population 225,100; and Cairo, population 7.7 million. Egypt as a whole had an estimated population of 77 million in 2005. There is also a Coptic Christian population in the country. Although for political reasons the Egyptian authorities do not reveal their exact number, it is estimated that they constitute 6–10% of the population. The majority of Copts live in Upper Egypt, particularly in Assyout and El-Minya. There is a high concentration of Copts in Cairo as well. Alexandria has the lowest concentration of Copts. The Egyptian survey was administered (from May 5 through June 30, 2005) to a representative sample of 928 youth (54% male), 289 (32%) from Cairo, 291 (32%) from Alexandria, and 325 (36%) from El-Minya. In terms of education, 320 (36 %) had at least some university education and 581 (65%) had below university education. Slightly more than 1% defined themselves as members of the upper class, 32% upper middle class, 49% lower middle class, 15% working class, and 3% lower class.

The Saudi survey (administered during July 10–25, 2005) also included three cities and rural surroundings: Jeddah, Riyadh and Dammam-Khobar. The kingdom had an estimated population of more than 26 million in 2005, of which more than 5 million are estimated to be non-nationals (CIA 2005:479). About 2.8 million live in Jeddah, 4 million in Riyadh, the capital, and fewer than 1 million in Dammam-Khobar. The latter has a large Shi'i population, as opposed to almost all Sunnis in Jeddah and Riyadh. The survey involved a representative sample of 954 youth (59% male), 473 (50%) from Jeddah, 321 (34%) from Riyadh, and 160 (17%) from Dammam-Khobar. In terms of education, 266 (28%) had at least some university education and 688 (72%) had less than a university education. About 11% identified themselves as members of the upper class, 37% upper middle class, 35% lower middle class, 15% working class, and 2% lower class.

FUNDAMENTALISM SCALE CONSTRUCTION

Item Selection and Reliability

Religious fundamentalism was measured using a Likert-scale to capture respondents' level of agreement or disagreement with a series of statements that operationalized the components of the construct described above. The statements were based on the fundamentalist and religious ethnocentrism scale devised by Altemeyer (2003:21), with some items modified and others added to accommodate the cultural and political conditions of the countries included in the present studies. After pretests, and taking into consideration recommendations from field researchers in the four countries, items were further modified or deleted. Due to time and space constraints, fewer fundamentalist items were included in the surveys conducted in Iran and Lebanon. Table 3.1 presents the items used in each of the countries. Also designated in this table are the items included in the fundamentalist scale published previously (Moaddel and Karabenick 2008). The table also groups the items according to the four components of fundamentalism: (a) nature of the deity; (b) inerrancy; (c) exclusivity; and (d) intolerance. Likert-scale response categories in Egypt, Lebanon, and Saudi Arabia were: strongly agree, agree, disagree, and strongly disagree (coded 4 to 1). A middle category was included in the Iran survey: strongly agree, agree, somewhat agree and somewhat disagree, disagree and strongly disagree (coded 5 to 1). As will be explained subsequently, the additional middle category had no discernible impact on the assessment of fundamentalism.

We began by selecting items (see items 7, 9, 14, 15, 16, 17, and 18 in Table 3.1) that were common across all countries. Analyses were then conducted to arrive at a final set of items that best satisfied the criteria of internal consistency (i.e., the existence of significant correlations among the scale items) and whether the scale items can be represented with a single dimension. Internal consistency was computed with Cronbach's alpha, which is considered an estimate of scale reliability. Alphas were computed both for the countries individually, and with Iran and Lebanon considered together, and Egypt and Saudi Arabia considered together. Items were retained if eliminating them reduced the alpha level, and items were eliminated if doing so increased alpha significantly. Unidimensionality was determined using exploratory factor analysis with principal component extraction and by determining whether the eigenvalue of an extracted factor was greater than one. The eigenvalue depends on the proportion of total variance accounted for by a factor, and is commonly used as a criterion for determining when a factor accounts for sufficient variance to represent the scale items. In the present instance, it is used to determine when a single factor will suffice to represent variation in the degree of fundamentalism.

The combined internal consistency and factor analysis procedure resulted in eliminating items 16 and 18 and arriving at the final set of five items (7, 9, 14, 15, and 17), the mean responses of which formed the fundamentalism scale score. Since the five items were a subset of the original set of 12 used in a previous analysis of the Egyptian-Saudi youth survey data (Moaddel and Karabenick 2008), we tested whether they were representative of the original scale by computing the correlation between the five selected items and the remaining seven. The correlation for the combined Egypt-Saudi-Arabia samples is .62 ($p <$. 00001), which indicates that the selected items provide an estimate of the fundamentalism construct that approximates the results that would have emerged from the larger set of items.

The presence of a middle category in the Iran survey, with its five response categories (and 5-point coding), would have precluded direct comparisons with the remaining countries that employed four response categories (and 4-point coding). Accordingly, we transformed the responses in Iran using the standard formula: Fundamentalism (4–pt.) = ((Fundamentalism (5 pt.) − 1) * .75 + 1). Since this is a linear transformation, the new scores correlate perfectly with the previous scores at the item level and for the total scale, and the internal consistency of the scale did not change (alpha = .68). The new scale resulted in the mean decreasing from 3.56 to 2.97, as did the variance (from SD = .78 to .59). The means for the Fundamentalism items and scale for Iran, Lebanon, Egypt, and Saudi Arabia are shown in Table 3.1.

Fundamentalism Scale Validity

According to Messick's (1989, 1995) comprehensive approach, validity incorporates multiple sources of evidence that bear on the interpretation or meaning of measures designed to operationalize constructs.

Table 3.1. Fundamentalism items included in Iran, Lebanon, Egypt & Saudi Arabia surveys.

Component	No.	Item	Iran	Lebanon	Egypt	Saudi Arabia	Social forces*
Nature of the Deity	1	The only acceptable religion to God is Islam.			✓	✓	
	2	God will punish most severely those who abandon his true religion.			✓	✓	✓
	3	The basic cause of evil in this world is Satan, who is still constantly and ferociously fighting against God.			✓	✓	✓
Inerrancy	4	There is a particular set of religious teachings in this world that are so true, you can't go any "deeper" because they are the basic, bedrock message that God has given humanity.			✓	✓	✓
	5	God has given humanity a complete, unfailing guide to happiness and salvation, which must be totally followed.			✓	✓	✓
	6	The Quran may have general facts, but the truth doesn't have to agree with it from beginning to end.			✓		
	7	Whenever there is a conflict between science and religion, *religion* is always right (religion is probably right for Lebanon and Iran).	✓	✓	✓	✓	
	8	The fundamentals of God's religion should never be tampered with, or compromised with others' beliefs.		✓	✓	✓	✓
	9	The religion of Islam is closer to God than other religions.[a] The only acceptable religion to God is Islam.[b]	✓	✓	✓	✓	✓

Table 3.1. (Cont.)

Component	No.	Item	Iran	Lebanon	Egypt	Saudi Arabia	Social forces*
Exclusivity	10	It is more important to be a good person than to believe in God and the right religion. (R)	✓	✓	✓	✓	
	11	When you get right down to it, there are basically only two kinds of people in the world: the Righteous, who will be rewarded by God; and the rest, who will not.			✓	✓	✓
	12	To lead the best, most meaningful life, one must belong to the one, fundamentally true religion.			✓	✓	✓
	13	Islam is the only religion on this earth that teaches, without error, God's truth.			✓	✓	✓
	14	Only good Muslims will go to heaven. Non-Muslims will not, no matter how good they are. [a] Muslims are the only ones who will go to heaven, and the rest of the people from other religions will not go no matter how good they are. [b]	✓	✓	✓	✓	✓
	15	Non-Muslim religions have a lot of strange beliefs and pagan ways.	✓	✓	✓	✓	✓
	16	People who belong to different religions are probably just as nice and moral as those who belong to mine.	✓	✓	✓	✓	
Intolerance	17	Islam should be the only religion taught in our public schools.	✓	✓	✓	✓	✓
	18	I would *not* mind to have teachers who are not religious. (R)	✓	✓	✓	✓	
	19	I would like my reli-gious leaders to meet with the leaders of other religions. (R)			✓	✓	
	20	If it were possible, I'd rather have a job where I worked with people with the same religious views I have rather than with people with different views.			✓	✓	

* from Moaddel and Karabenick (2008).
[a] Iran and Lebanon survey [b] Egypt and Saudi Arabia youth survey.

Applying this principle to the present assessment of fundamentalism, this would include whether the item content contains elements of the construct, the scale's internal consistency and whether the measure is associated in predictable ways with other variables. In view of the analyses conducted in this chapter, and substantially more to follow, there is suggestive evidence of validity for the current measure of fundamentalism. First, the item content represents dimensions of religious fundamentalism as previously operationalized, including evidence that the abbreviated five-item scale is strongly associated with its more extensive version (Moaddel and Karabenick 2008), as described above. Second, the internal consistency estimates (Cronbach alpha) suggest sufficient levels of reliability in each of the four countries represented. And perhaps most important, fundamentalism scores are related in predictable ways with the variation between countries and the association with levels of education, as will be shown below. Subsequent analyses, therefore, can be conducted with reasonable assurance that the scale construction successfully operationalizes the fundamentalism construct as currently construed.

Macro Comparisons

Macro comparisons address variation in religious fundamentalism as a function of national context (religiosity or secularism of the state, homogeneity or heterogeneity of the ruling elite, democracy or authoritarianism, pluralistic or monolithic religious context), religion, religious sects, and ethnicity. Table 3.2 presents the ethnic, religious, or religious-sect groups from each country that are included in these comparisons. In Egypt, the sample includes only the Sunni Arabs; in Iran the Shi'is, Sunnis, Azeri-Turks, Gilakis, Kurds, Lurs, and Persians; in Lebanon the Catholic, Maronites, Orthodox, Druze, Shi'is, and Sunnis; and in Saudi Arabia the Sunni and Shi'i [inferred from the Dammam-Khobar portion of the sample] Arabs (see the check marks in Table 3.2). Certainly, there are many other religious and ethnic groups in these countries. These specific groups were selected for analysis because their size in the sample from each country is large enough to allow for meaningful comparisons.

Cross-National Variations in Religious Fundamentalism

Table 3.3 presents the mean fundamentalism scale scores and standard deviations for each of the five items, and the total scale mean and standard deviation for each country. As was indicated earlier, higher

Table 3.2. Religious, sect, and ethnic groups sampled in each country.

		Egypt	Iran	Lebanon	Saudi Arabia
Christianity	Catholic			√	
	Maronite			√	
	Orthodox			√	
Islam	Druze			√	
	Shi'i		√	√	√
	Sunni	√	√	√	√
Ethnicity	Arab	√		√	√
	Azeri-Turk		√		
	Gilaki		√		
	Kurd		√		
	Lur		√		
	Persian		√		

Table 3.3. Item means (SDs) of fundamentalism scale items and total scale scores.

Item	Iran		Lebanon			
	Total Sample $n = 2,891$	18–25 Years $n = 1,047$	Total Sample $n = 3,037$	18–25 Years $n = 1,256$	Saudi Arabia $n = 954$	Egypt $n = 928$
Only good Muslims/ Christians will go to heaven. Non-Muslims/Christians will not, no matter how good they are.	2.06 (.91)	1.99 (.86)	2.48 (1.05)	2.53 (1.05)	3.45 (.80)	3.20 (.83)
Non-Muslim/non-Christian religions have a lot of weird beliefs and pagan ways.	2.42 (.89)	2.41 (.91)	2.23 (.79)	2.26 (.78)	3.58 (.63)	3.38 (.64)
The religion of Islam/Christianity is closer to God than other religions.	3.42 (.80)	3.46 (.80)	2.93 (.96)	2.89 (.93)	3.67 (.67)	3.66 (.58)
Whenever there is a conflict between science and religion, religion is probably right.	2.90 (.85)	2.93 (.90)	2.90 (.95)	2.94 (.87)	3.74 (.51)	3.71 (.50)
Islam/Christianity should be the only religion taught in our public schools.	2.85 (.92)	2.82 (.92)	2.05 (.75)	2.00 (.70)	3.77 (.53)	2.95 (.94)
Total Scale Mean	2.77 (.65)	2.74 (.65)	2.51 (.61)	2.52 (.58)	3.64 (.40)	3.38 (.44)
Cronbach alpha	.68	.74	.69	.68	.64	.56

Note: Response codes: 1 = Strongly Disagree 2 = Disagree 3 = Agree 4 = Strongly Agree.

scores mean stronger fundamentalist beliefs and attitudes. For Iran and Lebanon, the scores are reported for the country as a whole as well as for the 18–25 age groups. That is because, as noted earlier, for meaningful cross-national comparisons, the fundamentalism scores for Egypt and Saudi Arabia youth data must be compared with the same scores for the 18–25 age groups from Iran and Lebanon.

All fundamentalism scores are higher in Saudi Arabia and Egypt than in Iran and Lebanon. Likewise, the mean fundamentalism scores for Saudi Arabia and Egypt, 3.64 and 3.38, respectively, are higher than the mean fundamentalism scores for Iran and Lebanon, 2.77 and 2.74 respectively. We examined these overall country differences statistically. In addition, we simultaneously tested whether there were overall gender differences or differences due to level of education across the countries and whether gender or level of education differences varied by country. For this analysis, level of education was dichotomized according to whether respondents had no university education or at least some university education. In order to match the age distributions, only respondents less than 26 years of age were included in the Iran and Lebanon samples; accordingly, the analysis can be characterized as describing the fundamentalism status of youth in the four countries.

Table 3.4 shows cross-national variations in fundamentalism by gender and level of education. These data were analyzed using a three-way, Country (4) x Gender (2) x Education Level (2) univariate analysis of variance (ANOVA). ANOVA is used to test for between-groups differences on each dimension independently (a main effect), as well as whether between-group differences on one dimension depend on other dimensions (interaction effects). For example, we can test whether gender differences in fundamentalism vary by country. When there is a statistically significant main effect involving more thantwo groups (here, differences between the four countries), post-hoc paired comparisons (e.g., using Scheffe tests that compensate for conducting multiple comparisons on the same data set) are computed to determine which groups differ statistically from each other and which do not.

In the present instance, we found a strong main effect of country ($F_{3,4093}$ = 894.61, $p < .0001$); post-hoc comparisons indicated there were significant differences between all of the countries (Scheffe test at $p < .0001$). Thus, as shown in Table 3.4, Saudi Arabia is the highest, followed by Egypt, Iran, and Lebanon, which has the lowest fundamentalism score. The analysis also detected a much smaller but statistically significant main effect of education level ($F_{1,4093}$ = 33.00, $p < .0001$), such that those with less

Table 3.4. Mean fundamentalism (SD) as a function of country, gender and level of education.

Variable	Iran $n = 1{,}032$	Lebanon $n = 1{,}236$	Saudi Arabia $n = 949$	Egypt $n = 892$	Total
Male	2.62 (.56)	2.48 (.62)	3.63 (.40)	3.44 (.43)	3.01 (.72)
Female	2.73 (.56)	2.49 (.65)	3.64 (.38)	3.30 (.44)	3.00 (.70)
Less than university education	2.75 (.53)	2.58 (.64)	3.65 (.34)	3.39 (.44)	3.15 (.65)
Some university education	2.51 (.61)	2.45 (.63)	3.62 (.42)	3.35 (.44)	2.80 (.74)
Total	2.68 (.56)	2.49 (.64)	3.64 (.39)	3.38 (.44)	3.00 (.72)

education are higher in fundamentalism (*Mean* = 3.11) than those having some university education (*Mean* = 3.01). Interaction effects indicated that the gender and education differences also varied by country, although these effects are quite small. Inspection of the means in Table 3.4 suggests that the significant Country x Gender effect ($F_{3,4093}$ = 8.66, $p < .001$) is due to females being more fundamentalist than males in Iran, but the reverse in Egypt. The fact that there was no overall gender difference across counties can be attributed to these offsetting differences. There was no gender difference in fundamentalism among youth in Lebanon and Saudi Arabia. The Country x Education interaction ($F_{3,4093}$ = 6.07, $p < .0001$) appears due to the larger education differences in Iran and Lebanon than in Egypt or Saudi Arabia. The Country × Gender × Education Level was also statistically significant ($F_{3,4093}$ = 1.31, $p < .001$) but much too small to be considered important.

State Structures, State Cultures, and Religious Fundamentalism

On the national level, variation in fundamentalism seems to parallel the differences in the level of religious pluralism and the nature of a country's political structure. Lebanon is a democratic country. Politically organized in terms of religious confession, the country has a fairly strong tradition of religious pluralism. Under religious pluralism, there is a much higher possibility for the free exchange of religious ideas and interaction among the adherents of different religious sects. This exchange, in turn, tends to undermine religious exclusivity and enhance tolerance, and the presence of diverse religious institutions may weaken the belief in the comprehensiveness and absolute inerrancy of one's faith. At the same time, the Lebanese democratic environment tends to reduce political stress, which could be a factor contributing to lowering support for fundamentalism.

Egypt, Iran, and Saudi Arabia, on the other hand, are authoritarian countries. Egypt, at the time of the survey, was ruled by a secular government, whereas Iran and Saudi Arabia have Islamic governments. The effect of authoritarianism on people's cultural orientation, including the tendency to support religious fundamentalism, is apparently mediated by the nature of the political structure of the ruling regime. The Islamic Republic of Iran, despite its overall authoritarian nature and proven capacity and willingness to repress dissent, has a political structure that is heterogeneous, with considerable inter-elite rivalries and factionalism. This provides a favorable discursive space that has allowed the rise of a liberal trend among the country's intellectuals (Kamrava 2008) and the public at large (Moaddel 2009). This trend has undermined the religious and social influence of the fundamentalist ideology associated with the Islamic regime, particularly with its office of the absolutist ruler.

The political situation in Egypt and Saudi Arabia is quite different. Egypt has been ruled by a secular authoritarian regime, and the rise of religious oppositional discourse in the country has been largely in reaction to the state's secular authoritarianism (Moaddel 2005). This opposition seems to have promoted fundamentalist beliefs and attitudes among Egyptians. Although Saudi's religious authoritarianism may undermine support for the official religion (Moaddel 2010), in the absence of a heterogeneous political structure (unlike Iran), there is little social space for the rise of alternative cultural discourses. As a result, the public has remained vulnerable to the fundamentalist message of the oppositional religious movement in the country. In certain urban areas of Saudi society, like Dammam and al-Khobar (and presumably similar places on other parts of the kingdom), where there is a degree of religious pluralism, support for fundamentalism is much lower than in such other areas as like Riyadh and Jeddah.

The above argument points to the role of political structural heterogeneity—be this structure democratic like Lebanon or authoritarian like Iran—in undermining support for fundamentalism. This is so because structural heterogeneity is a more favorable context for dialogue and debates among different religious and cultural groups, and such debates tend to undermine fundamentalist beliefs and attitudes. Generally, however, the state tends to promote its own culture in society. In other words, the confessional state, whether it is democratically organized (Lebanon) or authoritarian (Iran and Saudi Arabia), tends to promote fundamentalist tendencies within its own confessional community, while a secular authoritarian state undermines fundamentalism. To put it differently, the stronger one's fundamentalist orientations, the greater that person's approval of the performance of the confessional state and less his/her approval of the secular state.

To assess this relationship, we focus on individual attitudes toward the government's performance. The respondents in were asked:

> People have different views about government in this country, by using this scale from 10 'steps' where the number (1) means very bad, and (10) means very good. What is the 'step' that you shall choose to express (your opinion) about the public sector?

Note that in Egypt and Saudi Arabia, the phrase "public sector" was used instead of "government." If our argument is correct, there will be positive relationships between fundamentalism and the ratings of government performance among Iranians as well as Lebanese Christians, Shi'is, and Sunnis, while this relationship will be negative among Egyptians. As shown in Table 3.5, in Iran, Saudi Arabia, and across all the three major religious groups in Lebanon, there are positive correlations between fundamentalism and ratings of their governments' performances, while in Egypt this relationship is negative.

Table 3.5. Correlations between fundamentalism and attitudes toward government performance.

Country	r
Egypt	−.11
Iran	.31
Lebanon-Christians	.08
Lebanon-Shi'is	.28
Lebanon-Sunnis	.14
Saudi Arabia	.09

All correlation are significant at $p < .01$.

Cross-Religion and Cross-Sect Variation in Religious Fundamentalism

Lebanon provides an opportunity to examine fundamentalism among Muslims and Christians as well as among different sects in each of these religions in the country. We compared these religious groups and assessed whether religious differences would be moderated by gender and level of education. A Religious Group (2) x Gender (2) x Education Level (2) analysis of variance detected statistically significant main effects of religion and education but no interactions, the means of which are shown in Table 3.6. Specifically, Muslims in Lebanon are more fundamentalist (*Mean* = 2.68) than are Christians (*Mean* = 2.29) ($F_{1, 2936}$ = 298.14, $p < .0001$), and those with less education are more fundamentalist (*Mean* = 2.63) than those with higher levels of education (*Mean* = 2.45) ($F_{1, 2936}$ = 45.76, $p < .0001$).

A follow-up analysis found no statistically significant differences in fundamentalism among the Christian sects (Maronites, Orthodox, and Catholics). However, there is a significant difference among the Muslim sects ($F_{2, 1901}$ = 6.54, $p < .001$). Post-hoc tests (Scheffé tested at $p < .01$) indicated that Sunni (*Mean* = 2.72) were more fundamentalist than the Druze (*Mean* = 2.58); there was no difference between the Lebanese Shi'is (*Mean* = 2.65) and either Sunnis or Druze.

So far, our analysis indicates that Lebanese youth were less fundamentalist than the youth from other countries, and that Lebanese Christians are less fundamentalist than Muslims. We can then ask to what extent the lower level of fundamentalism among Lebanese compared to Iranians is attributable to the influence of Christians in the sample. It is not possible to compare Christians in the two countries, but it is possible to compare Muslims. Detecting a difference would indicate that, to some extent at

Table 3.6. Mean (SD) fundamentalism in lebanon as a function of religion and level of education.

Level of education	Muslims $n = 1,883$	Christians $n = 1,061$	Total
Less than university education	2.75 (.54)	2.38 (.61)	2.63 (.59)
Some university education	2.61 (.55)	2.20 (.61)	2.45 (.61)
Total	2.67 (.55)	2.27 (.61)	2.53 (.60)

least, the Iran versus Lebanon difference is not solely attributable to the presence of Christians in Lebanon, but to such other factors as religious diversity and democratic structure of the state. To provide additional specificity, Shi'i and Sunni were considered separately.

The first analysis examined Shi'i versus Sunni differences in Lebanon and Iran simultaneously, with level of education added to check for possible moderation effects. A Country (2) x Shi'i-Sunni (2) x Level of Education (2) analysis of variance, with the proportion of Persians, Turks and Kurds (weighted to correct for the oversampling of the Kurds) in Iran, found significant main effects for each dimension. As reported in previous analyses, across countries, Iranians are more fundamentalist than Lebanese ($F_{1,4101}$ = 17.39, p < .0001), higher level of education is associated with lower levels of fundamentalism ($F_{1,4101}$ = 18.67, p < 0001), and the Sunnis are more fundamentalist than the Shi'is ($F_{1,4101}$ = 16.06, p < 0001). There was also a small Country x Shi'i-Sunni interaction effect ($F_{1,4101}$ = 8.72, p < 01). As shown in Table 3.7, this means that the Shi'i-Sunni difference for both countries combined (i.e., the main effect) is primarily attributable to the Shi'i-Sunni difference in Iran (*Mean Difference* = .39) compared to the relatively small difference between the sects in Lebanon (*Mean Difference* = .07). In fact, the Shi'i-Sunni difference in Iran was seven times greater than the gender difference in Lebanon. The results suggest, therefore, that the difference between Iran and Lebanon in fundamentalism is likely attributable to a difference between Muslims in the two countries, rather than just to the presence of Christians in Lebanon.

Next we assessed the Shi'i-Sunni difference within Saudi Arabia by comparing mean fundamentalism scores for the three cities—Jeddah, Riyadh, and Dammam-Khobar. Table 3.8 shows mean fundamentalism

Table 3.7. Mean (SD) fundamentalism of Shi'i and Sunni in Iran and Lebanon(using the entire sample).

Sect	Iran n = 2422	Lebanon n = 1687	Total
Shi'i	2.80 (.62)	2.65 (.51)	2.70 (.59)
Sunni	3.19 (.58)	2.72 (.59)	2.90 (.61)
Total	2.91 (.62)	2.70 (.55)	2.76 (.59)

Table 3.8. Mean (SD) fundamentalism of respondents in
Jeddah, Riyadh, and Damman-Khobar in Saudi Arabia.

Jeddah $n=473$	Riyadh $n=321$	Dammam-Khobar $n=160$	Total
3.73	3.60	3.50	3.64
(.33)	(.44)	(.41)	(.40)

scores for each of the three cities, which indicates that fundamentalism is
lowest for Dammam-Khobar and highest for Jeddah, with Riyadh's in
between. A one-way analysis of variance indicated statistically significant
variation among these cities ($F_{2,951}$ = 31.37, $p < .0001$), and post-hoc tests
(Scheffé tested at $p < .001$) verified, as shown in Table 3.8, that Jeddah was
most fundamentalist, followed by Riyadh and Dammam-Khobar.

It was not possible to specify the sectarian affiliations of the respondents from each of these cities, as there are no official statistics that break
down the population of Saudi Arabia by religious affiliation. We may
reasonably assume, however, that about 95% or more Saudi residents of
Jeddah and Riyadh are Sunnis, while those in Dammam-Khobar are part
of the Eastern Province of the kingdom where the majority of the estimated 1.5–2 million Saudi Shi'is live. Thus we cannot be certain that the
lower level of fundamentalism among Dammam-Khobar respondents is
the result of the influence of the Shi'i population. However, we may attribute this variation in fundamentalism across these three cities to the
influences of modernization and religious pluralism. Dammam-Khobar,
with a relatively large Shi'i population, may be religiously more pluralistic
than Jeddah, whereas Riyadh, a metropolitan area that grew from a small
town of a few thousand in the 1930s to more than 3 million in 2005, may
carry stronger elements of modern culture than Jeddah, which has historically been the center of Islamic orthodoxy and cultural tradition in the
kingdom (Moaddel and Karabenick 2008: 1699).

Inter-Ethnic Differences in Religious Fundamentalism among Iranians

The Iranian population provided a comparison among ethnic groups
(Kurds, Azeri Turks, Persians, Gilakis and Lurs). As shown in Table 3.9,
these groups varied in their levels of fundamentalism ($F_{4,2757}$ = 6.50,
$p < .0001$). Post-hoc paired comparisons (Scheffé tested at $p < .001$) found
no significant differences between Azeri Turks (*Mean* = 2.86) and Persians
(*Mean* = 2.79), both of which were significantly more fundamentalist than

Table 3.9. Mean (SD) fundamentalism among Iranians as a function of ethnicity, area of residence and level of education (entire sample).

Variable	Kurds $n = 297$	Persians $n = 1,516$	Turks $n = 560$	Total
Urban	2.44 (.72)	2.73 (.65)	2.76 (.62)	2.71 (.85)
Rural	2.66 (.88)	2.96 (.53)	3.05 (.56)	2.92 (.59)
Less than university education	2.61 (.67)	2.87 (.58)	2.92 (.57)	2.86 (.60)
Some university education	2.41 (.78)	2.58 (.59)	2.45 (.67)	2.54 (.70)
Total	2.55 (.71)	2.79 (.63)	2.86 (.61)	2.78 (.64)

the Kurds (*Mean* = 2.55). Gilakis (*Mean* = 2.71), and Lurs (*Mean* = 2.67) did not differ significantly from any other ethnic group. Because they were statistically differentiated and had sufficient numbers of respondents, Persians, Azeri Turks and Kurds were thus subject to further analysis, which included education and urban-rural residence to determine their independent effects as well as their potential moderating effects on fundamentalism. An Ethnicity (3) x Education Level (2) x Residence (2) analysis of variance detected significant main effects. There were no significant interaction effects, however, and thus the differences on each dimension (e.g., level of education) were the same for each level of the other dimensions (e.g., ethnic group). Means for the significant ethnicity main effect ($F_{2,2361}$ = 17.06, p < .0001) reflect the ethnic differences described above. That is, Persians, and Azeri Turks did not differ, and both were more fundamentalist than were Kurds. In addition, respondents in rural areas indicate being more fundamentalist than those in urban areas ($F_{1,2361}$ = 26.61 p < .0001). And, as in the other countries, those with more education were lower in fundamentalism ($F_{1,2936}$ = 29.40, p < .0001).

Sectarian Solidarity and Fundamentalism among Lebanese Religious Sects

To what extent is religious fundamentalism linked to in-group solidarity? We argue that trust is an important component of in-group solidarity and inter-group relationships. Trust among people is a *sine qua non* to stable social relationships and exchange, the core of social capital, and one of the key resources for the development of a democratic society. Social trust is said to reduce transaction costs, contribute to economic growth, help to solve collective action problems, promote an inclusive and open society, foster societal happiness and a general feeling of well-being, facilitate civic engagement, and create better government (Freitag and Bulhmann 2009; You 2012). Here, our objective is to assess the extent to which trust in the members of one's group and members of other groups is associated with fundamentalist attitudes.

To this end, respondents from different religious confessions were asked for the degree to which they trusted the members of their own as well as other confessions—that is, the Shi'is, Sunnis, Druze, Maronites, Catholics, and Orthodox—using a 4-point scale (a great deal of trust, some trust, not very much trust, or none at all). The results are reported in Table 3.10. As shown in this table, each religious group trusted in-group members more than those of other groups. Fully 72.0% of the Shi'is trusted other Shi'is a great deal, while only 16.9% trusted the Sunnis, 9.7% trusted the Druze, 21.7% trusted the Maronites, 20.9% trusted the Catholics, and 21.5% trusted the Orthodox. Likewise, 83.2% of the Sunnis trusted Sunnis a great deal. The level-of-trust figures the Sunnis gave for the Shi'is, Druze, Maronites, Catholics, and Orthodox were 32.5%, 24.4%, 31.7%, 33.0%, and 33.4%, respectively. The Druze also trusted other Druze a great deal—84.3% of the time—while they trusted the Shi'is, Sunnis, Maronites, Catholics, and Orthodox 31.8%, 56.4%, 10.9%, 9.3%, and 9.9% of the time. Maronites and Catholics also follow the same pattern, as 58% of the Maronites and 42.6% of the Catholics trusted a great deal the members of

Table 3.10. Percent members of different religious sects expressing "a great deal of trust" in members of their own sects and other sects.

Group Trusted	Religious Sect					
	Shi'i	Sunni	Druze	Maronite	Orthodox	Catholic
Shi'i	72.0	32.5	31.8	18.2	33.3	9.7
Sunnis	16.9	83.2	56.4	13.8	14.3	7.6
Druze	9.7	24.4	84.3	10.2	9.3	6.3
Maronite	21.7	31.7	10.9	58.2	24.8	27.8
Orthodox	21.5	33.4	9.9	41.7	43.9	32.6
Catholics	20.9	33.0	9.3	43.9	51.5	42.6

Note: Own sect trust in bold.

their own sects, while Maronites trusted a great deal the Shi'is 18.2%, the Sunnis 13.8%, the Druze 10.2%, the Catholics 43.9%, and the Orthodox 41.7% of the time. The Catholics felt the same about the Shi'i 9.7%, Sunnis 7.6%, Druze 6.3%, Maronites 27.8%, and Orthodox 32.6% of the time. The only exception to this pattern is among the Orthodox, who trusted the Catholics a great deal more than trusting themselves a great deal, 51.5% versus 43.9%, respectively. They trusted a great deal other groups—the Shi'is, Sunnis, Druze, and Maronites—33.3% 14.3%, 9.3%, and 24.8% of the time, respectively.

To assess the connection between religious fundamentalism and in-group solidarity, a measure of in-group solidarity was constructed for each of the six confessional groups, using the following formula:

In-Group solidarity of respondent I belonging to the religious confession J_i = the amount of trust member I has in group J_i – the average of the amount of trust this member has in other religious confessions (that is, in the religious confessions J_2 through J_6).

The correlation between this variable and religious fundamentalism is reported in Table 3.11 below. As this table shows, religious fundamentalism and in-group solidarity are significantly linked for five of the six religious confessions, including the Shi'is, Sunnis, Druze, Maronites, and Orthodox, but not the Catholics.

These findings are significant and consistent with the exclusivity component of fundamentalism discussed previously. These findings also indicate that fundamentalism and inter-group trusts are negatively linked. A measure of inter-group trust is computed by subtracting one's trust in his/her group from the average amount of trust one has in other groups:

Table 3.11. Correlations between fundamentalism and in-group solidarity.

Religious Confession	r
Shi'i	.34[b]
Sunni	.31[b]
Druze	.28[a]
Maronite	.23[b]
Orthodox	.42[b]
Catholic	.12

[a]$p < .001$ [b]$p < .0001$

> Inter-group trust= the average amount of trust respondent I belonging to the religious confession J_1 has in other religious confessions (that is, in the religious confessions other than his/her own; J_2 through J_6) – the amount of trust member I has in his/her own group J_1

In such a case, the stronger one's fundamentalist beliefs and attitudes, the lower is one's trust in those outside his/her own sects. Although it would be hard to advance a causal analysis with these correlational data, we could speculate that there is a reciprocal influence between religious fundamentalism and in-group solidarity.

Diversity of Lebanese Christians', Shi'is', and Sunnis' Regional Ties and Fundamentalism

The stability of the sectarian system in Lebanon is vulnerable to the diverse ties the different confessional groups have forged with regional forces and beyond, as well as to the crisscrossing pressures coming from these forces. For example, the Shi'is have strong ties with the Iranian regime, the Sunnis with the Kingdom of Saudi Arabia, and the Christians, mainly the Maronites, with Western countries, the French in particular. Since the Iranian and Saudis are purportedly Islamic regimes, we tested whether favorable attitudes toward the Iranian Islamic regime by the Shi'is and toward Saudi Arabia by the Sunnis are linked to religious fundamentalism among the Shi'is and Sunnis, respectively. We also assess the extent to which favorable attitudes toward the role of these countries are linked to fundamentalism among Christians.

To assess this linkage, we empirically evaluated the Christians', Shi'is', and Sunnis' ratings of the role of several foreign countries that have been actively involved in the internal affairs of Lebanon. The countries are Iran, Syria, Saudi Arabia, the U.S., Israel, and France. We then determined the relations between these ratings and religious fundamentalism among the Christians, Shi'is, and Sunnis in the country. The respondents were asked to rate, from very negative (1) to very positive (5), the impact of several countries on Lebanon, specifically:

> Some people believe that Lebanon is experiencing considerable political problems and violence nowadays, and some of these problems are caused by foreign countries. In your opinion, how do you rate the role of the following countries in affecting these conditions in Lebanon?

As shown in Table 3.12, both the Shi'is and Sunnis rated Syria, the U.S., Israel, and France below the midpoint, which indicates a negative

Table 3.12. Mean (SD) perceived role of a select foreign countries by Shi'is, Sunnis, and Christians in Lebanon (using the entire sample).

Country's Role in Lebanon	Shi'is n = 941	Sunnis n = 750	Christians n = 1075
Iran	3.49 (1.53)	1.38 (0.87)	1.51 (.95)
Syria	2.40 (1.38)	1.33 (0.73)	1.50 (.94)
Saudi Arabia	1.55 (0.89)	3.63 (1.58)	2.35 (1.43)
U.S.	1.53 (1.00)	1.70 (1.05)	2.01 (1.25)
Israel	1.22 (0.72)	1.10 (0.44)	1.32 (.80)
France	2.16 (1.24)	2.38 (1.31)	2.65 (1.34)

Rating Scale 1 = "Very negative" to 5 = "Very positive".

influence. However, they rated the role of Iran and Saudi Arabia quite differently. The Shi'is in Lebanon rated Iran as having the most positive influence on their country (3.49) compared to the negative influence attributed to Iran by the Sunnis (1.38). The Sunnis, on the other hand, considered Saudi Arabia as having the most positive influence (3.63) compared to that attributed to Saudi Arabia by the Shi'is (1.55). In other words, for the Shi'is, only Iran has played a predominantly positive role in Lebanon, while all other foreign countries mentioned on the list have played a predominantly negative role. For the Sunni, by contrast, only Saudi Arabia has played a predominantly positive role in the country, while all other countries have played a predominantly negative role.

Similarly, the Christians gave a higher rating (although below average) than the Shi'is or Sunnis to the role of France (2.65). Their next highest rating was given to the role of Saudi Arabia (2.35), followed by the U.S. (2.01). The average ratings of the role of Iran and Syria were almost as low as their average rating of the role of Israel (1.51, 150, and 1.32, respectively).

We argue that these ratings are linked to religious fundamentalism among the Christians, Shi'is, and Sunnis. We propose that the influence rating of Iran's role in Lebanon predicts religious fundamentalism among the Shi'is, and the influence rating of Saudi Arabia's role predicts religious fundamentalism among the Sunnis. Table 3.13 presents correlations between the rated roles of each country (negative to positive) in Lebanon and the fundamentalism scores of Shi'i and Sunni. As expected, Shi'i fundamentalism is strongly linked to the influence rating of Iran's role in Lebanon ($r = .43$) and Sunni fundamentalism to the influence rating of the role of Saudi Arabia in the country ($r = .45$). Christian fundamentalism, by contrast, displayed no significant linkage with attitudes toward France and the U.S.

This table also shows three significant correlations that need explanation. First, the link between fundamentalism among the Shi'is and favorable attitudes toward Syria ($r = .09$) is understandable, because the country is ruled by the members of the Alawite sect, which is a Shi'i offshoot, and because it also has close ties with the Hezbollah and the Islamic Regime in Iran. Second, the link between Shi'i fundamentalism and favorable attitudes toward the U.S. was unexpected. Our ad hoc explanation would be that for Lebanese Shi'is, the United States is a favorable destination to immigrate (there is a fairly large American-Lebanese Shi'i population in Michigan). Thus, the positive link between Shi'i fundamentalism and favorable attitudes toward the U.S. role in Lebanon may be a "spill-over" effect of positive attitudes of Shi'i fundamentalists toward their co-religionists in the U.S. Finally, the positive link between Christian fundamentalism and favorable attitudes toward Saudi Arabia ($r = .28$) may also be related to the complexity of their relationship with the kingdom. Although many Christians are concerned that Saudi Arabia may strengthen the Sunni brand of fundamentalism in their country,[3] they view this

Table 3.13. Correlations between Shi'is' and Sunnis' levels of fundamentalism and how they believe other countries affect conditions in Lebanon (using the entire sample).

Sect	Iran	Saudi Arabia	Syria	U.S.	Israel	France
Shi'i	.43[c]	.00	.09[a]	.10[b]	.04	.08
Sunni	−.04	.45[c]	−.08	.03	−.06	.00
Christians	−.05	.28[c]	−.03	−.06	.01	−.03

[a]$p < .01$ [b]$p < .005$ [c]$p < .0001$

---

[3] See Brian Palmer, "Why Would Lebanon's Christians Side with Iran?" http://www .slate.com/articles/news_and_politics/explainer/2009/06/why_would_lebanons _christians_side_with_iran.html. Retrieved June 24, 2012.

role as a counterweight to Iran and Syria. However, those who have stronger fundamentalist orientations are better prepared mentally to develop more favorable attitudes toward the Saudi role than those with weaker fundamentalist orientations. After all, as will be shown in Chapter Six, the more strongly Christian fundamentalists were the less they were in favor of gender equality, secular politics, and social individualism—orientations that are consistent with the dominant religious norms in Saudi Arabia.

The most notable aspects of these findings, however, are the existence of strong correlations between Shi'is fundamentalism and favorable attitudes toward Iran and between Sunni fundamentalism and favorable attitudes toward Saudi Arabia. These significant correlations support the connections between the strength of the religious ideas—here, religious fundamentalism—of a religious community and beliefs about its relationship with a foreign regime. The two religious regimes of Iran and Saudi Arabia, although rivals in the region, apparently contributed to different brands of religious fundamentalism in Lebanon. It may be speculated that in the pre-revolutionary period in Iran, when the country had a secular pro-Western regime, the Lebanese Shi'i ties to Iran in all likelihood promoted secularism or had no effect on their religious attitudes. Likewise, during the heyday of Arab nationalism, the Sunnis who had favorable attitudes toward Egyptian or Syrian regimes might have been drawn to Arab nationalism, and their attitudes toward Saudi Arabia might not have been so strongly linked to fundamentalism. Also speculative, insofar as the effect of regional factors on religious fundamentalism is concerned, the analysis just presented has shown one way in which a foreign regime may reinforce fundamentalist beliefs and attitudes among the members of the religious compatriots outside its borders.

The foregoing analysis also showed variations in fundamentalism by ethnicity, with the Druze and Kurds showing lower levels of fundamentalism than other ethnic groups among Lebanese Muslims and among Iranians, respectively. We attribute this lower level of support for fundamentalism to the Iranian Kurds' and Lebanese Druze's distinctive experience as ethnic groups. For the Iranian Kurds, like their counterparts in Iraq and Turkey, the most important issue has revolved on Kurdish identity, and the overarching goal has focused on the establishment of an autonomous republic for the Kurdish people. They have been led by secular leftist or liberal forces, and as a result there is little support for religious fundamentalism among them. Likewise, the Druze have acted in the Lebanese political scene as an ethnic rather than a religious group.

Their political organizations were secular left or liberal, which provide limited support for religious fundamentalism.

SUMMARY OF MACRO COMPARATIVE ANALYSIS

The foregoing macro comparative analysis revealed a pattern of similarities and differences in fundamentalism among youth across nations, religious sects, and ethnic groups. This pattern has displayed several features. First, on the national level, fundamentalism was lowest in Lebanon, followed by Iran, Egypt, and Saudi Arabia. This variation seems to parallel the differences in the level of religious pluralism and the nature of political structures of the ruling regimes. Lebanon is a democratic country with a fairly strong tradition of religious pluralism. Under religious pluralism, there is a much higher possibility for free exchange of religious ideas and interaction among the adherents of different religious sects. This exchange in turn tends to undermine religious exclusivity and enhance tolerance. At the same time, the presence of diverse religious institutions may weaken the belief in the comprehensiveness and absolute inerrancy of one's faith. Another factor contributing to lowering support for fundamentalism among the youth could be the Lebanese democratic environment, which tended to reduce political stress.

Egypt, Iran, and Saudi Arabia, on the other hand, have authoritarian regimes. Egypt was ruled by a secular government, whereas Iran and Saudi Arabia have Islamic governments. Generally, life under an authoritarian government is stressful. This stress may in turn provide favorable psychological and social conditions for the rise of fundamentalist beliefs and attitudes. This effect is, however, mediated by the nature of the political structure of the ruling regime. The Islamic Republic of Iran, despite its overall authoritarian nature and proven capacity and willingness to repress dissent, has a political structure that is heterogeneous, with considerable inter-elite rivalries and factionalism (Ehteshami 1995). This provides a favorable discursive space that has allowed the rise of a liberal trend among the country's intellectuals (Kamrava 2008) and the public at large (Moaddel 2009). We suggest that this trend has apparently undermined the religious and social influence of the fundamentalist ideology connected to the office of the absolutist ruler of the Islamic regime.

The political situation in Egypt and Saudi Arabia is quite different. Egypt had been ruled by a secular authoritarian regime. The rise of religious oppositional discourse in the country has been largely in reaction to the state's secular authoritarianism (Moaddel 2005). This opposition seems to have promoted fundamentalist beliefs and attitudes among Egyptians. Although Saudi Arabia's religious authoritarianism may undermine support for the official religion (Moaddel 2010), in the absence of a heterogeneous political structure (unlike Iran), there is little discursive space for the rise of alternative cultural discourses. As a result, the public has remained vulnerable to the fundamentalist message of the existing religious establishment (or fundamentalist religious oppositional movement) in the country. This is suggested by our finding that in Dammam-Khobar (and presumably similar places), where there is a degree of religious pluralism, support for fundamentalism is much lower than in such other cities as Riyadh and Jeddah.

With regard to religion, Christians tend to be less fundamentalist than are Muslims in Lebanon. It is premature, however, to attribute this difference to differences in primordial beliefs between the two religious faiths. Rather, they can be accounted for as outcomes of the contemporary experiences of the Christian, Shi'i, and Sunni communities in the country. In the modern period, Christian intellectuals have been among the harbingers of secularism and liberal ideas in the country and the region in general. Christian communities, the Maronites in particular, have maintained cultural relationships and favorable attitudes toward the West, France in particular. As a result, there is little cultural pressure from France or the U.S. that would favor religious fundamentalism among Christians. The Shi'is and Sunnis, on the other hand, are drawn toward fundamentalism by the very nature of their relationships with the Islamic regimes in the region in recent decades. Iran is the major patron of the Shi'is in Lebanon, and the Hezbollah, as the Shi'is' major Islamic political and military organization, has been founded and consistently supported by the Islamic Republic of Iran. The Sunnis, on the other hand, have received considerable support from Saudi Arabia. Thus the varying relationships of the Shi'i and Sunni communities with Iran and Saudi Arabia have shaped their perceptions of these countries, and these perceptions in turn are linked to more prevalent levels of fundamentalism. Interestingly, however, there is also evidence that Muslims in Lebanon are less fundamentalist than are those in Iran. This may be due potentially to the more democratic and pluralistic Lebanese society.

Finally, our findings have also demonstrated effects of gender, education, and rural-urban residence on fundamentalism. Gender differences in fundamentalism are country specific. In Iran, male youth tend to be less fundamentalist than female youth, while in Egypt it was just the opposite.

In Lebanon and Saudi Arabia, there was no significant gender difference in fundamentalism. University education is related to fundamentalism in Iran and Lebanon, while no such effect was detected in Egypt and Saudi Arabia. Finally, in Iran, there is a significant difference in fundamentalism between youth from rural and urban areas, the latter group being less supportive of fundamentalism.

CHAPTER FOUR

RELIGIOUS FUNDAMENTALISM AMONG YOUTH IN EGYPT AND
SAUDI ARABIA: EPISTEMIC AUTHORITY AND OTHER CORRELATES

This chapter examines fundamentalism and its correlates among youth in
Egypt and Saudi Arabia. It first focuses on epistemic authority (described
in the introductory chapter), which captures the sources of information/
knowledge that persons rely on in forming opinions or making decisions
on a variety of issues. We then analyze how youths' reliance on sources
of epistemic authority is related to fundamentalism and other sociological and social psychological variables that are potential correlates of
fundamentalism.

EPISTEMIC AUTHORITY

To examine epistemic authority, we selected a range of sources of knowledge from among those assumed to be closely related to fundamentalism—religious leaders, teachers of religion at school or university—and
those less likely—secular teachers, parents, friends, domestic TV and
newspapers, and satellite TV and the Internet (designated as international
media). Respondents were asked: "To what extent do you rely on, that is,
do you believe and trust, what the following people tell you about the following subjects?" (from 1 = "do not rely" to 5 = "completely rely"). The subjects or issues ranged from non-political and non-religious to clearly
political and religious issues, specifically: (a) the respondent's education
and career choice; (b) evolution: the explanation of how plants and animals have evolved; (c) the role of women in society and politics; (d)
Western societies and foreign culture; (e) politics and forms of government; and (f) the role of religion in politics and society. In all, respondents
provided 42 ratings of the degree of reliance on sources of epistemic
authority and issues.

The mean ratings for all issues and sources are provided in Table 4.1. For
descriptive purposes, the rank orders of the means across sources are also
provided, separately for each of the issues. Ranks were tied if they fell
within the 95% confidence interval of each mean (i.e., mean differences
< .07). Table 4.2 presents the means and ranks for the reliance on each of

Table 4.1. Mean reliance on epistemic sources for information/attitudes on all issues.

Issues	Parents	Religious Teachers	Secular Teachers	Friends	Religious Leaders	Domestic Media	Satellite/ Internet
				Sources			
				Saudi Arabia			
Role of women in society	3.96 (1)	3.76 (3)	3.32 (6)	3.49 (4)	3.86 (2)	3.40 (5)	3.12 (7)
Politics and government	3.93 (1)	3.69 (3)	3.37 (6)	3.52 (4.5)	3.86 (2)	3.47 (4.5)	3.27 (7)
Education & career choice	4.25 (1)	3.73 (2)	3.39 (5)	3.57 (3.5)	3.58 (3.5)	3.22 (6)	3.17 (7)
Evolution	3.70 (2)	3.72 (2)	3.56 (5.5)	3.41 (7)	3.74 (2)	3.66 (4)	3.50 (5.5)
The West	3.86 (2)	3.80 (2)	3.51 (6.5)	3.69 (4.5)	3.78 (2)	3.65 (4.5)	3.52 (6.5)
Role of religion in politics	4.10 (1)	4.00 (2)	3.47 (5.5)	3.62 (4)	4.08 (3)	3.51 (5.5)	3.24 (7)
				Egypt			
Role of women in society	3.03 (3)	3.12 (4)	2.52 (7)	2.72 (6)	3.27 (1)	3.17 (2)	2.86 (5)
Politics and government	2.95 (4.5)	2.90 (4.5)	2.63 (6.5)	2.69 (6.5)	3.00 (3)	3.55 (1)	3.24 (2)
Education & career choice	3.57 (1)	2.83 (2)	2.53 (6.5)	2.75 (3)	2.65 (3.5)	2.60 (3.5)	2.55 (6.5)
Evolution	2.78 (5)	2.90 (4)	3.15 (3)	2.46 (7)	2.54 (6)	3.44 (1)	3.29 (2)
The West	2.60 (7)	2.87 (3.5)	2.78 (5.5)	2.87 (3.5)	2.80 (5.5)	3.66 (1)	3.48 (2)
Role of religion in politics	3.47 (3)	3.70 (1.5)	2.71 (6.5)	2.69 (7.5)	3.72 (1.5)	3.34 (4)	3.00 (5)

Note: Values in ( ) represent the rank orders of the source means for each issue.

the sources of epistemic authority averaged over the six issues, and Table 4.3 shows the means and ranks for each of the issues averaged over the seven sources (and ranks were tied if means differed by < .05 within each country and by < .04 across countries).

A Country (2) x Source (7) x Issue (6) analysis of variance found all main and interaction effects to be statistically significant ($p < .0001$). With regard to the country main effect, summed across all sources and issues, respondents in Saudi Arabia reported greater reliance on epistemic authorities (3.62) than did those in Egypt (2.99) ($F_{1,1562} = 535.55$). The main effect of source ($F_{6,7392} = 95.29$) indicates that for both countries combined,

Table 4.2. Mean reliance on epistemic sources for information/attitudes: all issues combined.

Country	Sources							
	Parents	Relig. Teach.	Secular Teach.	Friends	Relig. Lead.	Dom. Media	Inter. Media	All
Saudi Arabia	3.97 (1)	3.78 (2.5)	3.44 (6)	3.55 (4)	3.79 (2.5)	3.48 (5)	3.30 (7)	3.62
Egypt	3.06 (3)	3.05 (3)	2.72 (6.5)	2.69 (6.5)	3.00 (5)	3.29 (1)	3.07 (3)	2.99
Both Countries	3.52 (1)	3.42 (2)	3.08 (6.5)	3.12 (6.5)	3.39 (3)	3.39 (4)	3.19 (5)	3.30

Note: Values in ( ) represent the rank orders of the means for all issues combined.

Table 4.3. Mean reliance on epistemic sources for information: all sources combined.

Issue	Egypt	Saudi Arabia	Combined
Role of women in society	2.96 (4.5)	3.56 (5)	3.26 (4)
Politics and government	2.99 (2.5)	3.56 (5)	3.28 (4)
Education & career choice	2.78 (6)	3.56 (5)	3.17 (6)
Evolution	2.94 (4.5)	3.61 (3)	3.28 (4)
The West	3.01 (2.5)	3.69 (1.5)	3.35 (2)
Role of religion in politics	3.23 (1)	3.72 (1.5)	3.48 (1)
All issues	2.99	3.62	3.30

Note: Values in ( ) represent rank orders of the means for all sources combined.

across all issues, as shown in Table 4.2, youth relied the most on parents, relied to a lesser extent on religious teachers, religious leaders and domestic media, relied somewhat less on international media, and relied the least on friends and secular teachers. According to the significant Country x Source interaction ($F_{6,9372} = 72.14$), however, the degree of reliance on the various sources of epistemic authority differed in Saudi Arabia and Egypt

As shown in Table 4.2, averaged across all issues, Saudi youth relied primarily on parents, less so on religious leaders and religious teachers, then on friends, even less on domestic media and secular teachers, and least on international media. By contrast, Egyptian youth relied the most on domestic media, even more so than on parents. They relied less on religious teachers and international media, slightly less on religious leaders, and the least on secular teachers and friends.

Regarding differences between issues ($F_{5,7810}$ = 62.27), as shown in Table 4.3, youth relied most on these sources for information and attitudes regarding the role of religion in politics and knowledge about the West, to a lesser extent about evolution, politics and role of women in society, and least about their education. The relatively small Country x Issue interaction ($F_{5,7810}$ = 28.07, p < .0001) implies that the magnitude of the between country differences in rated epistemic authority depended on the issue. For example, respondents in the two countries differed the most in regard to rated reliance on authorities for information about education (Saudi Arabia = 3.56 vs. Egypt = 2.78) and differed the least when it concerned the role of religion in politics (Saudi Arabia = 3.72 vs. Egypt = 3.23). A significant Source x Issue interaction ($F_{30,46860}$ = 104.53) indicates that how much respondents in the two countries relied on the various sources depended on the issue involved. In addition, the significant Country x Issue x Source interaction ($F_{30,46860}$ = 22.12) means that the Source of the Country x Issue interaction differed in the two countries; however, the effect is small, and inspection of the means reveals no readily interpretable pattern.

Taken together, it is quite evident that youth in Saudi Arabia and Egypt differed in the sources they considered credible. Although the degree of credibility depends somewhat on the issue involved, the overall pattern reflects the cultural, religious, political and social context in which they developed and that existed at the time the surveys were conducted. Specifically, on average, youth in Saudi Arabia tended to rely most on the traditional authorities in their world: parents, religious leaders and teachers. By contrast, Egyptian youth found domestic media the most credible source, which Saudi youth found one of the least credible. *Egyptian youth also rated international media as credible as they did parents and religious authorities.* The higher reliance of Saudi youth on the traditional sources of authority (parents and religion) may contribute to the maintenance of social continuity. This difference may be due to the difference in the structure of the religious market in the two countries. Because Egypt is both religiously and culturally more pluralistic than Saudi Arabia, Egyptian youth encounter more heterogeneous credible options than do Saudi youth when deciding which sources to rely on. As a result, Egyptian youth apparently relied less on any one source of knowledge than did their counterparts in Saudi Arabia. As recent events in Egypt have shown, the high credibility of information from the satellite and the Internet among Egyptian youth appears to have played a major role in the creation of social networks among these youth. These networks in turn might have contributed to the rise of nationwide protest movements that in the course of eighteen days (January 25–February 11, 2011) managed to push President Mubarak out of office.

Epistemic Authority and Fundamentalism

The next question concerns whether youths' reliance on authority is related to fundamentalism. To begin, we asked whether fundamentalist beliefs and attitudes were related to the general reliance on authority, predicting that there would be a positive association such that youth with stronger beliefs would rely more on such sources of information. To accomplish this, an overall reliance index was created by averaging the ratings of reliance on authority across all seven sources. The relationship between this index and fundamentalism was present in both countries, although it was somewhat higher in Saudi Arabia ($r = .19, p < .0001$) than in Egypt ($r = .12, p < .0001$). We then determined whether that relationship would vary depending on the source. It was expected that those with stronger fundamentalist attitudes and beliefs would tend to rely more on religious sources (religious leaders and teachers), but no prediction was advanced for non-religious sources. To test these predictions, a single score was calculated for each of the sources by averaging each respondent's ratings on the six issues (the aggregate scores for each source for Egypt and Saudi Arabia is reported in Table 4.2). Given that the ratings of reliance on religious sources (leaders and teachers) were very highly correlated in both countries ($r > .60$), they were combined (by averaging) to produce a single religious source index. Because the resulting six source scores were correlated with each other, multiple regression was used to determine their independent associations with fundamentalism.

Table 4.4 presents the standardized coefficients resulting from multiple regressions that were computed separately for each country. In Egypt, the only significant effect (not attributable to a probable artificial suppression effect) was the association ($\beta = .241, p < .0001$) between fundamentalism and the degree of reliance on religious sources (i.e., religious leaders and teachers combined). The same was true for youth in Saudi Arabia ($\beta = .185$,

Table 4.4. Fundamentalism and reliance on epistemic sources in Saudi Arabia and Egypt.

Epistemic source	Egypt	Saudi Arabia
Religious sources	.241[d]	.185[d]
Media-domestic	− .065	.152[b]
Parents	− .075[a]*	.071
Friends	− .059	− .044
Media-international	− .008	− .042
Secular teachers	− .020	− .046
Regression	$F_{6,885} = 6.29^d$	$F_{6,944} = 13.41^d$

[a]$p < .05$ [b]$p < .01$ [c]$p < .001$ [d]$p < .0001$
*Note: Discounted due to a likely suppression effect.

$p < .0001$). In addition, however, in Saudi Arabia, fundamentalism was also related to the degree of reliance on domestic media ($\beta = .152$, $p < .0001$). The difference between countries can be readily explained by the relative degree of control and contents of domestic media in the two countries. Specifically, in Saudi Arabia there was government ownership and operation of radio and TV, as well as censorship of material deemed offensive to Islamic mores; content that lent itself trusted more by those with fundamentalist beliefs. In comparison, the media in Egypt were relatively free of control and thus a variety of content that was relatively free and undoubtedly less relevant to fundamentalism. In sum, the stronger association in Saudi Arabia is attributable to the role of media trust by more fundamentalist youth in that country compared to that of youth in Egypt.

Islamic Orthodoxy and Religiosity

The content and scope of the *shari'a* is a subject of wide interpretations among Muslims. For Islamic modernists, the *shari'a* functions like common law, which can be changed according to changes in social conditions, in contrast to revealed laws, which are presumed unchangeable. In the nineteenth century, Muslim intellectual leaders such as Chiragh Ali (1883: xxvii) from India, for example, conceded that certain aspects of Islamic laws are irreconcilable with the conditions of modern life, whether in India or Turkey, and require modifications. "The several chapters of the Common Law, as those on political Institutes, Slavery, Concubinage, Marriage, Divorce, and the Disabilities of non-Moslem fellow-subjects are to be remodeled and re-written in accordance with the strict interpretations of the Koran [Qur'an]." He thus removed these laws from the level of religion (i.e., sacred laws to be discovered via exegesis) and placed them within the category of the secular (laws that were man-made). He did so by distinguishing between the Muhammadan revealed law of the Qur'an and the Muhammadan common law that had been developed over the course of Muslim history.

Likewise, Egyptian Muhammad Abduh distinguished between acts directed toward the worship of God (*ibadat*) and those directed toward other men and life in the world (*mu'amalat* [social exchange]), a distinction that paralleled Chiragh Ali's common law-revealed law dichotomy. He argued that while Islam laid down specific rules about worship, it contained only general principles about relations with other men, leaving it for men to apply them to all the circumstances of life (Hourani 1983; Adams 1933; Moaddel 2005). Islamic feminists like Indian Mumtaz Ali (Minault 1990) and Egyptian Qasim Amin (1992 [1899]) also reinterpreted the *shari'a* in order to advance Islamic arguments in favor of gender equality.

Islamic fundamentalists have also attempted to reinterpret the *shari'a* in a way that does not reveal its conformity and consistency with the modernist ideas of constitutionalism, democracy and gender equality, but rather to show the decadence of Western societies, the un-Islamic nature of gender equality, and the necessity of overthrowing the existing political order and establishing an Islamic state based on the unity of religion and politics (e.g., Khumayni 1981; al-Banna 1978; Qutb 1964, 1993). Islamic orthodoxy, on the other hand, gives a traditionalist interpretation of the *shari'a* as it was practiced before the modern period. Islamic orthodoxy vehemently resisted the modernist approach, while being attacked by the fundamentalists (Ahmad 1964; Marsot 1968; Adams 1933; Hourani 1983; Moaddel 2005).

In sum, for Islamic modernists, a good government is a democratic and constitutional government; for the fundamentalist, it is an Islamic government that is under the control of religious authorities; for the orthodox, it is a government that implements only the laws of the *shari'a*. In other words, support of the *shari'a* is primarily in line with the orthodox position in Islam. Support for the *shari'a*, therefore, is yet another potential correlate of religious fundamentalism rather than synonymous with it.

For the present study, Islamic orthodoxy was conceptualized according to what Davis and Robinson (2006) proposed as the orthodoxy/modernism continuum, assessed here as the degree to which respondents

Table 4.5. Mean (SD) religiosity and orthodoxy.

Variable	Egypt	Saudi Arabia	Difference p
Orthodoxy (*shari'a*)	3.64 (1.25)	4.56 (0.73)	< .0001
Mosque attendance	5.32 (1.87)	5.29 (2.29)	ns
Prayer	3.55 (0.79)	3.83 (0.48)	< .0001
Self-rated religiosity	.57 (0.50)	.66 (0.47)	< .0001

considered it important for a "good government" to implement only the laws of the *shari'a*. The survey measured support for the *shari'a* by asking respondents whether it was very important, important, somewhat important, least important, or not important (scaled from 5 to 1, respectively) for a good government to implement only the laws of the *shari'a*.

Next, three indicators measured individual religiosity: mosque attendance, daily prayer, and self-described religiosity. Respondents were asked how often (apart from funerals) they attended the mosque on a 7-point scale (from 1 = "never" to 7 = "more than once a week"), how often they prayed on a 4-point scale (from 1 = "at no time" to 4 = "five times a day"), and whether they would describe themselves as a religious person, with choices of "a religious person" (scaled = 1), "not a religious person" (scaled = 0) and "a convinced atheist (not believing in God)" (treated as missing)

Table 4.5 presents descriptive statistics for the religiosity and orthodoxy variables for Egypt and Saudi Arabia. Prayer and self-rated religiosity ratings are higher for youth in Saudi Arabia than in Egypt, but the same is not true for the frequency of mosque attendance that is virtually the same in both countries. Table 4.6 presents the correlations between the variables, with Egypt below and Saudi Arabia above the diagonal. As would be expected, mosque attendance and the frequency of prayer are related, although somewhat more so in Egypt. We then used multiple regression to determine which of the religiosity and orthodoxy variables predicted the degree of fundamentalism when controlling for influence of the remaining three. As presented in Table 4.7, orthodoxy (support for the *shari'a*) positively predicts fundamentalism both in Egypt (β = .217, p < .0001) and in Saudi Arabia (β = .227, p < .0001). The countries differ,

Table 4.6. Correlations between religiosity and orthodoxy predictors of fundamentalism in Egypt (below diagonal) and Saudi Arabia (above diagonal).

Variable	Mosque Attendance	Prayer	Self-Rated Religiosity	Orthodoxy (shari'a)
Mosque attendance		.11[b]	− .08[a]	.03
Prayer	.20[d]		.38[d]	.11
Self-rated religiosity	− .03	.29[c]		.01
Orthodoxy (shari'a)	.16[b]	.06	.03	

[a]$p < .05$ [b]$p < .01$ [c]$p < .001$ [d]$p < .0001$

Table 4.7. Religiosity and orthodoxy predictors of fundamentalism.

	Variable	Egypt	Saudi Arabia
Religion	Mosque attendance	.125[c]	− .004
	Prayer	− .049	− .062
	Self-rated religiosity	− .031	.256[d]
Orthodoxy (support for shari'a)		.217[d]	.227[d]
Regression		$F_{4,811} = 15.67^d$	$F_{4,889} = 26.69^d$

[c]$p < .001$ [d]$p < .0001$ Note: Standardized regression coefficients.

however, with regard to mosque attendance and religiosity. Specifically, mosque attendance positively predicts fundamentalism in Egypt ($\beta = .125$, $p < .001$) but not in Saudi Arabia, whereas self-rated religiosity predicts fundamentalism in Saudi Arabia ($\beta = .256$, $p < .0001$) but not in Egypt. Frequency of prayer did not predict fundamentalism in either country.

Fatalism, Powerlessness and Insecurity

There are two ways to measure fatalism from a Durkheimian perspective. First, because it is described "as one associated with feelings of personal helplessness and vulnerability, resulting from an overwhelming external force that has a total control over personal action" (Acevedo 2005:78), powerlessness remains at the core of the operational definition of fatalism. This is particularly true for those who suggest a parallel between fatalism and alienation (Lukes 1967; Lockwood 1992; Acevedo 2005). Second, considering that Durkheim's assessment of social regulation intended to demonstrate the pathological consequences of two extremes—deregulation on one end and excessive regulation on the other—for human happiness, and that the two extremes are conducive to unhappiness and suicide (Besnard 1993), an individual's perception of the possibility of happiness in this world becomes the key defining feature of fatalism.

Therefore, a measure that stresses the unrealizability of happiness in this life would be a better indicator of fatalism than one based on power-lessness. For respondents, powerlessness may be a fact of life rooted in the existing social and political arrangements that can be changed. On the other hand, the unrealizability of happiness in this world, while a cognitive understanding resulting from the individual submergence in an oppressive and overly regulated social environment, captures both the pessimism and inevitability component of fatalism. This measure is also more consistent with the fatalism measures common in the literature, although both have been used (Mayo, Ureda and Parker 2001; Powe 1995). In the present study, we used the unrealizability of happiness in this world as a measure of fatalism. However, a measure of powerlessness is also included as another indicator of the youth's subjective orientation that may correlate with fundamentalism. Unrealizability of happiness was measured by respondents' agreement (4-point Likert scale) "that it is not possible to be very happy in this world." To measure individuals' feeling of powerlessness, respondents were presented with the following scenario:

> Some people feel they have completely free choice and control over their lives, while other people feel that what they do has no real effect on what happens to them. Please use this scale where 1 means "none at all" and 10 means "a great deal" to indicate how much freedom of choice and control you feel you have over the way your life turns out.

Whereas some may consider insecurity as part of fatalism, it is more appropriate to treat these factors as conceptually distinct. Fatalistic attitudes in Durkheimian tradition are reflections of social structure. The feeling of insecurity, on the other hand, is often linked to difficult sociopolitical conditions, including lack of basic necessities, high unemployment and political violence—all shaping people's perception of the safety and certainty of life. Insecurity was measured in terms of the degree to which the respondents viewed life in their countries to be unsafe and unpredictable, by asking for their agreement (4-point Likert scale) "that in your country these days, life is unpredictable and dangerous." All three variables were recoded so that higher values indicate a higher level of powerlessness, a firmer belief that happiness may not be possible in this world, and greater insecurity.

The descriptive statistics for these variables presented in Table 4.8 reveal differences between the two countries. Thus youth in Saudi Arabia rated themselves as more fatalistic, but those in Egypt indicated being higher in powerlessness and insecurity. As shown in Table 4.9, with the exception of the correlation between fatalism and powerlessness in Saudi Arabia, all variables are significantly correlated with each other. Multiple regression was used to estimate how each of these variables independently predicted fundamentalism. As shown in Table 4.10, both fatalism

Table 4.8. Mean (SD) levels of fatalism, powerlessness and insecurity.

Variable	Egypt	Saudi Arabia	Difference p
Fatalism	2.31 (0.75)	2.77 (1.03)	< .0001
Powerlessness	4.82 (2.39)	4.31 (2.35)	< .0001
Insecurity	2.87 (0.84)	2.60 (0.98)	< .0001

Table 4.9. Correlations between fatalism, powerlessness and insecurity in Egypt (below diagonal) and Saudi Arabia (above diagonal).

Variable	Fatalism	Powerlessness	Insecurity
Fatalism		.00	.17[b]
Powerlessness	.14[b]		.12[b]
Insecurity	.12[b]	.19[c]	

[b]$p < .01$ [c]$p < .001$

Table 4.10. Fatalism, powerlessness and insecurity predictors of fundamentalism.

Psychological dimensions	Egypt	Saudi Arabia
Fatalism	.088[a]	.090[b]
Powerlessness	.079[a]	.004
Insecurity	.136[c]	− .004
Regression	$F_{3,840} = 12.05^{c}$	$F_{3,875} = 2.42$

[a]$p < .05$ [b]$p < .01$ [c]$p < .001$

(β = .088, p < .05), powerlessness (β = .079, p < .05) and insecurity (β = .136, p < .001) directly predicted fundamentalism in Egypt. However, only fatalism predicted fundamentalism in Saudi Arabia (β = .241, p < .0001).

Besieged Spirituality

We conceptualized besieged spirituality as a condition in which the faithful perceive that their religion is under serious attack, and that this perception prompts them to adopt fundamentalist beliefs and attitudes. Two questions were used as proxy measures of besieged spirituality. The first question asked respondents the seriousness for their country of "cultural invasion by the West" (from 1 = "not serious" to 5 = "very serious"). The second variable measured people's perception of the existence of conspiracies against their religious community. Respondents were asked for the extent to which they agreed (1 = "strongly disagree," 4 = "strongly agree") that there are "conspiracies against Muslim nations by Jews and Americans." The means and standard deviations for both variables are presented in Table 4.11. As this table indicates, youth in Egypt considered this issue more important (*Mean* = 4.47, *SD* = 0.99) than did those in Saudi Arabia (*Mean* = 3.92, *SD* = 1.35). The fact the Saudi youth are less concerned with Western cultural invasion than their Egyptian counterparts may be due to the fact that in Saudi Arabia the religious institutions enjoy considerable power and have extensive control over the country's cultural affairs and activities. In Egypt, on the other hand, religious institutions are not as powerful, and there has been a long cultural conflict between the religious and conservative groups on the one hand and supporters of liberal worldviews and secularism on the other hand. Thus, for Saudis, the issue of Western cultural invasion is less serious than for Egyptians. There was, however, no difference in the degree to which youth in the two

Table 4.11. Mean (SD) levels of besieged spirituality.

Variable	Egypt	Saudi Arabia	Difference p
Western cultural invasion	4.47 (0.99)	3.92 (1.35)	< .0001
Conspiracy against Muslim nations	3.65 (0.61)	3.68 (0.62)	ns

Table 4.12. Besieged spirituality predictors of fundamentalism.

Psychological Dimensions	Egypt	Saudi Arabia
Western cultural invasion	.087[a]	.107[c]
Conspiracy against Muslim nations	.284[d]	.217[d]
Regression	$F_{2,874} = 45.23$[d]	$F_{2,903} = 30.60$[d]

[a]$p < .05$ [b]$p < .01$ [c]$p < .001$ [c]$p < .001$[d]$p < .0001$

countries believed there was a conspiracy (*Mean* = 3.65, *SD* = 0.61 for Egypt, *Mean* = 3.68. *SD* = 0.62 for Saudi Arabia), as shown in Table 4.11.

Regarding the relationship between these two variables and fundamentalism, Table 4.12 shows that, for both countries, youth who considered that cultural invasion by the West was more important were higher in fundamentalism (Egypt: β= .087, $p < .05$; Saudi Arabia: β = .107, $p < .001$). Further, the table also shows that there is an association between fundamentalism and a perceived conspiracy (Egypt: β = .284, $p < .0001$; Saudi Arabia: β = .217, $p < .0001$), to a greater extent than the association between fundamentalism and the importance of cultural invasion by the West.

State Ideology and Muslim Identity

We proposed that people's conception of their identity is often developed in oppositional relations to the ideology of the authoritarian state. Secularist authoritarian states have contributed to the rise of Islamic identity among the public, whereas religious authoritarian states tend to elicit nationalist reactions from a discontented public—hence the rise of national identity. In the present study, the respondents were asked whether "above all" they considered themselves "a Saudi/Egyptian", "a Muslim", "an Arab", or "Other." A dummy variable of Muslim identity was created, where 1 = "Above all, I am a Muslim" and 0 = "Otherwise." The results are shown in Table 4.13. Using these data, we tested the relationship between identity and fundamentalist beliefs and attitudes. We predicted that youth who identified themselves as Muslim would subscribe to fundamentalist beliefs and attitudes more so than would those with non-Muslim identities. In these countries, most respondents self-identified as Muslim above all: 81% of the respondents in Saudi Arabia and 91% in Egypt. Self-identified Saudi Muslims were slightly higher in Fundamentalism (*Mean* = 3.66, *SD* = .39) than were others (*Mean* = 3.56, *SD* = .40) ($F_{1,952}$ = 10.14, $p < .001$), but that difference did not exist in Egypt

Table 4.13. Muslim identity and fundamentalism.

Variable	Egypt	Saudi Arabia	Difference p
Muslim identity	91%	81%	< .0001
Fundamentalism for those who identify themselves as...			
Muslims	3.88 (.42)	3.66 (.39)	
Non-Muslims	3.88 (.43)	3.56 (.40)	
Difference	$F < 1$	$F_{1,952} = 10.14^c$	

$^c p < .001$

(for both groups, *Mean* = 3.88). Thus, there is support for the identity-fundamentalism association, but whether it exists depends on the specific context.

Television Viewing

We also examined whether television viewing was related to religious fundamentalism. To measure television viewing, respondents were asked: "How much time do you usually spend watching television on an average weekday (not on weekends)?" Response categories were: (1) "I do not watch TV," (2) "1–2 hours per day," (3) "2–3 hours per day," (4) "More than three hours." Because the response scale is ordinal rather than interval, we used the rank-order correlation coefficient (rho) to compute the degree of association. The frequency distributions of TV viewing are provided in Table 4.14. For Egyptian respondents, the more television they watched,

Table 4.14. TV Viewing (%) and association with fundamentalism.

	Egypt	Saudi Arabia
Do not watch	4.5	1.2
1–2 hours/day	25.0	18.9
2–3 hours/day	24.0	30.5
> 3 hours/day	46.5	49.4
Correlation (rho) with fundamentalism	– .12^c	– .04

$^c p < .001$

Table 4.15. Self-assigned social class (%) and fundamentalism.

	Egypt	Saudi Arabia
Upper class	1.2	10.7
Upper middle class	32.3	37.3
Lower middle class	48.7	35.1
Working class	14.8	14.8
Lower class	3.0	2.1
Correlation (rho) with fundamentalism	−.01	.02

the lower their level of fundamentalism ($rho = -.12$, $p < .001$). The same was not the case for those in Saudi Arabia, however ($rho = -.04$).

Socioeconomic Status: Income and Social Class

Two indicators were used as measures of socioeconomic status. One was annual household income. Household income before taxes, counting all wages, salaries, pensions, and other income, was coded in deciles by the local investigators in each country. Results indicate that fundamentalism was inversely related income ($p < .01$) in both countries, at virtually the same magnitude: −.11 in Saudi Arabia and −.09 in Egypt. The other measure was self-assigned class membership. Respondents were asked: "People sometimes describe themselves as belonging to the working class, the middle class, or the upper or lower class. Would you describe yourself as belonging to the (1) upper class, (2) upper middle class, (3) lower middle class, (4) working class, or (5) lower class"? The frequency distribution of social class is presented in Table 4.15. In contrast to income level, self-assigned class membership appears to have no significant relationship with fundamentalism (both correlations < .03).

CONCLUSIONS

The foregoing analysis has revealed that Islamic fundamentalism in the world of young Muslims in Egypt and Saudi Arabia was linked positively to the epistemic role of religious authorities, Islamic orthodoxy, fatalistic attitudes, the perceptions that there was a conspiracy against Muslim nations, and attitudes toward Western cultural invasion (both used as measures of besieged spirituality) in both countries. In terms of socioeconomic status, fundamentalism was negatively linked to family income.

Table 4.16. Correlates of fundamentalism and effect sizes.

Variable		Egypt	Saudi Arabia
Epistemic authority	Religious sources	++	++
	Media-domestic	o	++
	Parents	o	o
	Friends	o	o
	Media-international	o	o
	Secular teachers	o	o
Religion	Mosque attendance	+	o
	Prayer	o	o
	Self-rated religiosity	o	++
Orthodoxy (support for *shari'a*)		++	++
Social psych. variables	Fatalism	+	+
	Powerlessness	+	o
	Insecurity	+	o
Besieged spirituality	Western cultural invasion	++	++
	Conspiracy against Muslim nations	+++	++
Muslim identify		o	+
TV viewing		–	o
Income		–	–
Self-assigned social class		o	o

o = No significant relationship Effect Sizes: +/– = Minor ++/– – = Small +++/– – – = Moderate

In addition, in Saudi Arabia, those who relied on domestic media and self-identified as Muslim were higher in fundamentalism. In Egypt, on the other hand, Mosque attendance and the feeling of insecurity, fatalism and powerlessness were positively while the frequency of watching TV was negatively linked to fundamentalism. While realizing that it is difficult to advance a causal argument with cross-sectional data, we may cautiously generalize about the social context of fundamentalism. A summary of these relations and the associated effect sizes (e.g., Valentine and Cooper, 2003) is shown in Table 4.16. Effect sizes are very small (+/–), small (++/– –), and moderate (+++/– – –). While there are certainly differences between countries, at a broad level, there is evidence that fundamentalism may play a role in the lives of youth in Egypt and Saudi Arabia.

CHAPTER FIVE

RELIGIOUS FUNDAMENTALISM IN IRAN AND LEBANON

The previous chapter analyzed the correlates of religious fundamentalism among young Muslims in Egypt and Saudi Arabia. It focused on the sources of epistemic authority and a comprehensive set of social, political and psychological variables. This chapter turns our attention to Iranian and Lebanese adults and advances a similar analysis in order to assess the significance of these variables in predicting fundamentalism in these two countries. Although resting on a common theoretical framework, as will be noted, several of the variables examined here were not operationalized in the same manner as in Egypt and Saudi Arabia. Every attempt was made, however, to preserve their meaning and relevance for elucidating the role of fundamentalist beliefs and attitudes in the social, political and historical context of Iran and Lebanon.

Correlates of Religious Fundamentalism

Epistemic Authority

The national surveys in Iran and Lebanon did not include the same questions on the sources of epistemic authority that were used in the youth survey in Egypt and Saudi Arabia. Nevertheless, the present analysis employs several other ways to gauge respondents' *confidence* in similar sources, such as confidence in religious institutions and the media. Also obtained in Iran and Lebanon was the extent of respondents' *access* to sources of news, including such digital sources of information and news as the Internet and email as well as the frequency of using personal computers. These variables are considered proxy measures of epistemic authority and are examined for their association with religious fundamentalism.

To assess the respondents' confidence in different sources of information, they were asked to provide their level of confidence (1 = "none at all," 2 = "not very much," 3 = "quite a lot," 4 = "a great deal of confidence") in religious institutions, the press, and television. In the Lebanon survey, the last item was divided into two questions: one about the level of confidence in Lebanese television and the other in non-Lebanese television. For the other set of items related to access to sources of information, respondents were prompted as follows: "People use different sources to learn what is going on in their country and the world. For each of the following sources, please indicate whether you used it last week or did not use it last week to obtain information." The sources were: daily newspaper, news broadcasts on radio or TV, books, Internet/email, and talks with friends or colleagues. Another item assessed how often they used a personal computer (1 = "never," 2= "occasionally," 3 = "frequently"). Descriptive statistics for each of these variables are shown in Table 5.1, which differentiates religious groups in Lebanon (Christians, Shi'is, and Sunnis) in addition to comparisons with Iran.

As this table shows, Iranians on average indicated having greater confidence in religious institutions and TV than did Lebanese, but lower confidence in the press. While they are similar in their use of daily paper, radio and TV and books, a much higher proportion of Lebanese reported to have used the Internet or email, used personal computers, or talked with friends or colleagues than did Iranians. There is also some variation between different Lebanese sects. For example, Christians reported having less confidence in their religious institutions than did members of the other two sects, whereas the Shi'is had less confidence in the press and TV than did the other two religious sects and were also less likely to read a newspaper. Christians indicated using the Internet or email and personal computers more often than did the Shi'is or Sunnis.

Table 5.2 presents the correlations of the confidence in and access to these sources with fundamentalism, separately for respondents in Iran (below the diagonal) and Lebanon (above the diagonal). The results reveal an interesting pattern of similarities and differences in the linkages between the sources of epistemic authority and fundamentalism among Iranians and Lebanese. First, except for talking to friends/colleagues as well as the use of radio and TV in Lebanon, all other sources of epistemic authority are significantly linked to fundamentalism. Confidence in the religious institutions has the strongest positive correlation and the frequency of using personal computers the strongest negative correlation with fundamentalism in both countries. Confidence in the press and TV is related to fundamentalist beliefs and attitudes in both countries as well. The use of radio and TV as a source of information is positively linked to fundamentalism among Iranians only. This is understandable given that these sources of information are controlled by

Table 5.1. Means (SD) for measures of source confidence and access in Lebanon and Iran.

Variable	Lebanon				Iran
	Christians	Shi'i	Sunni	Total	
Source Confidence[a]					
Religious institutions	4.34 (1.62)	4.48 (1.58)	4.52 (1.67)	4.38 (1.64)	4.98[d] (1.20)
Press	4.06 (1.53)	3.87 (1.58)	4.05 (1.56)	3.96 (1.57)	3.85[d] (1.22)
Television	3.77 (1.64)	3.64 (1.65)	3.86 (1.64)	3.75 (1.64)	4.14[d] (1.27)
Source Access[b]					
Read daily paper	.53 (.50)	.44 (.50)	.60 (.49)	.52 (.50)	.51 (.50)
Use radio and TV	.83 (.37)	.82 (.39)	.88 (.33)	.84 (.37)	.86 (.35)
Read books	.38 (.49)	.35 (.48)	.33 (.47)	.36 (.48)	.33 (.47)
Use Internet or email	.68 (.47)	.54 (.50)	.50 (.50)	.58 (.49)	.20[d] (.40)
Talk with friends and colleagues	.93 (.25)	.91 (.29)	.92 (.26)	.92 (.26)	.74[d] (.44)
Computer use[c]	2.76 (.74)	1.02 (.76)	2.09 (.80)	2.22 (.77)	1.66[d] (.75)

[a]Coding: 1 = Not at all...6 = A great deal.
[b]Coding for access: 0 = Not used last week, 1 = Used last week.
[c]Coding: 1 = Never, 2 = Occasionally, 3 = Frequently.
[d]$p < .0001$ between Lebanon and Iran.

the conservative Islamic regime. All other sources of news information where individuals have multiple sources of information from which to choose are negatively linked to fundamentalism. Again, across the two nations and religious sects (not shown), the factor that is consistently and positively linked to fundamentalism is confidence in the religious institutions, whereas reading books, the use of the Internet or email

Table 5.2. Correlations of fundamentalism, source confidence and source access in Iran (below diagonal) and Lebanon (above diagonal).

		1	2	3	4	5	6	7	8	9	10
						Source Confidence					
1.	Fundamentalism		$.30^d$	$.08^d$	$.08^d$	$-.06^c$	$-.01$	$-.11^d$	$-.18^d$	$-.01$	$-.21^d$
2.	Religious institution	$.40^d$		$.35^d$	$.33^d$	$.03$	$.06^c$	$-.09^d$	$-.06^b$	$.02$	$-.07^d$
3.	The Press	$.11^d$	$.18^d$		$.69^d$	$.05^a$	$.02$	$.02$	$.008$	$.01$	$-.02$
4.	TV	$.23^d$	$.35^d$	$.52^d$		$.03$	$.04$	$-.03$	$-.02$	$.03$	$-.05^b$
						Source Access					
5.	Read daily paper	$-.12^d$	$-.13^d$	$.01$	$-.06^b$		$.25^d$	$.23^d$	$.14^d$	$.11^d$	$.09^d$
6.	Use radio and TV	$.06^b$	$.03$	$.00$	$.04^a$	$.20^d$		$.07^d$	$-.01$	$.19^d$	$-.06^c$
7.	Read books	$-.08^d$	$-.10^d$	$-.01$	$-.06^b$	$.41^d$	$.09^d$		$.24^d$	$.06^b$	$.16^d$
8.	Use Internet/ email	$-.18^d$	$-.19^d$	$-.03$	$-.11^d$	$.25^d$	$.00$	$.32^d$		$.09^d$	$.66^d$
9.	Talk with friends	$-.03$	$-.06^c$	$-.09^d$	$-.05^b$	$.15^d$	$.11^d$	$.22^d$	$.15^d$		$.04^a$
10.	Computer use	$-.22^d$	$-.21^d$	$-.06^c$	$-.11^d$	$.30^d$	$.02$	$.26^d$	$.58^d$	$.14^d$	

$^a p < .05$ $^b p < .01$ $^c p < .001$ $^d p < .0001$.
Note: Highlighted (boldface) correlations are between variables that were combined for use in multiple regressions.

(except among the Shi'is), and the frequency of using personal computer are negatively related.

As in Egypt and Saudi Arabia, the nature of the data cannot determine the degree of directional influence between these variables; that is, the extent to which differences in fundamentalism influence beliefs about source credibility or source credibility influences fundamentalist beliefs and attitudes. Most likely these are reciprocal influences in which fundamentalist beliefs and attitudes affect source credibility and information from select sources reinforces fundamentalist beliefs.

Multiple regressions were computed to assess the independent predictive effects of source confidence and source access on fundamentalism. Since there are fairly strong correlations between the press and TV ($r = .52$ for Iran, $r = .69$ for Lebanon), reading daily newspapers and books

(r = .41 for Iran, = .23 for Lebanon), and the Internet or email and computer use (r = .58 for Iran, r = .66 for Lebanon), each of these pairs of variables were combined into single dimensions and labeled as Press and TV, reading papers and books, and the Internet and computer use, respectively. Computer use was binary coded ("not used" = 0; "occasionally or frequently" = 1) prior to combining it with access to the Internet and email.

The results of the regression estimates are presented in Table 5.3. Across all the three religious groups in Lebanon and in Iran, confidence in religious institutions is positively linked to fundamentalism, providing further evidence of its generality across, nations, religions, and religious sects. Confidence in the press & TV is significantly linked to fundamentalism only in Iran, however. This effect is understandable because the press, and more so TV, in Iran are controlled by the Islamic regime; thus people who have expressed confidence in these sources tend to have stronger fundamentalist beliefs and attitudes. In Lebanon, on the other hand, where the press and TV are not controlled by a single religious group, and thus there is a variety of epistemic sources, confidence in these sources is not linked to fundamentalism, since the information and attitudes expressed by those sources is less focused and restricted to content that is consistent with religious beliefs.

Access to other sources where respondents appear to be able to pick and choose tends to have either no or negative associations with fundamentalism. Thus the use of radio and TV did not predict fundamentalism among different religious groups in Lebanon, while it was significantly linked to fundamentalism among Iranians. Again, this relationship is understandable given that the radio and TV are controlled by the Iranian Islamic regime. Those who use these sources seem to have adopted fundamentalist beliefs or attitudes, or alternatively, people who have fundamentalist beliefs and attitudes tend to use these sources more often than those who do not. Access to such other sources as newspapers and books as well as the Internet and computer uses was inversely related to fundamentalism. As shown in Table 5.3, in Iran and among all religious groups in Lebanon, people who reported reading newspapers and books, and those who had access to the Internet or used personal computers tended to have weaker fundamentalist attitudes and beliefs than those who did not avail themselves of such resources. *Again, this finding is significant as it indicates that secular sources and access to modern technology of communication are negatively linked to fundamentalism across nations, religions, and sects.*

Table 5.3. Source confidence and access predictors of fundamentalism in Lebanon and Iran.

Variable	Lebanon				Iran
	Christians	Shi'i	Sunni	Total	
Source Confidence					
Religious institutions	.243^d	.281^d	.365^d	.287^d	.375^d
Press & TV	.011	.052	−.044	−.026	.093^d
Regression F	34.07^d	10.95^d	80.43^d	122.75^d	303.24^d
Source Access					
Read (paper & books)	−.110^d	−.079^a	−.077^a	−.072^d	−.056^b
Use radio and TV	−.050	.009	−.034	.003	.073^d
Internet/ computer use	−.133^d	−.185^d	−.149^d	−.176^d	−.206^d
Talk with friends and colleagues	.064	.009	−.035	.016	.013
Regression F	11.65^d	3.83^b	13.43^d	31.68^d	42.82

$^a p < .05$ $^b p < .01$ $^c p < .001$ $^d p < .0001$
Note: Standardized regression coefficients shown.

Religiosity

For the surveys conducted in Iran and Lebanon, three indicators were used to assess religiosity: mosque attendance, daily prayer, and self-rated religiosity. Similar to the youth surveys in Egypt and Saudi Arabia, respondents were asked how often (apart from funerals) they attended religious services at the mosque (for Christians, we asked how often they attended the church), how often they prayed, and whether they would describe themselves as a religious person. Descriptive statistics for these variables are presented in Table 5.4, which compares Muslims in Iran and Muslims and Christians in Lebanon. A one-way analysis of variance indicated there was statistically significant variation ($p < .0001$) among the groups on each religiosity variable. Specifically, attending religious services (mosque attendance for Muslims and church attendance for Christians) was highest among Muslims in Lebanon, somewhat less in Iran and lowest for Christians in Lebanon. By contrast, the frequency of prayer is lowest for

Table 5.4. Mean (SD) religiosity and orthodoxy.

Variable	Lebanon		Iran	F
	Christians	Muslims		
Mosque/Church attendance	3.85 (2.39)	4.63 (1.79)	4.16 (1.74)	43.81
Prayer	3.67 (1.63)	3.36 (1.38)	4.33 (1.35)	218.75
Self-rated religiosity	.69 (.46)	.66 (.47)	.83 (.38)	90.89

Note: Higher values indicate more frequent attendance, prayer and religiosity.
All row means vary significantly ($p < .0001$) and except for Christians' and Muslims' self-rated religiosity in Lebanon, are significantly different from each other at $p < .0001$ (Scheffé).

Muslims in Lebanon and highest in Iran. Self-rated religiosity is also highest in Iran and lowest both for Christians and Muslims in Lebanon.

Correlations between the three measures of religiosity within each group are shown in Table 5.5. All are statistically significant and of moderate magnitude, and separate multiple regressions for each group were computed to determine how each variable independently predicted fundamentalism. According to the standardized coefficients in Table 5.6, only self-rated religiosity predicted fundamentalism for Christians in Lebanon, but not church attendance or the frequency of prayer. All variables predicted fundamentalism for Muslims in both countries and Christians in Lebanon. The only outlier is the negative coefficient for Muslims' frequency of prayer in Lebanon. The positive correlation ($r = .14$, $p < .001$) between these variables, however, indicates that the negative regression coefficient can be attributed to a regression artifact. Taken together, therefore, fundamentalism in Iran is associated most consistently with the three indices of religiosity. By contrast, self-rated religiosity is the most important factor for Christians, rather than church attendance or the frequency of prayer.

Social Psychological Factors

The surveys in Iran and Lebanon included an assessment of powerlessness, as in Egypt and Saudi Arabia, but not fatalism (that was measured in terms of the unrealizability of happiness in this world), and the measure of insecurity was included only in the Lebanon survey. The Iran and

Table 5.5. Correlation of religious variables.

Variable	Mosque/Church Attendance	Prayer
	Iran	
Prayer	.44^d	
Self-rated religiosity	.29^d	.40^d
	Lebanon Muslims	
Prayer	.55^d	
Self-rated religiosity	.49^d	.56^d
	Lebanon Christians	
Prayer	.45^d	
Self-rated religiosity	.49^d	.38^d

$^a p <.05 \ ^b p < .01 \ ^c p < .001 \ ^d p < .0001$
Note: For orthodoxy—Muslims: Only laws of *shari'a*; for Christians:
Only laws inspired by Christian values

Table 5.6. Religious predictors of fundamentalism.

Variable	Lebanon		Iran
	Christians	Muslims	
Mosque/Church attendance	.036	.187^d	.219^d
Prayer	− .031	− .074^a	.137^d
Self-rated religiosity	.159^c	.198^d	.141^d
Regression F	10.02^d	56.53^d	149.04^d

$^a p < .05 \ ^b p < .01 \ ^c p < .001 \ ^d p < .0001$
Note: Standardized regression coefficients shown. Since the correlation between prayer and fundamentalism in Lebanon is significantly positive ($r = .14, p < .001$), the negative regression coefficient is likely due to a suppression effect.

Lebanon surveys, on the other hand, included one additional relevant variable: beliefs about fate versus freedom of choice. The present analyses, therefore, include measures of powerlessness, belief in fate versus freedom of choice, and insecurity (available only for Lebanon). For the assessment of powerlessness, respondents rated (from 1 = "none at all" to

10 = "a great deal") how much freedom of choice and control they had over what happens to them in their lives. To assess belief in fate, respondents were prompted with the statement that "some people believe that individuals can decide their own destiny, while others think that it is impossible to escape a predetermined fate" and were asked to rate (on a 10-point scale) the extent to which "everything in life is determined by fate" (1) or "people shape their fate themselves" (10). Finally, the degree of insecurity was assessed with a Likert scale for the degree to which they believed "that in Lebanon these days, life is unpredictable and dangerous." All variables were recoded so that the higher values represent higher levels of powerlessness, belief in fate, and insecurity.

Table 5.7 presents the means and standard deviations for powerlessness, fate versus choice, and insecurity in Lebanon and Iran. In each instance, Iranians on average had the lowest level of perceived powerlessness and were least fatalistic (4.05 and 4.32, respectively), whereas Lebanese Muslims on average perceived themselves as having the highest level of powerlessness and belief in fate (4.59 and 5.72, respectively). Lebanese Christians felt slightly less insecure than did Lebanese Muslims (3.01 versus 3.11).

Correlations between these variables are presented in Table 5.8. These correlations are significant and positively related, suggesting that powerlessness, belief in fate, and the feeling of insecurity tend to reinforce one another. But their relationships are moderate, indicating they are related but also somewhat independent of each other and reflect different aspects of this set of beliefs.

Table 5.7. Social psychological factors.

Variable	Lebanon		Iran	F
	Christians	Muslims		
Powerlessness	4.32	4.59	4.05	46.02
	(2.31)	(2.51)	(2.14)	
Belief in fate	4.87	5.72	4.32	132.61
	(2.84)	(2.94)	(2.79)	
Insecurity	3.01	3.11	—	7.89
	(.82)	(.82)		

Note: For the first three variables, row means vary significantly ($p < .0001$) and are significantly different from each other at $p < .001$ (Scheffé); for Security $p < .01$.

Table 5.8. Correlations between powerlessness, fatalism, and insecurity.

Variable	Powerlessness	Insecurity
Iran		
Belief in fate	.18	
Lebanon – Muslims		
Belief in fate	.18	
Insecurity	.10	.12
Lebanon – Christians		
Belief in fate	.26	
Insecurity	.14	.16

Note: $p < .001$ for all correlations.

These differences between Iran and Lebanon in powerlessness and fate versus choice are reflected by the way they predict fundamentalism, indicated by the pattern of regression coefficients in each country shown in Table 5.9. In Iran and for both religious groups in Lebanon, fundamentalism is positively linked to the belief in fate—that the more a person believes in fate rather than individual choice shaping one's life, the stronger that person's fundamentalist beliefs and attitudes. There are, however, variations in the association of powerlessness and fundamentalism. Among Lebanese Christians, this linkage is positive and significant, while that is not the case among their Muslim counterparts. Among Iranians, on the other hand, fundamentalism and powerlessness are negatively and significantly linked. This suggests that the more fundamentalist Iranians identify more strongly with the ruling religious fundamentalist regime and therefore feel more powerful than do those who are less fundamentalist. This finding is significant for understanding the relationship between dysphoric emotions and social structure, because it indicates that one's feeling of powerlessness is tied to one's lack of affinity with the ideological orientation of the state, rather than simply to one's conditions in and attitudes toward life in general. In other words, living under a fundamentalist regime, the feeling of empowerment is linked to having fundamentalist attitudes and orientation. On a broader philosophical and epistemological level, however, fundamentalism is still linked to fatalistic orientation, as shown across the two faiths and in both countries.

Table 5.9. Predictors of fundamentalism.

Variable	Lebanon		Iran
	Christians	Muslims	
Powerlessness	.094[b]	−.021	−.086[c]
Belief in fate	.070[a]	.067[b]	.073[c]
Insecurity	.005	.015	—
Regression F	6.00[c]	2.50[a]	12.70[c]

[a]$p < .05$ [b]$p < .01$ [c]$p < .001$
Note: Standardized regression coefficients.

Finally, the feeling of insecurity has no significant connection with fundamentalism among Lebanese Christians or Muslims. Given that Lebanese have experienced endemic political conflicts and violence, which also occurred during the survey period, the feeling of insecurity is real and felt by most Lebanese, fundamentalist or otherwise. As a result, it is not too surprising to see a lack of a significant linkage between fundamentalism and insecurity among the Lebanese public in 2008, where serious conflict occurred among major confession groups.

Rule Making According to the People's Wishes versus Religious Orthodoxy

Attitudes toward religious orthodoxy and rule making according to the people's wishes are used in the same way as the analysis in Chapter Four for young Egyptians and Saudis. Respondents were asked about their views of good government, specifically the extent to which they considered the following traits important for such a government to have (from 1 = "not important" to 5 = "very important"): (a) It should make laws according to the people's wishes, and (b) It should implement only the laws of the *shari'a*.

In analyzing the data, two important caveats in the way these two questions were asked in Iran and Lebanon and among Christians and Muslims must be taken into consideration. First, both questions in the Lebanon survey had five response categories as shown above, but in the Iran survey they had six response categories: (1) very important, (2) important, (3) to some extent important, (4) little important, (5) very little important, or (6) not at all important. Second, since the question about the significance of the *shari'a* law has no relevance to Lebanese Christians, this question was asked differently for Christian respondents: "A good government

Table 5.10. Attitudes toward rule making according to people's wishes and the shari'a among iranians and lebanese (% responding "very important").

Variable	Lebanon		Iran
	Christians	Muslims	
Laws according to people's wishes	50.0	49.0	32.0
Laws according to shari'a	6.5	6.4	24.0

should adopt only the laws inspired by Christian values." For statistical analysis, these variables were recoded so that the higher values indicate stronger support for laws according to the people's wishes or the shari'a laws. Because of the differences in the number of response categories, these two variables cannot be compared across the two countries in terms of their means and standard deviations. As an alternative, only those who responded "very important" are compared across countries and religions.

As shown in Table 5.10, there are major differences between the two countries but not between Lebanese Christians and Muslims. Both religious groups in Lebanon believe that laws should reflect people's wishes more so than do Iranian Muslims. Iranian Muslims are significantly different from the two Lebanese groups, and the Christian and Muslim Lebanese groups do not differ from each other. Consistently, Muslims in Iran are more likely to believe that laws should be formulated according to the subscribed orthodox beliefs than do both religious groups in Lebanon. Muslims are not statistically different from Lebanese Christians in this regard, however.

Table 5.11 clearly shows that these variables are relatively independent of each other. That is, the correlation coefficients between attitudes toward making laws according to the people's wishes and attitudes toward the shari'a law, or laws inspired by Christian values, are almost zero among Iranians or Lebanese Christians. Among the Lebanese Muslims, however, this relationship, albeit weak, is positive and significant.

The regression coefficients presented in Table 5.12 clearly reveal that support for Islamic orthodoxy—as measured in terms of attitudes toward the shari'a law—or Christian "orthodoxy"—as measured in terms of attitudes toward making only the laws that are inspired by Christian values—are consistently linked to religious fundamentalism. Attitudes toward

Table 5.11. Correlations between rule making, authority and fundamentalism in lebanon and iran.

Variable	Laws according to *Shari'a*
Lebanon Christian	
Laws according to people's wishes	.03
Lebanon Muslim	
Laws according to people's wishes	.10[d]
Iran	
Laws according to people's wishes	.01

[d]$p < .0001$

Table 5.12. Regression estimates of fundamentalism on laws according to people's wishes and the *shari'a* laws.

Variable	Lebanon		Iran
	Christians	Muslims	
Laws according to people's wishes	− .011	.052[a]	−.037[a]
Laws according to *shari'a*	.321[d]	.349[d]	.389[d]
Regression F	53.62[d]	105.64[d]	254.72[d]

[a]$p <. 05$ [b]$p < . 01$ [c]$p < . 001$ [d]$p < .0001$.

making laws according to the people's wishes are linked to fundamentalism in different ways across the two countries and religions. Among Iranians, this variable is negatively linked to religious fundamentalism, and is consistent with recent trends in culture and political values among Iranians toward democratic rule making and against the regime's fundamentalism (Moaddel 2010; Kamrava 2008). Among Lebanese Muslims the relationship is positive. However, when this regression estimate is computed for Lebanese Shi'is and Lebanese Sunnis separately, the linkage between attitudes toward making laws according to the people's wishes and religious fundamentalism is significant only among the Shi'is (for Shi'is β = .150, p <.0001). For the Sunnis, on the other hand, as with Christians, this value is negative but non-significant (β = −.041). That the a positive linkage between attitudes toward making laws according to the people's wishes and religious fundamentalism among Lebanese Shi'is is counter-intuitive, and may reflect the influence of the domination of Hezbollah's religious fundamentalism on the Lebanese Shi'i population, as some Lebanese Shi'is may not see a contradiction between their fundamentalist views and attitudes toward representative democracy.

Morality and Fundamentalism

To what extent are people's fundamentalist beliefs and attitudes shaped by their distinctive conception of morality? To assess this linkage, respondents were presented with three types of behavior—violence against other people, stealing other people's property, and pre-marital sex—and the linkages between their evaluations of the level of immorality of these behaviors and religious fundamentalism are assessed.

Morality questions were asked differently in Lebanon and Iran. Respondents in Lebanon were asked to choose which from among three behaviors was the most immoral: violence against others, premarital sex, or stealing. Table 5.13 presents the percentage of respondents who selected each of the alternatives as most immoral. Overall, both Christians and Muslims considered stealing the most immoral, followed by violence against others and premarital sex. That pattern was more pronounced among Christians than among Muslims, X^2 (2, n = 2960) = 67.95, p < .0001. For Christians, compared to Muslims, violence against others was considered more immoral than was premarital sex (considered the least immoral); whereas for Muslims, violence against others and premarital sex were more similar.

Table 5.13. Percentage of Lebanese christians and muslims who chose violence, premarital sex or stealing as being the most immoral.

Variable	Christians	Muslims	Total
Violence	38.9	26.2	30.8
Premarital Sex	14.7	24.4	20.9
Stealing	46.3	49.4	48.3
n	1079	1881	2960

The relation to fundamentalism was analyzed using a 2 (Christians vs. Muslims) x 3 (Type of Morality) analysis of variance. As shown in Table 5.14, fundamentalism was highest among those who considered premarital sex as more immoral than violence and stealing for both the Christian and Muslim religious groups combined (F = 45.74, p < .0001), as well as for each group separately. The small interaction effect (F = 3.81, p < .01) also provides some evidence that the relative difference between the level of fundamentalism for those who considered premarital sex most important, compared to those who selected violence or stealing, was somewhat more pronounced among Christians than among Muslims.

By contrast, respondents in Iran were asked to rate the degree to which they considered the three different types of behavior—violence against other people, stealing others' property, and premarital sex—to be immoral (ranging from 1 = "not necessarily immoral" to 10 = "totally immoral"). The mean immorality ratings and standard deviations for each behavior are reported in Table 5.15. As this table indicates, the variation among the means was statistically significant (p < .0001). This variation was primarily due to premarital sex, which by paired-comparison tests was considered less immoral than was either violence against others or stealing (p < .001) that did not differ from each other.

Although the immorality of these three different behaviors was measured differently in the two countries—that is, in case of Lebanon they are ranked vis-à-vis one another, while in Iran each one is separately rated by the respondents—the findings are remarkably consistent. Lebanese ranked stealing other people's property as the most immoral and Iranians

Table 5.14. Mean (SD) fundamentalism by Lebanese christians and muslims who consider one of three behaviors to be most immoral.

Variable	Christians	Muslims	Total
Violence	2.19 (.60)	2.62 (.54)	2.41
Premarital sex	2.61 (.55)	2.84 (.57)	2.89
Stealing	2.21 (.69)	2.61 (.52)	2.41
Total	2.50	2.77	2.61

Table 5.15. Mean (SD) morality ratings of dimensions of morality according to Iranians.

Variable	Iran
Violence	8.95 (2.68)
Premarital sex	8.66 (3.16)
Stealing	9.01 (2.20)
F	36.70^d

Note: 1= not necessarily to 10 = totally immoral
$^d p < .0001$

Table 5.16. Correlation between dimensions of morality in Iran.

Variable	Fundamentalism	Violence vs. Others	Premarital Sex
Violence	.09^d		
Premarital sex	.22^d	.73^d	
Stealing	.13^d	.63^d	.55^d

$^c p < .001$ $^d p < .0001$

gave on average the highest immorality rating to stealing. At the same time, Lebanese ranked the immorality of violence against other people and pre-marital sex about the same, while Iranians gave about the same average ratings to the immorality of violence and premarital sex.

As shown in Table 5.16, these views of immoral behavior are variously related to fundamentalism and strongly related to one another. Fundamentalism has the highest correlation with the immorality rating of premarital sex, followed by stealing and violence. Multiple regression was used to estimate the independent contribution of each immorality variable to predicting fundamentalism. As shown in Table 5.17, the findings are consistent with the correlations between premarital sex and fundamentalism and stealing. The negative regression coefficient should be discounted, however, since the sign is opposite to that of the correlation between those variables and can be attributed to a suppression effect.

Despite the different ways that immorality of the three types of behavior was measured and assessed in Lebanon and Iran, the results in both

Table 5.17. Dimensions of immorality predictors of fundamentalism among Iranians.

Variable	Iran
Violence	$-.168^{d}$*
Premarital sex	$.268^{d}$
Stealing	$.074^{b}$
Regression F	54.29^{d}

$^{b}p < .01$ $^{d}p < .0001$.
*Note: Due to a suppression effect.

countries are quite consistent, displaying a similar hierarchy in moral order insofar as these behaviors are concerned. Specifically, stealing other people's property was considered the most immoral behavior, and violence against other people was deemed slightly more immoral than was premarital sex. However, fundamentalism was higher for those who considered premarital sex as more immoral than for those who indicated they thought that violence against others and stealing were more immoral.

National Pride and National Identity

The assessment of national pride and national identity required a series of analyses that varied for the different countries and religions groups. First, respondents in both countries were asked to rate the how proud they were to be citizens of their country. As seen in Table 5.18, Iranians evidenced significantly higher levels of national pride than did Lebanese respondents. Correlation coefficients in the same table also show that for

Table 5.18. Mean national pride.

Variable	Lebanon		Iran	F
	Christians	Muslims		
Mean national pride	3.33	3.25	3.42	26.52^{d}
Correlation with fundamentalism	.01	.04	$.18^{d}$	

$^{d}p < .0001$
Note: Mean national pride is significantly higher in Iran (Scheffé at $p < .001$), but not between groups in Lebanon.

Iranians, but not for Lebanese, national pride was significantly related to fundamentalism: those with higher levels of fundamentalism were more likely to be more proud to be Iranian.

National identity was assessed by asking respondents to choose from among a set of alternatives, in response to the stem: "Above everything else, I am an Iranian or a Lebanese, a Muslim, Arab, Kurd, and other." The alternatives varied in the two countries, and by religious groups in Lebanon (an "other" category was always included). Iranians were asked to select between identifying themselves as Iranian, Muslim, or others, including Arab, Baluch, Kurd, Lur, Turk, or Tukman. As seen in Table 5.19, the respondents were split in Iran; and most Iranians opted to self-identify as non-Muslims (39.4% as Iranians and 13.6% as others), and the rest as Muslims (46.9%).Table 5.19 also shows that those who identified themselves according to their religion (i.e., Muslims) were higher in fundamentalism than were those who identified themselves as Iranians.

A very different identity pattern was found for Muslims in Lebanon compared to those in Iran, as most (64.8%) considered themselves to be Lebanese rather than Muslims or Arabs (Table 5.20). Similar to Iran, however, Lebanese Muslims who identified themselves according to

Table 5.19. Identity in Iran.*

	Iranian	Muslim	Other	Total
% of Total	39.4	46.9	13.6	2836
Mean fundamentalism	2.67	2.95	2.53	$F = 95.86^d$

$^d p < .0001$
Note: All means significantly different (Scheffé at $p < .001$).
* "Above everything else, I am a/an…"

Table 5.20. Lebanese muslim identity.*

	Lebanese	Arab	Muslim	Other	
% of Total	64.8	5.6	26.9	2.4	$n = 1886$
Mean fundamentalism	2.57	2.72	2.94	2.17	$F = 72.48^d$

$^d p < .0001$
Note: All means significantly different (Scheffé at $p < .001$).
* "Above everything else, I am a/an…"

Table 5.21. Lebanese christian identity.*

	Lebanese	Arab	Christian	Other	Total
% of Total	71.4	1.4	21.8	5.5	1079
Mean fundamentalism	2.26	1.56	2.42	1.87	$F = 20.00^d$

$^d p < .0001$
Note: All means significantly different (Scheffé at $p < .001$).
* "Above everything else, I am a/an..."

their religion were higher in fundamentalism (*Mean* = 2.94) than were those who identified themselves according to their nationality (*Mean* = 2.57). Lebanese Christians were offered a choice between self-identifying according to Arab ethnicity, their nationality or religion. As did Muslims, they chose to identify themselves primarily as Lebanese (71.4%) rather than according to their religion. As well, the 21.8% that thought of themselves primarily as Christians were higher in fundamentalism (*Mean* = 2.42) compared to those identifying themselves according to their nationality (*Mean* = 2.26), as shown in Table 5.21.

Besieged Spirituality

In the previous chapter, two measures of besieged spirituality were used. One measured the perception of an American/Jewish conspiracy against Muslim nations and the other attitudes toward Western cultural invasion. For the present analysis, data on only one of the variables—attitudes toward Western cultural invasion—are available, and only for Iran.

According to our analysis, the mean for this variable is 5.06 (*SD* = 1.30) (6 pt. scale from 1 = "Not at all important" – 6 = "Very important"), and is significantly linked to fundamentalism (correlation with fundamentalism: $r = .24$, $p < .0001$), which is consistent with findings from the youth survey in Egypt and Saudi Arabia. Again, the perception of besieged spirituality, which gives way to alarmist attitudes toward outsiders, is linked to religious fundamentalism in the three countries for which data on the proxy measures are available.

Socioeconomic Status and Fundamentalism

To assess the effect of socioeconomic status on fundamentalism, two indicators were used: reported family income and self-assigned class membership. To measure income, respondents were asked to specify the

Table 5.22. Correlations between fundamentalism, income and social class.

Variable Pair	Lebanon		Iran
	Christians	Muslims	
Income & fundamentalism	$-.13^d$	$-.07^a$	$-.09^b$
Subjective social class & fundamentalism	$-.19^d$	$-.03$	$-.11^c$
Income and social class	$.51^d$	$.45^d$	$.64^d$

$^a p <.05$ $^b p < .01$ $^c p < .001$ $^d p < .0001$

income decile they belonged in, from the lowest (= 1) to the highest (= 10), counting all wages, salaries, pensions and other incomes. To measure social class, respondents were asked to describe themselves as belonging to the lower class, working class, lower middle class, upper middle class, or upper class. Table 5.22 presents relations between fundamentalism, income and social class. For Lebanese Christians, and to a lesser extent Iranians, those with higher levels of income and subjective social class are lower in fundamentalism. For Lebanese Muslims, fundamentalism is related to income levels but not for subjective social class. This analysis thus lends support to the argument that fundamentalism may be a response to social inequality, measured both objectively in economic terms and subjectively (except among Lebanese Muslims) in terms of the perception of one's standing in the social hierarchy.

CONCLUSIONS

The forgoing analysis assessed the linkages between several sociological and social psychological variables and religious fundamentalism among Iranians, Lebanese Christians and Lebanese Muslims. These variables included respondents' confidence in the religious institutions, the press, and TV and access to such sources of epistemic authority as reading books and newspapers, listening to radio and TV, using the Internet and computer, and talking to friends or colleagues. Included in the analyses were also a host of other variables, such as the frequency of mosque attendance, individual prayer, and self-assigned religiosity; social psychological factors like measures of perceived powerlessness, fate versus freedom of choice, and insecurity; attitudes toward religious orthodoxy (i.e., the *sharïa*) and making rules according to the people's wishes; assessment of different types of immoral behavior, including violence against other people, stealing other people's property, and premarital sex; attitudes toward Western cultural invasion; and measures of national pride and identity. Measures of social class and income were also used to assess their linkages with fundamentalism. A summary of the relations of these variables with fundamentalism is presented in Table 5.23. Shown are the effects sizes based on regression estimates.

The range of variables that were linked to fundamentalism across the two countries and religious faiths were more impressive for their similarities than for the differences between countries. In terms of the linkages between the religious factors and fundamentalism, confidence in religious institutions, self-rated religiosity, favorable attitudes toward the religious orthodoxy—i.e., favorable attitudes toward the *sharïa* for Muslims and favorable attitudes toward the laws that were inspired by Christian values among Christians—and religious identity were all significantly and positively linked to religious fundamentalism among Iranians, as well as among Lebanese Christians and Lebanese Muslims. Among other factors that were also positively linked to religious fundamentalism were beliefs in the role of fate in shaping one's life and unfavorable attitudes toward premarital sex as an immoral behavior.

Among the common factors that were negatively linked to fundamentalism were such sources of epistemic authority as having read books and newspapers as well as using the Internet or email or the frequency of using a personal computer. Thus, among Iranians as well as Lebanese Christians and Lebanese Muslims, access to modern technology, books and newspapers tend to reduce people's belief in and attitudes toward religious fundamentalism. Likewise, annual family income also had an inverse relationship with fundamentalism across the two countries and the two faiths. Subjective class identification, on the other hand, was linked to fundamentalism only among Iranians and Lebanese Christians.

Although there are some cross-national and inter-faith variations in the predictors of fundamentalism, most of these variations are due to the influence of additional factors among Iranians in linking to fundamentalism. Favorable attitudes toward the institutions, activities, and cultural propaganda that are tied to the Islamic regime are also positively linked to fundamentalism. That is, having confidence in radio and TV, listening to radio and TV, attending mosque, and considering Western cultural invasion to be an important problem for Iran all are positively linked to

Table 5.23. Summary of correlates of fundamentalism and effect sizes.

	Variable	Lebanon	Iran
Epistemic authority (Confidence)	Religious institutions	C++/Sh++/ Su+++ Total ++	+++
	Press & TV	Co/Sho/Suo Total o	+
Epistemic authority (Access)	Read (paper & books)	C‐ ‐/Sh‐/Su‐ Total ‐	‐
	Use radio and TV	Co/Sho/Suo Total o	+
	Internet/computer use	C‐ ‐/Sh‐ ‐/ Su‐ ‐ Total ‐ ‐	‐ ‐
	Talk w/ friends/ colleagues	Co/Sho/Suo Total o	o
Religion	Mosque/Church attendance	Co/M++	++
	Prayer	Co/M‐	++
	Self-rated religiosity	C++/M++	++
Social psychological	Powerlessness	C+/Mo	‐ ‐
	Belief in fate	C+/M+	+
	Insecurity	Co/Mo	n
Morality	Laws according to people's wishes	Co/M+	‐
	Laws according to Shari'a	C+++/M++	+++
	Violence	n	n
	Premarital sex	n	++
	Stealing	n	+
National pride		Co/Mo	++
Islamic identity		C+/M+	++
Income		C‐ ‐/M‐	‐
Subjective social class		C‐/Mo	‐

Effect Sizes: o = no significant relationship +/‐ = Minor ++/‐ ‐ = Small +++/‐ ‐ ‐ = Moderate.
n = relationship not assessed.
C = Lebanese Christians M = Lebanese Muslims.
Sh = Lebanese Shi'i Su = Lebanese Sunni.

fundamentalism. Given that the domestic radio and TV are fully monopolized by the fundamentalist regime, that mosques are dominated by the pro-regime clerics, and that attack on the West is the key aspect of the regime ideology, it is thus expected that these factors would be positively linked to fundamentalism. Likewise, national pride, which may be indicative of the respondent's level of satisfaction with the regime, is positively linked to fundamentalism in Iran. Powerlessness, on the other hand, is negatively connected with fundamentalism, presumably because fundamentalist attitudes among Iranians signify identification with the ruling fundamentalist regime, which is therefore empowering. Among Lebanese Christians, on the other hand, perceived powerlessness is positively associated with fundamentalism.

The only religious factor that is linked to fundamentalism and is common to both Iranians and Lebanese Muslims is mosque attendance, which subjects the respondents to the fundamentalist messages often preached by Islamic clerics in the mosques. While individual prayer was negatively connected to fundamentalism among Lebanese Muslims, all the religious factors among Iranians were positively linked to fundamentalism. Favorable attitudes toward making rules according to the people's wishes—something that is contrary to the dominant religious fundamentalist view of rules to be based on religion and the *shari'a*—is negatively linked to fundamentalism among Iranians. This factor, however, is positively related to fundamentalism only among Lebanese Shi'is.

All in all, religious fundamentalism across the two countries and among the Christians and Muslims were commonly enhanced by the level of confidence in religious institutions, fatalism, and morality governing sexual relations. Fundamentalism is negatively linked to income and access to modern technology. Among Iranians, in addition, fundamentalism is reinforced by various institutions and processes connected to the Islamic regime.

CHAPTER SIX

FUNDAMENTALISM AS DISCOURSE VERSUS BELIEFS
ABOUT AND ATTITUDES TOWARD RELIGION

We have discussed two conceptions of religious fundamentalism. One conceptualized religious fundamentalism as a discourse, constituting a set of positions on significant issues. This conception was then applied to the analysis of historical cases of fundamentalist movements in the Muslim world, focusing on the diachronic relationships between Islamic movements and changing social contexts. The other conception considered fundamentalism as a set of beliefs about and attitudes toward religion. We examined data from single-wave cross-national survey data in order to analyze the synchronic relationships between fundamentalism and several sociological and social psychological factors on the macro and micro levels. These two approaches are different in terms of not only the methodology and the type of evidence used but in conceptualization of the construct as well. In this chapter, we attempt to link empirically these two conceptions and thus further validate the two different ways in which fundamentalism is conceptualized.

In the first approach, fundamentalism was conceptualized as a religious discourse formulated by the intellectual leaders of the movements to address and resolve significant issues facing their faith and community. Included among these issues were: (1) the relationship between religion and politics, (2) form of government, (3) the nature of the outside world, Western culture in particular, (4) the basis of identity, and (5) the social status of women. Religious fundamentalists were not the only group that addressed these issues, for sure. These issues were also the concerns of intellectual leaders of diverse cultural movements in the contemporary Middle East that promoted Islamic modernism, nationalism, liberalism, secularism, Arabism, and pan-Arab nationalism. These movements were distinguished from one another in terms of their positions on these issues.

As indicated in Chapter One, the intellectual leaders of fundamentalist movements generally rejected constitutional government in favor of the unity between religion and politics in an Islamic government, gave priority to religious laws drawn from the scripture (the *shari'a*) over man-made laws, portrayed Western culture as decadent, asserted the Islamic identity of their community and rejected nationalism, and supported the institutions of male domination and gender segregation. Religious fundamentalism as a set of distinctive beliefs about and attitudes toward religion was viewed as a multi-component concept. One component consisted of a disciplinarian conception of the Deity who commands absolute obedience to His rule and severely punishes those who have engaged even in a minor infraction of His laws. Another component is inerrancy that considers the scriptures as a comprehensive system of absolute truth, which is both infallible and literally accurate. This belief thus supports the view that there is no need for man-made laws. The third is religious centrism and exclusivity that asserts one's own religion to be superior to the religions of others. The fourth is religious intolerance, which rests on the belief that in order to maintain the purity of the faith the believers must maintain little contact with the followers of other faiths, whom, in the fundamentalists' view, should not be given the same rights as those given to the followers of one's own faith.

The challenge was to demonstrate convergence of these conceptions of fundamentalism by means of the extent to which they adequately represent the construct either within the national-historical context or with data from the comparative cross-national surveys. *As stated at the outset, the proposition here is that while we cannot access public beliefs and attitudes during those historical periods, their legacies may be reflected in the beliefs and attitudes among contemporary populations, and that those who have stronger fundamentalist beliefs and attitudes also display stronger orientations toward the sociopolitical, cultural, and religious issues in a way that is similar to the orientations of the religious fundamentalist movements.* In other words, we are demonstrating empirically that in contemporary contexts, fundamentalist beliefs and attitudes are linked in predictable ways with positions on issues that we can assume would be advanced by religious fundamentalist leaders and activists.

Assessing such empirical relationships has also implications for theoretical developments in the social-scientific studies of religion. The resolutions of historically significant issues offered by the intellectual leaders and activists of religious fundamentalism project a certain normative modality of social life that governs politics, patriarchy and gender relations, identity, and the relationship with the outside world. Fundamentalism as a discourse on sociopolitical and cultural issues thus constitutes a *model for* social reality. It guides the construction of the sociopolitical order that is deemed to be religious. Fundamentalism as a set of beliefs and attitudes toward religion represents individuals' conceptions about the nature and role of the Supreme Being or God, His relationship with humans, and the significance of His laws in human affairs. It also projects a form of religious hierarchy in which some religions are viewed to be closer to God than other religions. This conception provides a *model of* religion—one of the many ways in which the supernatural phenomena are perceived and understood.

These two conceptions thus parallel the distinction Geertz has made between an ethos and a worldview as different aspects of any culture. For Geertz, an ethos represents a people's moral and aesthetic style and mood, and the other the picture of the way things are in nature, self, and society. According to Geertz:

> The moral (and aesthetic) aspects of a given culture, the evaluative elements, have commonly been summed up in the term "ethos," while the cognitive, existential aspects have been designated by the term "world view." A people's ethos is the tone, character, and quality of their life, its moral and aesthetic style and mood; it is the underlying attitude toward themselves and the world that life reflects. Their world view is their picture of the way things in sheer actuality are, their concept of nature, of self, of society. It contains their most comprehensive ideas of order. Religious belief and ritual confront and mutually confirm one another; *the ethos is made intellectually reasonable by being shown to represent a way of life implied by the actual state of affairs of which the world view describes, and the world view is made emotionally acceptable by being presented as an authentic expression.* This demonstration of a meaningful relation between the values a people holds and the general order of existence within which it finds itself is an essential element in all religions, however those values or that order be conceived (Geertz 1973: 126–127, italics added).

In the same way that Geertz relates an ethos to worldviews, people's understanding of their religion shapes their orientations toward issues. Nonetheless, insofar as Geertz' conception of and approach to cultural analysis is concerned, the following caveats must be considered. First, Geertz' conceptualization of culture, of which ethos and worldview are two complementary symbolic orders, is totalistic and portrays an image of culture that is uniform. It thus fails to capture the varied ways in which cultural elements shape people's worldviews. He considers culture as an integrated whole, consisting of a unified system of beliefs, norms, symbols, and rituals. In reality, societies or even "a people" adhere to a diversity of cultural elements that often clash. Given this diversity, different modalities of religion—conservatism, religious orthodoxy, modernism, and fundamentalism—are available to individuals in a society, and these modalities are linked to a diversity of worldviews. Second, people are also heterogeneous in terms of their ethos and worldviews. Third, proposed harmony between an ethos and a worldview is hard to sustain empirically. This is true because this relationship is potentially moderated by a host of historical and political factors. For example, as we have shown in Chapter 3 (Table 3.5), the fundamentalist perception of the government's performance—that is, the relationship between religious fundamentalist attitudes and beliefs, on the one hand, and their perception of government performance (i.e., reality), on the other—is moderated by the nature of the state itself. Under such religious authoritarian regimes as Iran and Saudi Arabia, or a democratic confessional regime like Lebanon, there is a positive link between the fundamentalist ethos and the perception of the real, that is, the government's performance. On the other hand, under the secular authoritarian regime of President Mubarak in Egypt, this relationship is negative.

Nonetheless, Geertz's classification of cultural elements into two groups and his proposition regarding the relationship between the two groups are instructive for our understanding of the relationship between the two conceptions of religious fundamentalism. We thus suggest that there may be a degree of harmony between religious fundamentalism as a cognitive model of religion and religious fundamentalism as a normative model for reality that reflects a particular worldview. That is, fundamentalist attitudes toward and beliefs about religion are linked to fundamentalist orientations toward issues. On a higher level of abstraction, this implies that people's modality of religion and their conception of the appropriate way to live, or model for social life, mutually reinforce each other.

Relevant also to the present discussion is the Weberian notion of the relationship between human conception of the Divinity and their concrete actions and social relationships. In the present context, this relationship means that people's beliefs and attitudes about their religion are linked to their specific orientations toward historically significant social issues. In other words, for example, the more strongly one adheres to a disciplinary conception of Deity, the stronger that person supports the system of male domination and patriarchy, and the less strongly he/she is oriented toward the liberal values of political democracy and gender equality. Or, the more strongly people believe in the superiority of their religion, the less strongly they support the principles of social equality among all ethnic and racial groups in society.

To operationalize this thesis, we conducted additional analyses to test whether there are predictable links between fundamentalist beliefs and attitudes and positions on issues that were adopted by the leaders and activists of religious fundamentalist movements in the second half of the twentieth century. We first specify these issues and construct composite measures of such attitudes. Then, we assess the relationship between fundamentalism and these measures on the macro level, where the group is the unit of analysis—religion, religious sect, ethnicity, and country—followed by relations within each of the groups.

HISTORICALLY SIGNIFICANT ISSUES AND RELIGIOUS FUNDAMENTALISM

The variables measuring attitudes toward historically significant issues can be captured by five constructs. These constructs are social individualism, gender equality, the form of government, identity, and Western culture. Social individualism, gender equality, form of government, and attitudes toward the Western culture are composite variables that are measured by combining one or more indicator variables. We first discuss and describe these constructs, then empirically evaluate their linkages with religious fundamentalism across the four countries, religions, religious sects, and ethnic groups on the macro level, and within each of these groups on the micro level as well.

Social Individualism

Social individualism is conceptualized as the degree to which the autonomy of individuals and their rights to make choices as they see fit are recognized. Modern democratic societies rest on the recognition of the individual as an autonomous entity having rights and responsibilities. A patriarchal culture, on the other hand, gives priority to the role of authority and emphasizes obedience to authority in the family and society. Islamic fundamentalist movements have historically favored authority, in particular the authority of the male parent or male guardian in the family and have disapproved of individualistic values.

The construct of social individualism may be viewed broadly to cover its theoretical and practical meanings in various contexts of politics, economics, gender relations, marriage and family. Here, however, we have employed a narrower definition of social individualism to apply only to marriage and child-rearing practices. We treat gender relations and forms of government as separate categories, and we measure them as such. We deleted the concept of economic individualism from the analysis because of the complexity of defining the practical meanings of the term—whether it is equality of economic opportunity, economic equality, or support for laissez-faire capitalism. One measure of economic individualism, however, is used in the construction of the composite measure of gender equality (i.e., equal treatment of men and women in the job market).

The composite measures of social individualism in the context of marriage and child-rearing practices include attitudes toward the basis for marriage and favorable qualities for children to have. Four indicators are considered. All have a dummy-variable format. The first indicator is constructed from the respondents' answer to the question regarding the basis for marriage: "In your view, which of the following is the more important basis for marriage: parental approval, or love?" (with "love" coded as 1 and "parental approval" as 0). Regarding the significance of this variable for measuring social individualism, we should note the rich historical pedigree of debate over this choice in different fields of culture. Scholars have used the expression of "Romeo and Juliet revolution" in recognition of the freedom of the individual to choose a spouse, which has as its basis the humanism movement in Europe during the sixteenth and seventeenth centuries that gave priority to individual choice over religious dogma and tradition (Deutsch 1981). We thus propose that people who consider love as a more important basis for marriage than parental approval are more supportive of social individualism.

The other three indicators are selected from among the list of the characteristics that respondents selected as favorable qualities for children to have. The respondents were instructed to choose up to five among ten qualities: independence, hard work, feeling of responsibility, imagination, tolerance and respect for other people, thrift/saving money and things, determination/perseverance, religious faith, unselfishness, and obedience. The three indicators that are considered as measures of social individualism are independence (1 = selected, 0 = otherwise), imagination (1 = selected, 0 = otherwise), and obedience (1 = not selected, 0 = selected). We propose that people who selected independence and imagination but not obedience as favorable qualities of children to have are more in favor of social individualism than those who made other selections. A composite measure of social individualism was constructed as a linear combination of these four dummy variables: Social Individualism = independence + imagination + obedience + love. This variable thus ranges from "least individualistic" = 0 to "most individualistic" = 4. Accordingly, the most individualistic people are those who selected independence and imagination but not obedience as favorable qualities for children to have and who consider love as a more important basis for marriage than parental approval. If our argument regarding the positive linkage between fundamentalist attitudes and beliefs, on the one hand, and one's social orientation against social individualism, on the other, is correct, then there must be a negative correlation between the fundamentalism factor and the composite measure of social individualism.

Gender Equality

One of the cornerstones of modern democratic politics is the quality of all political voices. This includes equality between men and women. In the Islamic modernist movements, people have displayed favorable attitudes toward gender equality. The Islamic fundamentalists, on the other hand, favored the idea of male domination, gender hierarchization, and gender segregation. A gender-equality composite measure was constructed to examine this link, which combines attitudes toward equality between men and women in family, politics, and the job market. These indicators are constructed in Likert-scale format and measure whether respondents (1) strongly agree, (2) agree, (3) disagree, or (4) strongly disagree that a wife must always obey her husband (obedience),that men make better political leaders than women do (political leadership), and that when jobs are scarce, men should have more right to a job than women (job market). Response codes were averaged to provide a composite measure of gender equality: Gender equality = (obedience + political leadership + job market)/3. Accordingly, the minimum value is "1", where the respondents agree strongly with gender hierarchization, and the maximum is "4" where the respondents strongly disagree with gender inequality. Higher values on this variable indicate stronger support for gender equality than lower values and thus a negative relation with fundamentalism is predicted.

Form of Government

Variables related to form of government include attitudes toward democracy, secular politics, the role of religious laws in the formation of government policies, the significance of the religiosity of the people running for public office, and the role of religious leaders in politics. Here also, composite measures are constructed using these indicators. However, it should be noted that the variable measuring attitudes toward democracy was excluded in the construction of the composite measures of form of government. The reason for this exclusion is that in some countries like

Lebanon, more than 95% of the public "strongly agrees" or "agree" that democracy is the best form of government, which provides insufficient variation among Lebanese respondents on this variable for a meaningful analysis.

Two composites were created to represent the preferred form of government. The first consists of orientations toward secular politicians in response to whether they (1) strongly agree, (2) agree, (3) neither agree or disagree, (4) disagree, or (5) strongly disagree that politicians who do not believe in God are unfit to work for government in high offices (atheist politicians), that it would be better for your country if more people with strong religious beliefs held public office (no religious politicians), and that religious leaders should not interfere in politics. Responses to the question, "Religious leaders should not interfere in politics," were recoded so that higher values indicated stronger agreement with the statement (religious leaders refrain from politics). The fourth indicator (*shari'a*/Christian value) asked respondents whether they considered it (1) very important, (2) important, (3) somewhat important, (4) least important, or (5) not important for a good government to implement only the *shari'a* law (for Muslim respondents) or only the laws inspired by Christian values (for Christian respondents). The secular-politicians variable is constructed by averaging these four indicators. The secular politicians scale was constructed by averaging responses to these four variables: Secular Politicians = (atheist politicians + no religious politicians + religious leaders refrain from politics + *shari'a*/Christian values unimportant)/4.

This variable ranges between 1 and 5, with a higher value indicating stronger support for secular politicians. That is, people who more strongly supported secular politicians were those who tended to more strongly disagree that atheist politicians were unfit for public office, to more strongly disagree that people with strong religious beliefs held public office, to more strongly agree that religious leaders should not interfere in politics, and to attach less importance to the statement that a good government implemented only religious laws.

The second composite combined two variables to assess attitudes toward secular politics. One variable—separation of religion and politics—asked whether respondents (1) strongly agree, (2) agree, (3) disagree, or (4) strongly disagree that Lebanon would be a better place if religion and politics are separated. The second variable—no religious government—asked whether it was (1) very good, (2) fairly good, (3) fairly bad, or (4) very bad for Lebanon to have an Islamic government where religious authorities have absolute power (for Muslim respondents), or to have a Christian government where religious authorities have absolute power (for Christian respondents). Answers to the first question were recoded so that higher values indicate stronger support for the separation of religion and politics. This composite variable is constructed also in the same manner. Secular politics consists of the average of these two variables: Secular Politics = (separation of religion and politics + no religious government)/2.

This variable ranges between 1 and 4; higher values indicate stronger supports for secular politics. Consistent with the previous two variables, we propose that the fundamentalism factor is negatively correlated with the composite measures of secular politicians and secular politics. Negative relations are interpreted as support for the argument that fundamentalist attitudes and beliefs shape one's orientations toward politics.

Secular Identity

Generally, the participants in religious fundamentalist movements do not recognize nationalism, either in the form of ethnic, linguistic, or territoriality. Instead, they adhere to an image of a universal community of the faithful that are bounded together by a common adherence to and observance of *shari'a* law under an Islamic government. On the personal level, they adhere to religious identity: Muslim identity among Islamic fundamentalists and Christian identity among their Christian counterparts. To measure this variable, respondents were asked, "Which of the following best describes you?" Depending on the country, religion, or ethnicity, respondents were instructed to answer only one of the following: (1) "I am an Egyptian, Iranian, Lebanese, Saudi, above all"; (2) "I am a Muslim (for Muslim respondents), Christian (for Christian respondents), above all"; (3) "I am an Arab, Kurd, Azeri-Turk, Gilaki, Lur, above all"; or (4) "Other." A dummy variable is created where 0 = Religious identity ("Muslim above all" for Muslim respondents, or "Christian above all" for Christian respondents), and 1 = otherwise.

Western Culture

Criticisms of Western culture feature prominently in the discourse of the leaders of religious fundamentalism. These leaders portray Western culture as morally decadent. We used a proxy measure of attitudes toward Western culture whereby respondents were asked to rate the morality of the public from several countries: "Now, I would like you to rate several countries on a scale of morality, where '1' means that society is culturally decadent with a very low level of morality, where '10' means that people in that society have a high level of morality, and where '5' means a middle level of morality. Where would you rate [country name]?" Since the survey did not ask respondents to rate Western culture in terms of morality, we used ratings for the morality of the people from the U.S. and France as proxy measures for attitudes toward the Western culture. We combined the two ratings as a composite measure representing respondents' attitudes toward Western culture. The indicator, Western morality, is the average of the two variables: Western morality = (rating of the morality of the U.S. public + rating of the morality of the French)/2. We expected that the fundamentalism factor would be negatively linked to this measure, indicating that the stronger people's fundamentalist attitudes and beliefs, the lower is their rating of the morality of the U.S. and French public.

Liberalism-Fundamentalism Index

Higher levels of support for social individualism, gender equality, secular politicians, secular politics, and secular identity as well as higher ratings of the morality of the U.S. and French publics indicate liberal orientation, while lower levels of support show religious fundamentalist orientation. Based on these measures, we also created a single liberalism-fundamentalism index. People with higher scores on this measure within each group are considered to have stronger attachments to liberal values and people with lower scores have a stronger fundamentalist orientation.

MODEL AND FINDINGS

Figure 6.1 summarizes the relationship between the fundamentalism factor, on the one hand, and the liberal-fundamentalism index, on the other. The fundamentalism factor summarizes beliefs about and attitudes toward religion. The liberal-fundamentalism index represents a composite measure of attitudes toward issues that ranges from liberalism (higher values) to fundamentalism (lower values). The measures for each of the two factors are also shown in the figure. This figure is not intended to be a formal model to be estimated for each group and country separately, using structural equation modeling. It is rather a heuristic model to further illuminate the relationship between the religious fundamentalist factor and value orientations toward the historically significant issues described above. Although cross-sectional data limits causal inference, the degree to which the evidence supports the relations between fundamentalism individually and as a set provides evidence for a link between these two manifestations of fundamentalism. Nonetheless, we assess specifically the extent to which the fundamentalism factor predicts measures of social individualism, gender equality, secular politicians, secular politics, religious identity, Western culture, and the liberal-fundamentalism index for each of the countries, religions, religious sects, and ethnic groups that are discussed in this book.

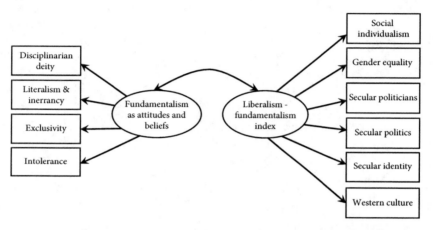

Figure 6.1. Relationship between fundamentalism as attitudes and as orientations toward significant issues.

Tables 6.1a and 6.1b present the means and standard deviations of the measures of social individualism, gender equality, secular politicians, secular politics, secular identity, and Western culture for each religious sect, religion, ethnicity group, and country. As these tables show, generally Lebanese have the highest and Saudis the lowest scores on all these measures. In between are Iran and Egypt on these values. This pattern inversely corresponds to fundamentalism scores across the countries and different groups, with the Saudis having the highest mean fundamentalism scores and Lebanese the lowest on these measures. Again, Egypt and Iran fall in between.

Between-Group Variation in Linkages between Fundamentalism and Attitudes toward Issues

On the macro level, we assess how group variation in the mean fundamentalism scores is associated with group variation in the mean scores for

Table 6.1a. Means (SD) for religious fundamentalism, variables measuring attitudes toward issues, and religious identity (KSA, Egypt, and Iran).

| | KSA | Egypt | Iran | | | |
	Youth		Persian	Kurd	Azeri Turk	Total
Religious fundamentalism	3.64 (.40)	3.38 (.44)	2.75 (.56)	2.52 (.68)	2.82 (.56)	2.72 (.59)
Social individualism	.36 (.48)	.46 (.50)	.56 (.24)	.62 (.25)	.53 (.26)	.57 (.25)
Gender equality	1.78 (.66)	1.80 (.61)	2.47 (.87)	2.94 (1.07)	2.32 (.84)	2.52 (.92)
Secular politicians	1.32 (.55)	2.24 (.53)	2.52 (.68)	2.95 (.99)	2.42 (.68)	2.57 (.76)
Secular politics	1.85 (.69)	2.19 (.67)	2.48 (.95)	2.99 (.99)	2.30 (.97)	2.52 (.99)
Secular identity	.20 (.40)	.09 (.28)	.50 (.50)	.77 (.42)	.46 (.50)	.53 (.50)
Western morality	4.69 (2.67)	2.61 (2.04)	4.84 (2.36)	5.76 (2.12)	4.61 (2.46)	4.94 (2.37)
Liberalism-fundamentalism index	1.11 (.32)	1.37 (.28)	1.73 (.41)	2.08 (.54)	1.62 (.40)	1.76 (.45)

CODING SCHEME:

Religious fundamentalism: As discussed and measured in chapter 3.

Social Individualism: For Egypt and KSA, only one variable is used (love as the basis for marriage); for Iran and Lebanon, all the four indicators were used.

Gender equality: All countries: Wife obedience, political leadership, job market. Higher value is strong disagreement with gender inequality.

Secular politicians: For Egypt, Atheists unfit for office, religious leaders shouldn't influence politics, *shari'a* law. Higher value is in favor of secularism. For KSA, *shari'a* law. Higher value is in favor of secularism. For Iran and Lebanon, Atheists unfit for office, better if people w/ strong religious beliefs in office, religious leaders shouldn't influence vote, *shari'a* law. Higher value is in favor of secularism.

Secular politics: For Egypt and KSA, Country better if religion and politics separated, having an Islamic govt. Higher value favors secularism. For Iran and Lebanon, Country better if religion and politics separated. Higher value favors secularism.

Secular identity: Secular (nationality/other=1) above all (vs. Muslim=0).

Western morality: Mean of US and France morality rating. Higher values are higher morality.

Liberalism-fundamentalism index: Linear combination of social individualism, gender equality, secular politicians, secular politics, and secular identity. People with higher scores on this measure have stronger liberal orientations.

Table 6.1b. Means (SD) for religious fundamentalism, variables measuring attitudes toward issues, and religious identity (Lebanon).

| | Lebanon | | | | | | | | |
| | Muslims | | | | Christians | | | | |
	Sunni	Shi'a	Druze	Muslim Total	Catholic	Maronite	Greek Ortho.	Christian Total	Total
Religious fundamentalism	2.72 (.59)	2.65 (.51)	2.58 (.55)	2.67 (.55)	2.23 (.58)	2.27 (.60)	2.28 (.64)	2.27 (.61)	2.53 (.61)
Social individualism	.58 (.28)	.62 (.28)	.66 (.25)	.61 (.28)	.64 (.24)	.67 (.25)	.66 (.26)	.67 (.25)	.63 (.27)
Gender equality	2.73 (1.10)	2.85 (1.06)	3.11 (.95)	2.83 (1.07)	3.48 (1.02)	3.24 (1.06)	3.23 (1.13)	3.27 (1.08)	2.99 (1.09)
Secular politicians	3.00 (.84)	3.00 (.89)	4.35 (.69)	3.15 (.94)	3.38 (.91)	3.31 (.90)	3.75 (.91)	3.46 (.92)	3.27 (.95)
Secular politics	2.74 (1.16)	2.90 (1.15)	3.61 (.54)	2.91 (1.13)	3.61 (.65)	3.50 (.70)	3.63 (.58)	3.56 (.66)	3.16 (1.03)
Secular identity	.69 (.46)	.71 (.46)	.97 (.16)	.73 (.44)	.74 (.44)	.77 (.42)	.82 (.39)	.78 (.41)	.75 (.43)
Western morality	5.64 (2.54)	4.79 (2.50)	4.22 (2.07)	5.06 (2.52)	5.58 (2.16)	5.75 (2.45)	5.25 (2.42)	5.57 (2.41)	5.24 (2.49)
Liberalism-fundamentalism index	1.93 (.51)	1.96 (.48)	2.54 (.31)	2.01 (.51)	2.37 (.41)	2.30 (.40)	2.42 (.36)	2.35 (.39)	2.13 (.50)

CODING SCHEME:
Religious fundamentalism: As discussed and measured in chapter 3.
Social Individualism: For Egypt and KSA, only one variable is used (love as the basis for marriage); for Iran and Lebanon, all the four indicators were used.
Gender equality: All countries: Wife obedience, political leadership, job market. Higher value is strong disagreement with gender inequality.
Secular politicians: For Egypt, Atheists unfit for office, religious leaders shouldn't influence politics, *shari'a* law. Higher value is in favor of secularism. For KSA, *shari'a* law, higher value is in favor of secularism. For Iran and Lebanon, Atheists unfit for office, better if people w/ strong religious beliefs in office, religious leaders shouldn't influence vote, *shari'a* law. Higher value is in favor of secularism.
Secular politics: For Egypt and KSA, Country better if religion and politics separated, having an Islamic govt. Higher value favors secularism. For Iran and Lebanon, Country better if religion and politics separated. Higher value favors secularism.
Secular identity: Secular (nationality/other=1) above all (vs. Muslim=0)
Western morality: Mean of US and France morality rating. Higher values are higher morality.
Liberalism-fundamentalism index: Linear combination of social individualism, gender equality, secular politicians, secular politics, and secular identity. People with higher scores on this measure have stronger liberal orientations.

Table 6.2. Correlations between mean fundamentalism and social issues across all groups.

Social individualism	− .96
Gender equality	− .96
Secular politicians	− .82
Secular politics	− .90
Secular identity	−.87
Western morality	− .67
Liberalism-fundamentalism index	− .92

each variable measure of social individualism, gender equality, secular politicians, secular politics, religious identity, and the Western culture. For a more effective assessment of this relationship, across all the fifteen groups (four countries, three ethnic groups, two religions, and six religious sects, as shown in the fifteen columns in Tables 6.1a and 6.1b), Pearson correlation coefficients between group means, fundamentalism scores and group means for these variables are computed and reported in Table 6.2.

As this table shows, the correlation coefficients between fundamentalism and each of these variable measures for the fifteen cases are significant on the macro level. That is, those groups with a higher fundamentalism mean tend to have lower means in social individualism, gender equality, secular politicians, Western morality, and secular identity. The fundamentalism factor and liberal-fundamentalism index are also negatively linked. Thus, on the macro level, fundamentalist attitudes and beliefs predict attitudes toward social issues.

Within-Group Variation in Linkages between Fundamentalism and Attitudes toward Issues

Tables 6.3a and 6.3b present the correlations between religious fundamentalism and each of the variables within each of the fifteen groups. As indicated, the religious fundamentalism factor is significantly inversely linked to social individualism across religions, religious sects, ethnic groups, and countries. The only exception is among Egyptian youth and Lebanese Druze. That is, except for the latter two groups, the higher respondents' fundamentalist attitudes and beliefs, the lower their support for social individualism. The magnitude of this relationship is higher among Iranians compared to the other three countries, among the Kurds compared to Persians and Azeri-Turks, among the Shi'is compared to the

Sunnis and Druze, and among Catholics compared to other religious
sects. Likewise, except for the Druze, attitudes toward gender equality are
significantly inversely linked to religious fundamentalism. That is, the
stronger the respondents' religious fundamentalist attitudes and beliefs,
the weaker is their attitudes in favor of gender equality. Again, similar to
the two social-individualism and gender-equality variables, religious fundamentalism is significantly inversely linked to both of the composite
measures of form of government. As these tables show, fundamentalism
is inversely linked to attitudes toward favoring secular politicians across
all the groups and countries, except for among the Druze, for which the
correlation is positive and significant, and the Orthodox, for which it is
not significant. Likewise, fundamentalism is significantly inversely linked
to attitudes toward secular politics across all the groups and countries,
except for among the Saudi youth and Lebanese Catholics. The relatively
larger of size of the correlation coefficients within each group may

Table 6.3a. Correlations between religious fundamentalism and variables measuring
attitudes toward issues and religious identity (KSA, Egypt and Iran).

	KSA	Egypt	Iran			
	Youth		Persian	Kurd	Azeri Turk	Total
Social individualism	$-.10^b$	$-.04$	$-.20^d$	$-.31^d$	$-.16^c$	$-.23^d$
	923^*	857	1530	422	563	2515
Gender equality	$-.22^d$	$-.23^d$	$-.29^d$	$-.16^b$	$-.23^d$	$-.27^d$
	953	893	1530	422	563	2515
Secular politicians	$-.23^d$	$-.21^d$	$-.47^d$	$-.65^d$	$-.43^d$	$-.53^d$
	930	894	1530	422	562	2514
Secular politics	$-.06^a$	$-.15^d$	$-.25^d$	$-.36^d$	$-.17^c$	$-.28^d$
	948	893	1509	410	552	2471
Secular identity	$-.10^c$	$.00$	$-.25^d$	$-.29^d$	$-.21^d$	$-.27^d$
	954	893	1522	421	561	2504
Western morality	$-.05$	$-.13^d$	$-.26^d$	$-.34^d$	$-.25^d$	$-.29^d$
	920	881	1400	371	501	2274
Liberalism-fundamentalism index	$-.252^d$	$-.281^d$	$-.47^d$	$-.54^d$	$-.37^d$	$-.49^d$
	954	894	1530	422	563	2515

$^a p < .05$ $^b p < .01$ $^c p < .001$ $^d p < .0001$
*Sample size

Table 6.3b. Correlations between religious fundamentalism and variables measuring attitudes toward issues and religious identity (Lebanon).

| | Lebanon | | | | | | | | |
| | Muslims | | | | Christians | | | | |
	Sunni	Shi'a	Druze	Muslim Total	Catholic	Maronite	Greek Ortho.	Christian Total	Total
Social individualism	$-.14^d$ (749)*	$-.22^d$ (952)	.01 (198)	$-.17^d$ (1899)	$-.33^d$ (149)	$-.09^b$ (597)	$-.17^d$ (332)	$-.15^d$ (1078)	$-.18^d$ (2977)
Gender equality	$-.22^d$ (753)	$-.23^d$ (953)	$-.07$ (198)	$-.22^d$ (1904)	$-.31^d$ (149)	$-.17^d$ (597)	$-.31^d$ (338)	$-.24^d$ (1084)	$-.27^d$ (2988)
Secular politicians	$-.43^d$ (728)	$-.43^d$ (857)	$.15^a$ (198)	$-.37^d$ (1783)	$-.46^d$ (149)	$-.09^a$ (594)	$-.02$ (338)	$-.11^d$ (1081)	$-.30^d$ (2864)
Secular politics	$-.39^d$ (711)	$-.32^d$ (827)	$-.15^a$ (194)	$-.35^d$ (1732)	$-.15$ (148)	$-.13^c$ (592)	$-.22^d$ (328)	$-.16^d$ (1068)	$-.36^d$ (2800)
Secular identity	$-.33^d$ (749)	$-.27^d$ (940)	$-.17^a$ (197)	$-.30^d$ (1886)	$-.17^a$ (148)	$-.10^a$ (594)	$-.19^d$ (335)	$-.14^d$ (1077)	$-.24^d$ (2963)
Western morality	$-.17^d$ (697)	$-.08^a$ (925)	$-.17^d$ (191)	$-.11^c$ (1813)	$-.10$ (146)	$-.26^d$ (567)	$-.19^c$ (320)	$-.22^d$ (1033)	$-.18^d$ (2846)
Liberalism-fundamentalism index	$-.45^d$ (753)	$-.38^d$ (953)	$-.05$ (198)	$-.38^d$ (1904)	$-.49^d$ (149)	$-.22^d$ (598)	$-.34^d$ (338)	$-.29^d$ (1085)	$-.42^d$ (2989)

$^a p < .05$ $^b p < .01$ $^c p < .001$ $^d p < .0001$
*Sample size

indicate that fundamentalists more sharply disfavor secularism than other issues like social individualism or gender equality.

Religious fundamentalists are identified less with such secular bases of identity as the territorial nation or ethnicity and more with religion (Christianity or Islam) across all the groups except among Egyptian youth. The variable is also significantly negatively linked to the morality ratings of the US-French public (as a composite proxy measure of attitudes toward Western culture) across all the groups, except among the Saudi youth and Lebanese Catholics. Finally, the fundamentalism factor is significantly negatively linked to the liberalism-fundamentalism index across all the groups, except for among the Druze.

The empirical analysis of the data thus indicates strong linkages between fundamentalist beliefs about and attitudes toward religion, on the one hand, and fundamentalism as particular resolutions of a set of historically significant issues, including those related to social individualism, gender equality, secular politics and politicians, secular identity, and Western culture. Across countries, ethnicity, religions, and almost all religious sects, fundamentalist beliefs and attitudes are linked to fundamentalist orientations toward historically significant issues. The presence of such strong linkages between the two manifestations of the same phenomenon further validates the conceptualizations of fundamentalism advanced in this book.

CONCLUSIONS

In Chapter One, we presented an overview of Islamic fundamentalism within a different historical context. In that overview, we defined religious fundamentalism as a discourse that offered distinctive resolutions of a set of historically significant issues. In the following chapters, we defined, measured, and analyzed religious fundamentalism as a set of interrelated beliefs about and attitudes toward religion across country, religion, religious sect, and ethnicity, using findings from values survey carried out in Egypt, Iran, Lebanon, and Saudi Arabia. In this chapter, we attempted to show that these two sets of attitudes—attitudes toward one's religion and attitudes toward social issues—are related and that thus the two conceptions of fundamentalism measure aspects of the same phenomenon.

The foregoing analysis empirically linked religious fundamentalism as beliefs and attitudes to the type of value orientations promoted by the intellectual leaders of religious fundamentalist movements. In the same way that the discourse of these leaders rested on the rejection of the Western liberal values, fundamentalists treated the West as culturally decadent, abandoned secular politics, supported Islamic government, Islamic identity, and gender inequality. As our analysis has shown, people with stronger fundamentalist beliefs and attitudes also tended to be less in favor of social individualism, gender equality, secular politics, secular identity, and Western culture than people with weaker fundamentalist orientations. Because these two sets of attitudes and beliefs are significantly linked, we may suggest that religious fundamentalism reinforces people's support or even participation in the religious fundamentalist movements and vice versa; that participation in religious fundamentalist movements reinforces fundamentalist beliefs and attitudes. We may thus conclude that the two different conceptualizations of the construct reflected different aspects of the same reality.

Furthermore, this analysis suggests that fundamentalist beliefs and attitudes do not simply indicate the degree of people's commitment to their faith. Such beliefs and attitudes have also social consequences, as they tend to support a certain modality of social life that rested on religious government, patriarchy, religious identity, and rejection of the Western modality of politics and culture. On a higher level of abstraction, our findings also support a modified version of Geertz' view of the relationship between the ethos and the world-views aspects of a culture as well as the Weberian notion of the connection between people's conception of divinity and the type of social relationships they tend to support and desire. Our analysis thus demonstrated a significant connection between fundamentalism as a distinctive cognitive modality of religion and fundamentalism as normative modality of social life. Thus, the fundamentalist religious beliefs and attitudes have far reaching implications for the organization of social life.

APPROACHES TO FUNDAMENTALISM AND THE CYCLE
OF SPIRITUALITY

The conceptual framework constituting the organizing theme of this book in order to describe and analyze religious fundamentalism is drawn from two complementary approaches: one historical and the other based on contemporary beliefs and attitudes toward religion. The way fundamentalism was conceptualized in the historical approach was intended to distinguish religious fundamentalism from other cultural movements that have emerged in the Muslim world. The historical approach covered the period between 1700s, when the three Muslim empires of the Mughals, Ottomans, and Safavids were on the course of disintegration, and the second half of the twentieth century, when Muslim-majority countries were mostly dominated by various forms of authoritarian regimes. During that period, we identified two major episodes of religious fundamentalism. The first was the reformist fundamentalism of Shah Waliallah in India and Muhammad Ibn Abdul Wahhab in Arabia in the eighteenth century. The other was the Sunni and Shi'i fundamentalism of the twentieth century. In between, there was a secular cultural episode that was manifested in the rise of various forms of modern cultural movements.

We interpreted this sequence of fundamentalism-secularism-fundamentalism as reflecting a broader cycle of spirituality that alternated between sacred and secular sources. Our interpretation of the historical processes that contributed to the rise of religious fundamentalism highlighted the diachronic relations among the factors that prompted intellectual leaders to focus on religion as a framework to address and resolve the sociopolitical and cultural issues facing their faith and societies.

The second approach assessed and analyzed variations in fundamentalist orientations among the ordinary public, using findings from surveys carried out in Egypt, Iran, Lebanon, and Saudi Arabia. These analyses highlighted the variables that were similar to these historical factors as well as a set of other sociological and social psychological variables in order to assess empirically the strength of their synchronic relations with an attitudinal measure of religious fundamentalism. The analyses provided evidence that the two approaches were complementary in that the attitudinal measure of fundamentalism correlated with variables measuring orientations toward significant sociopolitical and cultural issues across nations, religions, religious sects, and ethnicities. The direction of these correlations was consistent with the beliefs and attitudes displayed by the leaders and activists of religious fundamentalist movements toward these issues. That is, people with stronger fundamentalist beliefs and attitudes display orientations toward sociopolitical and cultural issues that were similar to the orientations displayed by the leaders and activists of these movements.

In parallel fashion, both approaches showed that religious fundamentalism is weakened under pluralistic cultural conditions, the state's structural heterogeneity, or elite diversity and conflict, and enhanced by a monolithic culture imposed from above by the secular authoritarian state and by in-group solidarity. Further, fundamentalism has been negatively linked to the introduction or the usage of new communications technologies. Historically, the introduction of the press to the Muslim world in the nineteenth century contributed to the expansion of secular discourses and Islamic modernism. Likewise, on the individual level, our survey data showed that the use of the Internet, personal computer, and Satellite TV was inversely related to fundamentalist attitudes and beliefs.

Our interpretation of the historical context in which religious fundamentalism emerged and of the expressions of the intellectual leaders of this movement supported the view that fundamentalism was reinforced by a perception of besieged spirituality—that the faith was under attack and the solidarity of the religious communities was being undermined by secular and un-Islamic currents. Likewise, considering people's assessment of the significance of Western cultural invasion or the belief in a U.S. or Jewish conspiracy against Muslims as proxy measures of the perception of besieged spirituality, findings from the surveys showed that these measures were directly linked to religious fundamentalism.

In the same way that the fundamentalist movements aimed at restoring the rule of the *shari'a* in people's lives, the link between fundamentalism and attitudes toward a good government as one that implements only the *shari'a* law was significant and positive across the four countries. Finally, such factors as fatalism, the feeling of powerlessness, and the perception that happiness may not be realized in this world were linked to fundamentalist beliefs and attitudes. This connection is consistent with the interpretations that fundamentalism resonates with such psychological conditions under state authoritarianism. Under such fundamentalist regimes as the Islamic Republic of Iran, the feeling of powerlessness is, however, inversely related to fundamentalism.

Equally significant in linking the two approaches to religious fundamentalism is the effectiveness of the measure in predicting people's orientations toward the same sociopolitical issues that were the concerns of the fundamentalist movements historically. The twentieth century fundamentalist movements displayed a typical pattern of value orientation. This pattern was an abstraction from the individualized totality of religious fundamentalism, to paraphrase Parsons' explication of Weber's concept of the ideal type (1964, xxxiii). This value orientation consisted of the desirability of an Islamic government based on the unity between religion and politics, support for gender hierarchization and patriarchy (which also entails the rejection of social individualism), promotion of religious identity, and a view of the West as culturally decadent. We constructed measures of these value orientations in terms of social individualism; attitudes toward gender equality, secular politicians, and secular politics; secular identity; and attitudes toward Western morality.

As our analysis showed, across all the four countries, religious sects, and ethnic groups, fundamentalism was negatively linked to almost all these measures. This finding also supports the Weberian notion that people's conception of the divinity has social consequences, which in the current analysis means that it shapes their orientations toward sociopolitical and cultural issues. It was also consistent with a modified version of Geertz's theory on the relationship between ethos and the worldviews aspects of a culture. As our analysis has shown, the fundamentalist model of religion was linked to a distinctive orientation toward sociopolitical and cultural issues (i.e., a model for social reality).

KEY FINDINGS

Religious Fundamentalism as an Orientation toward Religion

As a set of distinctive beliefs about and attitudes toward religion, fundamentalism was proposed to have four separable but interrelated components. The first is a disciplinarian conception of God who requires absolute obedience from the faithful. The second component is inerrancy and literalism, which considers the scriptures as a comprehensive system of absolute truth that is both infallible and literally accurate. The belief supports the view that there is no need for man-made laws. The third is religious centrism and exclusivism that considers one's own religion to be superior to the religions of others. The fourth is religious intolerance, which rests on the belief that in order to maintain the purity of the faith, the believers must maintain little contact with the followers of other faiths, who should not be given the same rights as those given to the followers of one's own faith.

These components of fundamentalism were operationalized by Likert-scale items that comprised a psychometrically reliable and valid scale based on data from youth surveys carried out in Egypt and Saudi Arabia in 2005, as well as from national surveys of adults in Iran in 2005 and Lebanon in 2008. Included among these items were:

– Whenever there is a conflict between science and religion, religion is always right.
– The religion of Islam [Christianity for Christian respondents] is closer to God than other religions.
– The only acceptable religion to God is Islam [Christianity for Christian respondents].
– Only good Muslims [Christians for Christian respondents] will go to heaven. Non-Muslims [non-Christians for Christian respondents] will not no matter how good they are.
– Islam [Christianity for Christian respondents] should be the only religion taught in our public schools.

These items constituted the scale that was used to determine relations between fundamentalism and theoretically relevant variables on the macro and micro levels. On the macro level, fundamentalism was used for cross-country, inter-faith, and inter-ethnic comparative analysis. The four countries were similarly compared in terms of variations in attributes of the state and national-historical context, religious background (Christianity and Islam), religious sects (among Lebanese Christians: the Maronites, Catholics, and Orthodox; and Muslims: the Shi'is, Sunnis, and Druze), and ethnicity (among Iranians: the Azeri-Turks, Gilakis, Kurds, Lurs, and Persians). Although there were many other religious sects and ethnic groups in these countries, the selection of the above groups for analysis was based on the sufficient representation in the samples. Variations on this level were also analyzed in terms of education and gender as well as urban-rural differences. On the micro level, the analysis focused on such factors as the sources of information people relied on, level of confidence in the religious institution and the media (the press and TV), the use of the Internet and satellite TV, frequency of computer use, religiosity and religious orthodoxy, social psychological factors, the feeling of besieged spirituality, identity, morality, and demographics.

On the *macro* level, comparative analysis of these groups showed that:

- Fundamentalism was lowest in Lebanon, followed by Iran, Egypt, and Saudi Arabia.
- Lebanese Christians on average were less fundamentalist than Muslims.
- There were no significant differences in fundamentalism among Lebanese Christians. Among the Muslim sects, however, the Druze were less fundamentalist than either the Shi'is or Sunnis.
- The Iranian Kurds were less fundamentalist than the other ethnic groups in Iran that were included in this analysis. There were no significant differences in the level of fundamentalism among the other ethnic groups in Iran, although Azeri Turks tended to be slightly more fundamentalist than the rest.
- Gender differences in fundamentalism were country specific. In Iran, males tended to be less fundamentalist than females, while in Egypt it was just the opposite. In Lebanon and Saudi Arabia, there was no significant gender difference in fundamentalism.
- University education was inversely related to fundamentalism in Iran and Lebanon, while no such effect was detected in Egypt and Saudi Arabia.
- Finally, in Iran, those in urban areas were lower in fundamentalism than those in rural areas of the country.

Our macro analysis thus showed that cross-national differences in fundamentalism parallel the differences in the cultural and religious context, the form of the state, the religiosity of the state, and the homogeneity-heterogeneity of the ruling elite. Among the four countries, Lebanon's relatively lower level of fundamentalism was attributed to the country having a stronger tradition of religious pluralism, cultural diversity, elite heterogeneity, and democratic politics. A higher level of fundamentalism in Saudi Arabia, by contrast, was related to the relative absence of these factors. Further, fundamentalism on the aggregate level appeared to have been affected by the nature of the political structure of the ruling regime. The Islamic Republic of Iran, despite its overall authoritarian nature and proven capacity and willingness to repress dissent, has a heterogeneous political structure, with considerable inter-elite rivalries and factionalism. This provided a favorable political space that has allowed the rise of a liberal trend among the country's intellectuals (Kamrava 2008) and the public at large (Moaddel 2009). This trend in turn has undermined the religious and social influence of the fundamentalist ideology associated with the Islamic regime, particularly with the office of the absolutist ruler.

The political situation in Egypt and Saudi Arabia was quite different. Egypt has been ruled by a secular authoritarian regime, and the rise of religious oppositional discourse in the country has been largely in reaction to the state's secular authoritarianism (Moaddel 2005). This opposition seems to have contributed to fundamentalist beliefs and attitudes among Egyptians. Although Saudi Arabia's religious authoritarianism may undermine support for the official religion (Moaddel 2010), in the absence of a heterogeneous political structure (unlike Iran), there was little discursive space for the rise of alternative cultural discourses. And such events as the outbreak of the Iranian Revolution and the Soviet invasion of Afghanistan in 1979 appeared to have energized individuals and groups favorable to political Islam and religious fundamentalism. As a result, the public remained vulnerable to the fundamentalist message of the oppositional religious movement in the country. In certain urban areas of Saudi society, such as Dammam and al-Khobar, where there is a degree of religious pluralism, support for fundamentalism is much lower than in such other areas as like Riyadh and Jeddah.

At the same time, the attitude of religious fundamentalists toward the state, whether democratically organized (Lebanon) or authoritarian (Egypt, Iran, and Saudi Arabia), may be attributed to the state's culture or religiosity. To put it differently, the state culture, whether religious or secular, moderates the relationship between fundamentalism and favorable attitudes toward the state. As a moderator, the state culture serves as a context that affects the direction of the relationship between fundamentalism and attitudes toward the state. Under a confessional democratic (Lebanon) or religious authoritarian (Iran and Saudi Arabia) state, there was a positive relationship between fundamentalism and perception of state performance, whereas under the secular authoritarian regime (Egypt), on the other hand, this relationship was negative.

With regard to religion, Lebanese Christians were less fundamentalist than were Muslims. It is premature, however, to attribute this difference to differences in the primordial beliefs between the two faiths. Rather, they can be accounted for, as least in part, as an outcome of the contemporary experiences of the Christian, Shi'i, and Sunni communities. In the modern period, Christian intellectuals have been among the harbingers of secularism and liberal ideas in the region. Furthermore, Christian communities, primarily the Maronites, have maintained cultural relationships and favorable attitudes toward the West, France in particular, which might have attenuated the tendency toward religious fundamentalism among them. The Shi'is and Sunnis, on the other hand, are drawn toward fundamentalism by the very nature of their relationships with the Islamic regimes in the region in recent decades. Iran is the major patron of the Shi'is in Lebanon, and the Hezbollah, as their chief Islamic political and military organization, has been founded and consistently supported by the Islamic Republic of Iran. The Sunnis, on the other hand, have received considerable support from Saudi Arabia. As shown by our analysis, fundamentalism among the Shi'is was reinforced by their favorable attitudes toward Iran and among the Sunnis by their favorable attitudes toward the Kingdom of Saudi Arabia.

On the micro level, two sets of factors were linked to fundamentalism. The first set consists of those that are common across all the four countries and religious groups. The other set consists of the variables that are linked to fundamentalism only among a subset of the countries or religious groups. As for the first set, across all the four countries and the two religious groups—Christians and Muslims—fundamentalism was related in the following ways:

- Positively to religious sources of epistemic authority (in Egypt and Saudi Arabia) or when respondents expressed confidence in these sources (Iran and Lebanon);
- Positively to religious orthodoxy;
- Positively linked to fatalism—whether fatalism was measured in terms of the belief in the unrealizablility of happiness in this world (in Egypt and Saudi Arabia), or in terms of the belief that fate would shape one's life (in Iran and Lebanon);
- Positively to besieged spirituality, where such measures were available as attitudes toward Western cultural invasion (in Iran, Egypt, and Saudi Arabia) or the belief in an American and Jewish conspiracy against Muslim nations (Egypt and Saudi Arabia); and
- Negatively to annual family income.

The following describes variables related to fundamentalism among individuals in only a subset of these countries or religious groups:

- Mosque attendance is positively associated with fundamentalism only in Egypt, Iran, and Lebanon. Church attendance is not related to fundamentalism among Christians.
- Confidence in the media or the use of the media as the source of epistemic authority is positively related to fundamentalism in Iran and Saudi Arabia.

- The use of the Internet or email or the frequency and the use of personal computer are negatively related to fundamentalism (these questions were not included in the youth surveys in Egypt and Saudi Arabia).
- Self-rated religiosity was positively associated with fundamentalism across the two religions in Lebanon, in Iran, and Saudi Arabia, but not in Egypt.
- Frequency of prayer was negatively linked to fundamentalism among only Lebanese Muslims but positively among Iranians.
- The feeling of powerlessness was positively related to fundamentalism among Lebanese Christians, but negatively to fundamentalism among Iranians.
- Attitudes toward premarital sex as an immoral behavior were linked to fundamentalism across all the religious groups in Iran and Lebanon.
- National pride was linked to fundamentalism among Iranians.
- Attitude toward making rules according to the people's wishes was negatively related to fundamentalism among Iranians but positively so among Lebanese Shi'is.
- Subjective class identification was negatively linked to fundamentalism among Lebanese Christians and Iranians.
- Religious identity was directly related to fundamentalism among Iranians and Lebanese Christians and Muslims.
- Among Lebanese Shi'is, fundamentalism was positively correlated with favorable attitudes toward the role of Iranians and Syrian regimes in Lebanon. Among Lebanese Sunnis, fundamentalism was positively linked to favorable attitudes toward the role of Saudis in the country.
- Finally, in Lebanon, fundamentalism was positively associated with in-group solidarity (negatively linked to inter-group trust) among all the confessional groups, except the Catholics.

CYCLE OF SPIRITUALITY AND SECULAR FUNDAMENTALISM

The cycle of spirituality is conceived as an outcome of historical altercations between the forces favoring sacred spirituality and those supporting secular spirituality. This cycle, as we argued, reflected a sequence of religious fundamentalism, modernism, and fundamentalism that emerged in the Muslim world between the eighteenth and twentieth centuries. While we realize that the usage of religious fundamentalism is controversial and some scholars prefer to abandon the term altogether, there are people, as our data have demonstrated, with fundamentalist beliefs and

attitudes in society and such beliefs and attitudes have social consequences, as this book attempted to demonstrate. Nonetheless, as attitudes
and beliefs, fundamentalism may not be confined only to religion. During
the hey-day of secular ideologies, there have been peoples and movements who displayed secular attitudes that were similar in orientation to
those of religious fundamentalists. In fact, not all fundamentalists are religious (Summer 2006). Although the literature predominantly focuses on
the former, secular fundamentalist movements have been no less conse-
quential in shaping state policies and historical events. Such secular ideological movements as Nazism, Fascism, some forms of nationalism,
Stalinism, Maoism, and leftist terrorist groups have displayed features
that are remarkably similar to religious extremism. The stress on heroism,
the glorification of death, and the anti-liberal and anti-materialist orientations that have informed these movements display considerable affini-
ties with contemporary religious fundamentalism. For example, in his
exposition of philosophy of fascism, Palmieri (1936, 33) says:

> Fascism turns toward the individual and tells him: Thy life has no absolute,
> no eternal value whatsoever; thy life can assume worth only inasmuch as it
> is devoted and, if necessary, sacrificed to the triumph of an idea. Men live
> today, die tomorrow, but ideas live forever. And the one who will seek to save
> his own life shall truly lose it, because only by offering it in holocaust to
> an everlasting Idea does individual life partake of the character of
> immortality.

It is the fascist "ambition to place ideals above wants, sacrifice above
desires, heroism, martyrdom and death above cowardice, safety and well-
being" (Palmeiri 1936, 39, Marcuse 1968). Nationalist ideologues have also
used similar expressions in defending the sanctity of their homeland and
in rallying the public to the cause of national liberation. Like other forms
of fundamentalism, liberalism and individual freedom are glossed over in
order to sacrifice individuality for the sake of the glorified nation. An
exemplar of this position is one of the ardent spokespeople of Arab
nationalism, Sati' al-Husri (1880–1968), who subordinates the idea of freedom to the necessity of self-sacrifice for the liberation of Arab land. He
proclaims that:

> I wish it realized that freedom is not an end unto itself, but is a means to a
> higher life. The patriotic interests, which may sometimes demand a person
> to sacrifice his life and soul, may also demand the sacrifice of his freedom.
> He who does not sacrifice his personal freedom in the cause of his nation's
> freedom when the situation demands it, may then lose his personal freedom

along with the freedom of his nation and his fatherland. He who does not consent to "lose" (*yufni*) himself in the nation to which he belongs, may then be "absorbed" (*al-fana*) by a foreign nation which could someday conquer his fatherland. Therefore, I say continuously and without hesitation: "Patriotism and nationalism above and before all else, even above and before freedom" (Cleveland 1971, 169–70; Haim 1958, 283).

In a parallel fashion, the ideas of martyrdom, the glorification of death, and heroism featured prominently in the mobilization efforts of Shi'i fundamentalism during the Iranian Revolution of 1977–1979 and later in the Islamic regime's mobilization of the public in the Iran-Iraq war. In the words of a prominent ideologue of Iran's revolutionary Shi'ism, Ayatollah Motahhari, martyrdom (*shahadat*) "is heroic and admirable, because it results from a voluntary, conscious and selfless action. It is the only type of death which is higher, greater and holier than life itself" (cited in Moaddel 1993, 258).

In the Marxian tradition, fundamentalism has also been a predominant feature of vulgar Marxism and leftist authoritarianism. Stalin justified his pogroms on the grounds that he was returning the country to the dictatorship of the proletariat. The Chinese Gang of Four that came to prominence during the Cultural Revolution (1966–1976), Pol Pot and the Cambodian communist movement known as the Khmer Rouge (1976–1979), and the Italian Revolutionary Red Brigade were all inspired by an extremist form of Marxist fundamentalism.

Adherence to secular fundamentalism, like religious fundamentalism, however, does not necessarily imply support for political extremism and violence. The concept of Marxist fundamentalism, for example, has been used to indicate distinctive orientations toward some of the core beliefs in Marxism. Fundamentalists are those who advanced "a very strong and uncompromising criticism of the existing system," believed "in genuine Marxism," and were ideological and dogmatic (Klaus and Jezek 1991, 31; Lindsay 1961, 57–58). They also relied exclusively on a literal reading of "classical, nineteenth-century texts and ignore the later development of Marxist theory" (Blaut, Haring, O'Keefe, and Wisner, 1997, 126). Finally, they were "scornful of civil liberties" and believed that abstract concepts can be applied directly to the analysis of concrete historical conjunctures (Hall 1985, 117–118). It has been argued that Marxist fundamentalists tend to espouse revolutionary politics, are obsessed with the notion of the imminent crisis of capitalism, and reject compromise. They are also criticized for adopting an image of the proletariat as a secular equivalent of

Hegel's Absolute Spirit, the protagonist of an eschatological philosophy of history whose culmination is the revolution (Hassard et al. 2006, 343–351).

From these observations, we may thus suggest that fundamentalism may exist in other belief systems that are secular as well. As such, we may generalize as fundamentalist any belief and orientation that rests on:

- The inerrancy of the sacred text (whether it's the *Torah, Bible, Quran,* or *Das Capital,* or *What Is to Be Done*),
- Accessibility of its truth through a literal reading of the text,
- The universality of its truth and unchanging character,
- A splitting of the world into the truth and falsehood (good and evil),
- Stereotypical thinking—the employment of rigid and inflexible categories,
- The presence of a narrow interstitial capacity in the belief system, and
- A lack of acknowledgment of inconsistencies in the belief system.

Fundamentalism thus tends to overlook or dismiss the existence of an overlap between one's position and that of one's opponent (i.e., the gray area between one's 'truth' and another's 'falsehood'), showing little interest in any compromise with the followers of other belief systems. It supports exclusivity; that is, the benefits of a better life are reserved only for the true believers. It claims the superiority and centrality of one's beliefs over others' beliefs. It is also committed to the consistency and coherence of the principles of the faith, and cognitive consonance.[1] In that sense, it has much in common with dogmatism, which is (a) a relatively closed cognitive organization of beliefs and disbeliefs about reality, (b) organized around a central set of beliefs about absolute authority which, in turn, (c) provides a framework for patterns of intolerance and qualified tolerance toward others (Rokeach 1954; also Altemeyer 2002; Crowson 2009).

---

[1] We use this concept in a sense just the opposite of the concept of "cognitive dissonance" (Festinger 1957). It is the feeling of comfort that comes when all the elements of one's belief system appear coherent and remarkably consistent with one another.

SPIRITUALITY AND THE ARAB SPRING

By conceptualizing the historical opposition between the forces favoring sacred and those favoring secular spirituality in terms of a cycle of spirituality, we are not suggesting that history repeats itself and that, for example, religious fundamentalism in the eighteenth century was identical to the fundamentalism of the twentieth. The religious and intellectual problems the two movements faced and the solutions they offered were quite different from one another. Rather, they were similar in terms of their orientations toward the sacred, their rejection of the secular, and the type of attitudes they displayed toward their religion, on the one hand, and toward outsiders, on the other, as both considered the faith being contaminated by cultures other than Islamic and displayed intolerant attitudes toward other religions.

Furthermore, as we argued, the shift from one type of spirituality to another may be event-driven and the intensity of the opposition between sacred and secular spirituality is certainly historically a variable. For example, nineteenth-century religious reformers and Westernizers displayed by and large tolerant attitudes toward one another in Egypt. Secularists in the twentieth century, on the other hand, displayed a fairly strong anti-religious orientation. Perhaps in response, the religious activists also displayed equally strong alarmist attitudes toward secular discourses. There are, however, indications that the Arab Spring signifies the ushering in of a new era in the Middle East where the relationship between secular and religious movements rests on a negotiated accommodation between these two major social forces. First, the Arab Spring occurred within the context of a shift in values among Arab countries. For example, in such countries as Egypt, Iraq, and Saudi Arabia, where longitudinal survey data are available, the dominant trend has been toward national identity, the decline in support for the *shari'a*, increase in support for the separation of religion and politics, and gender equality (except for Egypt). Second, the movements that unseated entrenched dictators in Egypt, Libya, Tunisia, and Yemen and in such places as Bahrain and Syria where people are still struggling for change have thus far been predominantly pragmatic and non-ideological. Findings from the surveys carried out in Egypt, Lebanon, and Pakistan in 2011 support this interpretation. As shown in Figure 8, an overwhelming majority of the public from these countries perceived that the Arab Spring constituted a movement for democracy and economic prosperity, and only a minority of about less than 10% in Egypt and Lebanon and 16% in Pakistan believed that it was

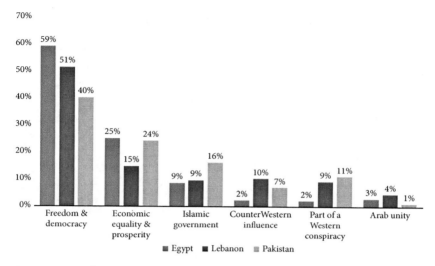

Figure 7.1. Explanations for the Arab Spring in Egypt, Lebanon, and Pakistan.

for the formation of an Islamic government. Another small minority rejected the movements of the Arab Spring as a part of Western conspiracy (2% among Egyptians, 9% Lebanese, and 11% Pakistanis) or considered them as movements to counter Western influence (2% Egyptians, 10% Lebanese, and 7% Pakistanis).

Finally, findings from a 2011 values survey in Egypt have also provided further evidence indicating the predominantly secular nature of the type of people who participated in the movement against President Hosni Mubarak. The respondents were asked to rate their participation in the movement on the scale of "1", being none or minimum participation, to "10", being utmost participations. Accordingly, those who rated their participation higher tend to be male, age 18–45 (formative years under President Mubarak), urban residents, of higher socioeconomic status, newspaper readers, internet users, less trusting of their government, or less satisfied with the government's performance. They also displayed stronger support for liberal values, were less fatalistic, felt more empowered but less secure, and did not mind having Westerners as neighbors.[2]

---

[2] For more information on the recent surveys carried out by Moaddel and associates, see www.mevs.org, and "What Do Arabs Want?" *Project Syndicate*, http://www.project -syndicate.org/commentary/what-do-arabs-want, retrieved April 17, 2012.

Such measures of religiosity as mosque attendance, daily prayer, self-described religiosity, and the importance of God in one's life did not have a significant effect on participation. At the same time, the major political beneficiaries of the Arab Spring appear to have been Islamic political parties; the candidates connected to the Freedom and Justice Party, the political wing of the Muslim Brothers, and the al-Nour party, the political wing of a coalition of ultraconservative Islamic groups, together garnered about 70% of the votes in the 2011–2012 parliamentary elections.

Thus, it appears that the people who led the movement against President Hosni Mubarak and those who gained the majority of the seats in the parliament had diverse cultural orientations, the first having secular and the second religious. This paradox may be an outcome of the fact that religious activists benefitted from years of political organizing and were thus better able to bring their supporters to the polls, while the secular groups, being continuously under attack for decades from both religious extremists and the authoritarian government, did not have a nationwide network that would have enabled them to translate their newly acquired political capital into votes. Nonetheless, this paradox provides a context for a negotiated accommodation between religious parties and secular activists, which in turn may bring into relief a new distinctive conception of spirituality that is neither distinctly secular nor religious. We may speculate that insofar as political debates revolve on how to rebuild the economy, the context for a negotiated new form of spirituality that transcends the existing conceptions of both the sacred and secular may become strengthened. On the other hand, if the Islamic groups push forward the idea of the Islamization of society, then one may witness considerable cultural conflict and discords in post-authoritarian Egypt and other Arab-majority countries.

REFERENCES

Abrahamian, Ervand. 1982. *Iran between Two Revolutions*. Princeton: Princeton University Press.

Abrahamian, Ervand. 2008. *A History of Modern Iran*. Cambridge: Cambridge University Press.

Abu-Izzeddin, Nejla M. 1984. *The Druzes: A New Study of Their History, Faith and Society*. Leiden: Brill.

Acevedo, Gabriel A. 2005. "Turning Anomie on its Head: Fatalism as Durkheim's Concealed and Multidimensional Alienation Theory." *Sociological Theory* 23: 75–85.

Adamiyat, Fereydoun. 1976/1355. *Idi'olozhi-ye Nahzat-i Mashrutiyat-i Iran* [The Ideology of the Constitutional Movement in Iran]. Tehran: Payam Publications.

Adamiyat, Fereydoun. 1978/1357. *Andishaha-yi Mirza Aqa Khan Kirmani* [The Ideas of Mirza Aqa Khan Kirmani]. Tehran: Zar.

Adamiyat, Fereydoun. 1970. *Andishaha-yi Mirza Fath Ali Akhundzadah*. Tehran: Kharazmi.

Adorno, Theodor W., Else Frenkel-Brunswik, Daniel Levinson, and Nevitt Sanford. 1950. *The Authoritarian Personality*. New York: Harper & Row.

Afary, Janet. 1996. *The Iranian Constitutional Revolution, 1906–1911: Grassroots Democracy, Social Democracy, and the Origin of Feminism*. New York: Columbia University Press.

Ahmad, Aziz. 1964. *Studies in Islamic Culture in the Indian Environment*. Oxford: Oxford University Press.

Ahmad, Qeyamuddin. 1966. *The Wahabi Movement in India*. Calcutta: Firma K.L. Mukhopadhyay.

Ahmed, Jamal Mohammad. 1960. *The Intellectual Origins of Egyptian Nationalism*. Oxford: Oxford University Press.

Ajami, Fouad. 1986. *The Vanished Imam: Musa al Sadr and the Shia of Lebanon*. Ithaca: Cornell University Press.

al-Banna, Hasan. 1978. *Five Tracts of Hasan al-Banna (1906–1949)*. Translated by Charles Wendell. Berkeley: University of California Press.

Algar, Hamid. 1969. *Religion and State in Modern Iran*. Berkeley: University of California Press.

al-Ghazali, Zainab. 2006. *Return of the Pharaoh*. Leicestershire: The Islamic Foundation.

Allport, Gordon W. 1954. "The Historical Background of Modern Social Psychology." In *Handbook of Social Psychology*, edited by Gardner Lindzey, vol. 1, 3–56. Cambridge: Addison-Wesley.

al-Rasheed, Madawi. 1998. *Iraqi Assyrian Christians in London: The Construction of Ethnicity*. Lewiston: Edwin Mellen Press.

al-Rasheed, Madawi. 2002. *A History of Saudi Arabia*. Cambridge: Cambridge University Press.

Aldridge, Alan. 2000. *Religion in the Contemporary World: A Sociological Introduction*. Cambridge: Polity Press.

Altemeyer, Bob, and Bruce Hunsberger. 1992. "Authoritarianism, Religious Fundamentalism, Quest, and Prejudice." *International Journal for the Psychology of Religion* 2: 113–133.

Altemeyer, Bob. 2003. "Why Do Religious Fundamentalists Tend to Be Prejudiced?" *The International Journal for the Psychology of Religion* 13: 17–28.

Altemeyer, Bob, and Bruce Hunsberger. 2004. "A Revised Religious Fundamentalism Scale: The Short and Sweet of It." *International Journal for the Psychology of Religion* 14: 47–54.

Ammerman, Nancy. 1987. *Bible Believers: Fundamentalists in the Modern World*. New Brunswick: Rutgers University Press.

Antoun, Richard T. 2008. *Understanding Fundamentalism: Christian, Islamic, and Jewish Movements.* Plymouth: Rowman & Littlefield.

Arendt, Hannah. 1958. *The Origin of Totalitarianism.* New York: Meridian Books.

Arjomand, Said Amir. 1984. *The Shadow of God and the Hidden Imam.* Chicago: University of Chicago Press.

Assaad, Sadik A. 1974. *The Reign of Al-Hakim Bi Amr Allah.* Beirut: The Arab Institute for Research and Publishing.

Atran, Scott, and Joseph Henrich. 2010. "The Evolution of Religion: How Cognitive By-Products, Adaptive Learning Heuristics, Ritual Displays, and Group Competition Generate Deep Commitments to Prosocial Religions." *Biological Theory* 5: 18–30.

Ayubi, Nazih Nassif M. 1980. *Bureaucracy and Politics in Contemporary Egypt.* London: Ithaca Press.

Baer, Gabriel. "Urbanization in Egypt, 1820–1907." In *Beginnings of Modernization in the Middle East: The Nineteenth Century,* edited by William R. Polk and Richard L. Chambers, p. 147. Chicago: The University of Chicago Press.

Baljon, Jr., Johannes Marinus Simon. 1970. *The Reforms and Religious Ideas of Sir Sayyid Ahmad Khan.* Lahore: Sh. Muhammad Ashraf.

Barelvi, Sayyid Ahmad. n.d. *Correspondence of Sayyid Ahmad of Barelvi.* London: India Office Library and Records, British Museum Oriental 6635.

Bayly, Christopher Alan. 1988. *Indian Society and the Making of the British Empire.* Cambridge: Cambridge University Press.

Bellin, Eva. 2004. "The Robustness of Authoritarianism in the Middle East: Exceptionalism in Comparative Perspective." *Comparative Politics* 36: 139–157.

Bergesen, Albert J. 2008. *The Sayyid Qutab Reader.* New York: Routledge.

Besnard, Philippe. 1993. "Anomie and Fatalism in Durkheim's Theory of Regulation." In *Émile Durkheim: Sociologist and Moralist,* edited by S.P. Turner, 169–186. London: Routledge.

Betts, Robert Brenton. 1988. *The Druze.* New Haven: Yale University Press.

Blaut, James Morris, Kirsten Haring, Phil O'Keefe, and Ben Wisner. 1997. "Theses on Peasantry." *Antipode* 9: 125–127.

Blaydes, Lisa, and Drew A. Linzer. 2008. "The Political Economy of Women's Support for Fundamentalist Islam." *World Politics* 60: 576–609.

Bruce, Steve. 2002. *God is Dead: Secularization in the West.* Oxford: Blackwell.

Bruce, Steve. 2006. "Secularization and the Impotence of Individualized Religion." *The Hedgehog Review* 8: 35–45.

Cheragh Ali, Moulavi. 1883. *The Proposed Political, Legal, and Social Reforms in the Ottoman Empire and Other Mohammadan States.* Bombay: Education Society Press.

Chevallier, Dominique. 1968. "Western Development and Eastern Crisis in the Mid-Nineteenth Century: Syria Confronted with the European Economy." In *Beginnings of Modernization in the Middle East,* edited by William R. Polk and Richard L. Chambers, 205–222. Chicago: University of Chicago Press.

CIA. 2005. *The World Factbook.* Washington: The Office of Public Affairs, Central Intelligence Agency.

Clark, Elizabeth A. 1991. "Sex, Shame, and Rhetoric: En-Gendering Early Christian Ethics." *Journal of the American Academy of Religion,* 59: 221–245.

Cleveland, William L. 1971. *The Making of an Arab Nationalist: Ottomanism and Arabism in the Life and Thought of Sati' al-Husri.* Princeton: Princeton University Press.

Cordesman, Anthony H. 2003. *Saudi Arabia Enters the Twenty-First Century.* Westport: Praeger Publishers.

Cragg, Kenneth. 1957. "The Tests of 'Islamicity.'" *Middle East Forum* 32: 15–17, 33.

Crawford, Robert W. 1955. "William of Tyre and the Maronites." *Speculum,* 30: 222–228.

Cromer, Evelyn Baring. 1908. *Modern Egypt.* New York: Macmillan Co.

Darnell, Alfred, and Darren E. Sherkat. 1997. "The Impact of Protestant Fundamentalism on Educational Attainment." *American Sociological Review,* 62: 306–315.

Davies, James Chowning. 1969. "The J-Curve of Rising and Declining Satisfaction as a Cause of Some Great Revolutions and a Contained Rebellion." In *Violence in America*, edited by Hugh D. Graham and Ted R. Gurr, 671–709. New York: Signet.

Davis, Nancy J., and Robert V. Robinson. 2006. "The Egalitarian Face of Orthodox Islam: Support for Islamic Law and Equality in Seven Muslim-Majority Nations." *American Sociological Review* 71: 167–190.

DeJong, Gordon, and Thomas Ford. 1965. "Religious Fundamentalism and Denominational Preference in the Southern Appalachian Region." *Journal for the Scientific Study of Religion* 5: 24–43.

Dekmejian, R. Hrair. 1994. "The Rise of Political Islamism in Saudi Arabia." *Middle East Journal* 48: 627–643.

Dekmejian, R. Hrair. 1998. "Saudi Arabia's Consultative Council." *Middle East Journal* 52: 204–218.

Deutsch, W. Karl. 1981. "On Nationalism, World Religion and the Nature of the West." In *Mobilization, Center-Periphery Structures and National Building*, edited by Per Torsvik, 51–93. Bergen: Universitestsvorlaget.

Dick, Ignatios. 2004. *Melkites: Greek Orthodox and Greek Catholics of the Patriarchates of Antioch, Alexandria and Jerusalem.* Boston: Sophia Press.

Dina'nie, Gholamhosein Ibrahimi. 1991/1370. *Mantiq va Marifat dar Nazar-i Ghazali* [Ghazali's View on Logic and Knowledge]. Tehran: Amir Kabir.

Dohrenwend, Bruce P. 1959. "Egoism, Altruism, Anomie, and Fatalism: A Conceptual Analysis of Durkheim's Types." *American Sociological Review* 24: 466–473.

Downs, Anthony. "An Economic Theory of Political Action in a Democracy." *The Journal of Political Economy* 65: 135–150.

Durkheim, Émile. 1965. *The Elementary Forms of Religious Life.* New York: Free Press.

Du Toit, Cornel W. 2006. "Secular Spirituality versus Secular Dualism: Towards Post-Secular Holism as Model for a Natural Theology." *HTS Teologiese Studies/Theological Studies* 62: 1251–1268.

Ehteshami, Anoushiravan. 1995. "The Politics of Economic Restructuring in Post-Khomeini Iran." Working paper. Durham: University of Durham, Centre for Middle Eastern and Islamic Studies.

Ellis, Shmuel, and Arie W. Kruglanski. 1992. "Self as an Epistemic Authority: Effects on Experiential and Instructional Learning." *Social Cognition* 10: 357–375.

Esposito, John. 1992. *The Islamic Threat.* Oxford: Oxford University Press.

Evans, John H. 2010. *Contested Reproduction: Genetic Technologies, Religion, and Public Debate.* Chicago: University of Chicago Press.

Evans, John H. 2011. "Epistemological and Moral Conflict Between Religion and Science." *Journal for the Scientific Study of Religion* 50: 707–727.

Exline, Julie Juola and Ephraim Rose. 2005. "Religious and Spiritual Struggles." In *Handbook of the Psychology of Religion and Spirituality*, edited by Raymond F. Paloutzian and Crystal L. Park, 315–330. New York: The Guilford Press.

Fandy, Mamoun. 1999. "CyberResistance: Saudi Opposition between Globalization and Localization." *Comparative Studies in Society and History* 41: 124–147.

Faulk, Edward, 2007. *101 Questions and Answers on Eastern Catholic Churches.* New York: Paulist Press.

Festinger, Leon. 1957. *A Theory of Cognitive Dissonance.* Stanford: Stanford University Press.

Ford, Thomas. 1960. "Status, Residence, and Fundamentalist Religious Beliefs in the Southern Appalachians." *Social Forces* 39: 41–49.

Freitag, Markus, and Marc B. Bühlmann. 2009. "Crafting Trust: The Role of Political Institutions in a Comparative Perspective." *Comparative Political Studies* 42: 1537–1566.

Geertz, Clifford. 1973. *The Interpretation of Cultures.* New York: Basic Books.

Gershoni, Israel, and James P. Jankowski. 1995. *Redefining the Egyptian Nation, 1930–1945.* Cambridge: Cambridge University Press.

Gibb, Hamilton Alexander Rosskeen. 1937. "Al-Mawardi's Theory of the Khilafah." *Islamic Culture* 11: 291–302.

Gibb, Hamilton Alexander Rosskeen. 1947. *Modern Trends in Islam.* Chicago: University of Chicago Press.

Gibb, Hamilton Alexander Rosskeen, ed. 1960. *The Encyclopaedia of Islam.* Leiden: Brill.

Goldstein, Warren S. 2009. "Patterns of Secularization and Religious Rationalization in Émile Durkheim and Max Weber." *Implicit Religion* 12: 135–163.

Goldstein, Warren S. 2011. "The Dialectics of Religious Conflict: Church-Sect, Denomination and the Culture Wars." *Culture and Religion* 12: 77–99.

Gopal, Surendra. 1972. "Nobility and the Mercantile Community in India, XVI–XVIIth Centuries." *Journal of Indian History* 50: 793–802.

Grassow, Peter S. 1991. "Spirituality and the Struggle." In *We Shall Overcome: Spirituality of Liberation,* edited by Michael Worship and Desmond van der Water, 52–58. Hilton: Cluster Publications.

Grunebaum, Gustave von. 1954. *Medieval Islam: A Study in Cultural Orientation.* Chicago: University of Chicago Press.

Gurr, Ted Robert. 1970. *Why Men Rebel.* Princeton: Princeton University Press.

Haim, Sylvia G. 1958. "Islam and the Theory of Arab Nationalism." In *The Middle East in Transition,* edited by Walter Z. Laqueur, 280–307. New York: Praeger.

Hairi, Hadi. 1977. *Shi'ism and Constitutionalism in Iran.* Leiden: E. J. Brill.

Hallaq, Wael B. 1984. "Was the Gate of Ijtihad Closed?" *International Journal of Middle East Studies* 16: 3–41.

Hall, David D. 1997. *Lived Religion in America: Toward a History of Practice.* Princeton: Princeton University Press.

Hall, Stuart. 1985. "Authoritarian Populism: A Reply to Jessop et al." *New Left Review,* I/151: 115–124.

Hanson, Brad. 1983. "The 'Westoxication' of Iran: Depictions and Reactions of Behrangi, Al-e Ahmad, and Shariati." *International Journal of Middle East Studies* 15: 1–23.

Hardy, Peter. 1972. *The Muslims of British India.* Cambridge: Cambridge University Press.

Harvey, David. 1990. *The Condition of Postmodernity.* Oxford: Blackwell.

Hassanpour, Amir. 2005. "Kurds." *Encyclopedia of Genocide and Crimes Against Humanity,* edited by Dinah L. Shelton. New York: MacMillan Reference USA.

Hassard, John, John Hogan, and Michael Rowlinson. 2001. "From Labor Process Theory to Critical Management Studies." *Administrative Theory & Practices* 23: 339–362.

Hatch, William. 1946. *An Album of Dated Syriac Manuscripts.* Reprint, Piscataway: Gorgias Press, 2002.

Hendryx, John. 2009. "Fundamentalism vs. Reformed Theology." Accessed October 1. http://www.monergism.com/thethreshold/articles/onsite/FundyReform.html.

Heyworth-Dunne, James. 1968. *An Introduction to the History of Education in Modern Egypt.* London: Frank Cass & Co.

Hinnebusch, Raymond A. 1981. "Egypt Under Sadat: Elites, Power Structure, and Political Change in a Post-Populist State." *Social Problems* 28: 442–464.

Hitti, Philip. 1967. *The History of Arabs.* New York: St. Martin's Press.

Holland, Joe. 1988. "A Postmodern Vision of Spirituality and Society." In *Spirituality and Society: Postmodern Visions,* edited by David Ray Griffin, 41–62. New York: State University of New York.

Hood, Jr., Ralph W., Peter C. Hill, and W. Paul Williamson. 2005. The Psychology of Religious Fundamentalism. New York: The Guildford Press.

Hourani, Albert Habib. 1983. *Arabic Thought in the Liberal Age 1789–1939.* Oxford: Oxford University Press.

Hourani, Albert Habib. 1991. *A History of the Arab Peoples.* New York: Warner Books.

Hunter, James Davison. 1991. *Culture Wars: The Struggle to Define America.* New York: Basic Books.

Hunter, Sir William Wilson. 1876. *The Indian Musalmans.* London: Trubner and Co.

Hussein, Taha. 1938. *The Future of Culture in Egypt.* Reprint, Washington, DC: American Council of Learned Societies, 1954.

Ibn Khaldun, Abd al-Rahman. 1967. *The Muqaddhimah: An Introduction to History.* Translated by Franz Rosenthal. Princeton: Princeton University Press.

Ibrahimi Dina'nie, Gholamhosein. 1991/1370. *Mantiq va Marifat dar Nazar-i Ghazali* [Ghazali's View on Logic and Knowledge]. Tehran: Amir Kabir.

Inglehart, Ronald, Mansoor Moaddel, and Mark Tessler. 2006. "Xenophobia and In-Group Solidarity in Iraq: A Natural Experiment on the Impact of Insecurity." *Perspective on Politics* 4: 495–505.

International Crisis Group. 2005. "The Shiite Question in Saudi Arabia." *Crisis Group Middle East Report* 45: 9–15.

Iqbal, Muhammad. 1934. *The Reconstruction of Religious Thought in Islam.* London: Oxford University Press.

Issawi, Charles, ed. 1966. *The Economic History of the Middle East 1800–1914: A Book of Readings.* Chicago: University of Chicago Press.

Jalbani, Ghulam Husain. 1967. *Teachings of Shah Waliyullah.* Lahore: Sh. Muhammad Ashraf.

Johnson, Chalmers A. 1964. *Revolution and the Social System.* Stanford: Stanford University.

Johnson, Chalmers A. 1966. *Revolutionary Change.* New York: Little, Brown and Company.

Jones, Toby. 2009. "Embattled in Arabia: Shi'is and the Politics of Confrontation in Saudi Arabia." *Combating Terrorism Center at West Point,* June 3. http://www.ctc.usma.edu/posts/embattled-in-arabia-shiis-and-the-politics-of-confrontation-in-saudi-arabia.

Kamrava, Mehran. 2008. *Iran's Intellectual Revolution.* Cambridge: Cambridge University Press.

Karpat, Kemal H. 1982. "Millets and Nationality: The Roots of the Incongruity of Nation and State in the Post-Ottoman Era." In *Christians and Jews in the Ottoman Empire, The Functioning of a Plural Society,* vol. 1, edited by Benjamin Brad and Bernard Lewis, 141–170. New York: Holmes & Meier Publishers.

Katz, Steven. 1985. *Post-Holocaust Dialogues.* New York: New York University Press.

Kellstedt, Lyman, and Corwin Smidt. 1991. "Measuring Fundamentalism: An Analysis of Different Operational Strategies." *Journal for the Scientific Study of Religion* 30: 259–278.

Kerr, Malcolm. 1966. *Islamic Reform: The Political and Legal Theories of Muhammad 'Abduh and Rashid Rida.* Berkeley: University of California Press.

Khoury, Philip S. 1987. *Syria and the French Mandate: The Politics of Arab Nationalism, 1920–1945.* Princeton: Princeton University Press.

Kinder, Donald R., 1998. "Communication and Opinion." *Annual Review of Political Science* 1: 167–197.

Klaus, Václav, and Tomás Jezek. 1991. "Social Criticism, False Liberalism, and Recent Changes in Czechoslovakia." *East European Politics and Societies* 5: 26–40.

Kourie, Celia. 2006. "The 'Turn' to Spirituality." *Acta Theologica Supplementum* 8: 219–238.

Kramer, Martin. 1996. "Fundamentalist Islam at Large: The Drive for Power." *Middle East Quarterly* 3: 37–49.

Kramer, Martin. 2003. "Coming to Terms: Fundamentalists or Islamists?" *Middle East Quarterly* 10: 65–77.

Kruglanski, Arie W. 1989. *Lay Epistemics and Human Knowledge: Cognitive and Motivation Bases.* New York: Plenum Press.

Kruglanski, Arie W. 1990. "Motivations for Judging and Knowing: Implications for Causal Attribution." In *Handbook of Motivation and Cognition,* vol. 2, edited by Edward Tory Higgins and Richard M. Sorrentino, 333–368. New York: Guilford Press.

Kruglanski, Arie W., Antonio Pierro, Lucia Mannetti, and Eraldo De Grada. 2006. "Groups as Epistemic Providers: Need for Closure and the Unfolding Group-Centrism." *Psychological Review* 113: 84–100.

La Fontaine, Jean Sybil. 1998. *Speak of the Devil: Tales of Satanic Abuse in Contemporary England.* Cambridge: Cambridge University Press.

Lambton, Ann Katharine Swynford. 1962. "Justice in the Medieval Persian Theory of Kingship." *Studia Islamica* 17: 91–119.

Lapidus, Ira M. 2002. *History of Islamic Societies.* Cambridge: Cambridge University Press.

Lapidus, I.M. 1992. "The Golden Age: The Political Concepts of Islam." *Annals of the American Academy of Political Science* 524: 13–25.

Layish, Aharon. 1987. "Saudi Arabian Legal Reform as a Mechanism to Moderate Wahhabi Doctrine." *Journal of the American Oriental Society* 107: 279–92.

Leonard, Thomas M., ed. 2006. *Encyclopedia of the Developing World.* London: Routledge Taylor & Francis Group.

Levy, Reuben. 1933. *An Introduction to the Sociology of Islam.* London: Williams & Norgate.

Lewis, Bernard D. 1988. *The Political Language of Islam.* Chicago: University of Chicago Press.

Lewis, Bernard D. 1993a. "Islam and Liberal Democracy." *Atlantic Monthly* 271: 89–98.

Lewis, Bernard D. 1993b. *Islam and the West.* Oxford: Oxford University Press.

Lewis, M. Paul, ed. 2009. "Azerbaijani, South." *Ethnologue: Languages of the World,* sixteenth edition. Dallas: SIL International. http://www.ethnologue.com.

Lindsay, Lord. 1961. "Is Cleavage Between Russia and China Inevitable?" *The Annals of the American Academy of Political and Social Science* 336: 53–61.

Lockwood, David. 1992. *Solidarity and Schism: The Problem of Disorder in Durkheimian and Marxist Sociology.* Oxford: Oxford University Press.

Louer, Lawrence. 2008. *Transnational Shia Politics: Religious and Political Networks in the Gulf.* New York: Columbia University Press.

Lukes, Steven. 1967. "Alienation and Anomie." In *Philosophy, Politics, and Society: Third Series,* edited by Peter Laslett and Walter Garrison Runciman, 134–156. Oxford: Basil Blackwell.

Lyden, John. 1995. *Enduring Issues in Religion.* San Diego: Greenhaven Press.

Macedo, Stephen 1995. "Liberal Civic Education and Religious Fundamentalism: The Case of God versus Johan Rawls." *Ethic* 105: 468–496.

MacKenzie, David Neil. 1961. "The Origin of Kurdish." *Transactions of the Philological Society* 60: 68–86.

Magnarella, Paul, ed. 1999. *Middle East and North Africa: Governance, Democratization, and Human Rights.* Aldershot: Ashgate.

Mann, Michael. 1993. "The Emergence of Modern European Nationalism." In *Transition to Modernity,* edited by John A. Hall and I.C. Jarvie, 137–166. Cambridge: Cambridge University Press.

Mann, Michael. 1993. *The Sources of Social Power, Vol. 2: The Rise of Classes and Nation-States, 1760–1914.* New York: Cambridge University Press.

Ma'oz, Moshe. 1968. *Ottoman Reform in Syria and Palestine 1840–1861.* Oxford: Oxford University Press.

Maehr, Martin L., and Stuart A. Karabenick. 2005. *Advances in Motivation and Achievement Vol. 14: Motivation and Religion.* United Kingdom: Elsevier.

Makarem, Sami Nasib. 1974. *The Druze Faith.* Delmer: Caravan Books.

Malik, Hafeez. 1981. *Sir Sayyid Ahmad Khan and Muslim Modernization in India and Pakistan.* New York: Columbia University Press.

Marcuse, Herbert. 1968. "The Struggle against Liberalism in the Totalitarian View of the State." In *Negations: Essays in Critical Theory,* 3–42. Middlesex: Penguin Books.

Marsden, George M. 2006. *Fundamentalism and American Culture,* second edition. Oxford: Oxford University Press.

Marsden, George M. 1980. *Fundamentalism and American Culture: The Shaping of Twentieth Century Evangelicalism.* New York: Oxford University Press.

Marsot, Afaf Lutfi al-Sayyid. 1968. "The Role of the Ulama in Egypt during the Early 19th Century." In *Political and Social Change in Modern Egypt,* edited by P.M. Holt, 264–280. London: Oxford University Press.

Marsot, Afaf Lutfi al-Sayyid. 1972. "The Ulama of Cairo in the Eighteenth and Nineteenth Century." In *Scholars, Saints, and Sufis,* edited by Nikki Keddi, 275–305. Berkeley: University of California Press.

Marsot, Afaf Lufti Sayyid. 1977. *Egypt's Liberal Experiment: 1922–1936.* Los Angeles: University of California Press.

Marty, Martin E., and Appleby, R. Scott. 1994. *Accounting for Fundamentalisms: The Dynamic Character of Movements.* Chicago: University of Chicago Press.

Messick, Samuel. 1989. "Validity." In *Educational Measurement,* edited by Robert L. Linn, 13–104. New York: Macmillan.

Meyer, Birgit. 1995. "Delivered from the Powers of Darkness' Confessions of Satanic Riches in Christian Ghana." *Journal of the International African Institute* 65: 236–255.

Mikulincer, Mario, and Phillip R. Shaver. 2007. *Attachment in Adulthood: Structure, Dynamics, and Change.* New York: The Guilford Press.

Miller, Arthur, and Martin Wattenberg. 1984. "Politics from the Pulpit: Religiosity and the 1980 Election." *Public Opinion Quarterly* 48: 301–317.

Mitchell, Richard D. 1969. *The Society of the Muslim Brothers.* New York: Oxford University Press.

Moaddel, Mansoor, and Hamid Latif. 2006. "Events and Values Change: The Impact of the September 11, 2001, on the Worldviews of Egyptians and Moroccans." *Interdisciplinary Journal of Research on Religion* 2: 1–48.

Moaddel, Mansoor, and Kamran Talattof. 2000. *Contemporary Debates in Islam: An Anthology of Modernist and Fundamentalist Thought.* New York: Macmillan.

Moaddel, Mansoor. 1993. *Class, Politics, and Ideology in the Iranian Revolution.* New York: Columbia University Press.

Moaddel, Mansoor. 2001. "Conditions for Ideological Production: The Origins of Islamic Modernism in India, Egypt, and Iran." *Theory and Society* 30: 669–731.

Moaddel, Mansoor: 2002. "The Study of Islamic Culture and Politics: An Overview and Assessment." *Annual Review of Sociology* 28: 359–386.

Moaddel, Mansoor. 2005. *Islamic Modernism, Nationalism, and Fundamentalism: Episode and Discourse.* Chicago: The University of Chicago Press.

Moaddel, Mansoor, and Stuart A. Karabenick. 2008. "Religious Fundamentalism among Young Muslims in Egypt and Saudi Arabia." *Social Forces* 86: 1675–1710.

Moaddel, Mansoor. 2009. "The Iranian Revolution and Its Nemesis: The Rise of Liberal Values among Iranians." *Comparative Studies of South Asia, Africa, and the Middle East* 29: 126–136.

Moaddel, Mansoor, 2010. "Religious Regimes and Prospects for Liberal Politics: Futures of Iran, Iraq, and Saudi Arabia." *Futures* 42: 532–544.

Ma'oz, Moshe. 1968. *Ottoman Reform in Syria and Palestine, 1840–1861: The Impact of the Tanzimat on Politics and Society.* Oxford: Oxford University Press.

Moin, Baqer. 2000. *Khomeini: Life of the Ayatollah.* New York: St. Martin's Press.

Momen, Moojan. 1985. *An Introduction to Shi'i Islam.* New Haven: Yale University Press.

Mortimer, Edward. 1982. "Haig and the Palestinians." *Journal of Palestine Studies* 11: 187–189.

Mühlbacher, Fakhoury Tamirace. 2009. *Democracy and Power-Sharing in Stormy Weather: The Case of Lebanon.* Wiesbaden: Vs Verlag.

Munson, Jr., Henry. 1988. *Islam and Revolution in the Middle East.* Binghamton: Yale University Press.

Musallam, Adnan Ayyub. 1983. "The Formative Stages of Sayyid Qutb's Intellectual Career and His Emergence as an Islamic Da'iyah, 1906–1952." Ph.D diss., University of Michigan.

Najjar, Abdallah. 1973. *The Druze: Millennium Scrolls Revealed.* Translated by Fred I. Massey. New York: Columbia University Press.

Nickel, Gordon. 1987. "'The Grand Opening': Shah Wali Allah's [Waliallah's] Principles of Exegesis." M.A. thes., School of Oriental and African Studies, University of London.

Nomani, Farhad, and Sohrab Behdad. 2006. *Class and Labor in Iran: Did the Revolution Matter.* Syracuse: Syracuse University Press.

Norris, Pippa, and Ronald Inglehart. 2011. *Sacred and Secular: Religion and Politics Worldwide,* second edition. Cambridge: Cambridge University Press.

Obaid, Nawaf. 2006. "Stepping Into Iraq; Saudi Arabia Will Protect Sunnis If the U.S. Leaves." *The Washington Post,* November 29.

Okruhlik, Gwenn. 2002. "Networks of Dissent: Islamism and Reform in Saudi Arabia." *Current History* 101: 22–28.

Okruhlik, Gwenn. 2003. "Saudi Arabian-Iranian Relation: External Rapprochement and Internal Consolidation." *Middle East Policy* 10.

Palmieri, Mario. 1936. *The Philosophy of Fascism.* Chicago: Dante Alighieri Society.

Paloutzian, Raymond F., and Crystal L. Park, eds. 2005. *Handbook of the Psychology of Religion and Spirituality.* New York: Guilford.

Parry, Ken, and David Melling, eds. 1999. *The Blackwell Dictionary of Eastern Christianity.* Malden: Blackwell Publishing.

Peshkin, Alan. 1986. *God's Choice: The Total World of a Fundamentalist Christian School.* Chicago: University of Chicago Press.

Petran, Tabitha. 1972. *Syria: A Modern History.* London: Benn.

Pew Research Center. 2009. "Mapping the Global Muslim Population: A Report on the Size and Distribution of the World's Muslim Population." Accessed January 19, 2011. http://www.pewforum.org/uploadedfiles/Topics/Demographics/Muslimpopulation.pdf.

Popkin, Samuel L. 1991. *The Reasoning Voter: Communication and Persuasion in Presidential Campaigns.* Chicago: University of Chicago Press.

Pratt, Douglas. 2007. "Exclusivism and Exclusivity: A Contemporary Theological Challenge." *Pacifica* 20: 291–306.

Prokop, Michaela. 2003. "Saudi Arabia: The Politics of Education." *International Affairs* 79: 77–89.

Quinney, Richard. 1964. "Political Conservatism, Alienation, and Fatalism: Contingencies of Social Status and Religious Fundamentalism." *Sociometry* 27: 372–381.

Qutb, Sayyid. 1964. *Ma'alim fi al-Tariq.* Cairo: Maktabat Wahbah.

Rahman, Fazlur. 1968. *Islam.* New York: Doubleday.

Ranstorp, Magnus. 1997. *Hizb'Allah in Lebanon.* London: Palgrave Macmillan.

Raviv, Amiram, Daniel Bar-Tal, Alona Raviv, Braha Biran, and Zvia Sela. 2003. "Teachers' Epistemic Authority: Perceptions of Students and Teachers." *Social Psychology of Education* 6: 17–42.

Reid, Donald Malcolm. 1990. *Cairo University and the Making of Modern Egypt.* Cambridge: Cambridge University Press.

Rice, Nicole. 2010. "'Temples to Christ's Indwelling' Forms of Chastity in Barking Abbey Manuscript." *Journal of the History of Sexuality,* 19: 115–132.

Rizvi, Saiyid Athar Abbas. 1975. "Islam in Medieval India." In *A Cultural History of India,* edited by Arthur Llewellyn Basham. Oxford: Clarendon Press.

Rokeach, Milton. 1954. "The Nature and Meaning of Dogmatism." *Psychological Review.* 61: 194–294.

Rosenthal, Erwin I.J. 1958. *Political Thought in Medieval Islam: An Introductory Outline.* Cambridge: Cambridge University Press.

Ruedy, John. 1992. *Modern Algeria: The Origins and Development of a Nation.* Bloomington: Indiana University Press.

Sageman, Marc. 2004. *Understanding Terror Networks.* Philadelphia: University of Pennsylvania Press.

Said, Abdul Aziz. 1977. *Pursuing Human Dignity. Society* 15: 34–38.

Saseen, Sandra M. 1990. "The Taif Accord and Lebanon's Struggle to Regain its Sovereignty." *American University International Law Review* 6: 57–75.

Schwartz, Stephen. 2002. *The Two Faces of Islam: The Houses of Sa'ud from Tradition to Terror.* New York: Doubleday.

Schwartz, J.P. and L.D. Lindley. 2005. "Religious Fundamentalism and Attachment: Prediction of Homophobia." *International Journal for the Psychology of Religion* 15: 145–157.

Sewell, Jr., William H. 1996. "Historical Events as Transformations of Structures: Inventing Revolution at the Bastille." *Theory and Society* 25: 841–881.

Sewell, Jr., William H. 1997. "Geertz, Cultural Systems, and History: From Synchrony to Transformation." *Representations* 59: 35–55

Shari'ati, Ali. 1980. *Marxism and Other Western Fallacies: An Islamic Critique.* Translated by Robert Campbell. Berkeley: Mizan Press.

Sharp, Lynn L. 2006. *Secular Spirituality: Reincarnation and Spiritism in Nineteenth-Century France.* Lexington Books.

Shaw, Stanford J. 1977. *History of the Ottoman Empire and Modern Turkey,* vol. 1. Cambridge: Cambridge University Press.

Sivan, Emmanuel. 1985. *Radical Islam: Medieval Theology and Modern Politics.* New Haven: Yale University Press.

Smith, Christian. 1998. *American Evangelicalism: Embattled and Thriving.* Chicago: The University of Chicago Press.

Sniderman, Paul M., Richard A. Brody, and Philip E. Tetlock. 1991. *Reasoning and Choice: Exploration in Political Psychology.* Cambridge: Cambridge University Press.

Stark, Rodney, and William Sims Bainbridge. 1985. *The Future of Religion: Secularization, Revival, and Cult Formation.* Berkeley: University of California Press.

Stark, Rodney, and Roger Finke. 2000. *Acts of Faith: Explaining the Human Side of Religion.* Berkeley: University of California Press.

Summers, Frank. 2006. "Fundamentalism, Psychoanalysis, and Psychoanalytic Theories." *Psychoanalytic Review* 93: 329–353.

Taheri, Amir. 1986. *The Spirit of Allah: Khomeini and the Islamic Revolution.* Bethesda: Adler and Adler.

Toynbee, Arnold. 1931. *A Journey to China.* London: Constable.

Traboulsi, Fawwaz. 2007. *A History of Modern Lebanon.* London: Pluto Press.

Troll, Christian W. 1978. *Sayyid Ahmad Khan: A Reinterpretation of Muslim Theology.* New Delhi: Vikas Publishing House.

Turner, Victor W. 1967. *The Forest of Symbols: Aspects of Ndembu Ritual.* Ithaca: Cornell University Press.

Valentine, Jeff C., and Harris Cooper. 2003. *Effect Size Substantive Interpretation Guidelines: Issues in the Interpretation of Effect Sizes.* Washington, DC: What Works Clearinghouse.

Vatikiotis, Panayiotis J. 1980. *The History of Egypt,* second edition. Baltimore: Johns Hopkins University Press.

Voll, John O. 1994. *Continuity and Change in the Modern World,* second edition. New York: Syracuse University Press.

Watt, W. Montgomery. 1960. "Shi'ism under the Umayyads." *Journal of the Royal Asiatic Society* 92: 158–172.

Weber, Max. 1964. *The Sociology of Religion.* Boston: Beacon.

Wikipedia. 2012. "1988 Executions of Iranian Political Prisoners." Last modified July 1. http://en.wikipedia.org/wiki/1988_executions_of_Iranian_political_prisoners.

Wikipedia. 2012. "Fada'iyan-e Islam." Last modified June 4. http://en.wikipedia.org/wiki/Fada%27iyan-e_Islam.

Wills, Garry. 1990. *Under God: Religion and Politics in America.* New York: Simon and Schuster.

Wolpe, David. 1997. "Hester Panim in Modern Jewish Thought." *Modern Judaism* 17: 25–56.

Wuthnow, Robert. 1998. *After Heaven: Spirituality in America Since the 1950s.* Berkeley: University of California Press.

Yapp, Malcolm E. 1991. *The Near East Since the First World War.* Harlow: Longman.

You, Jong-sung. 2012. "Social Trust: Fairness Matters More than Homogeneity." *Political Psychology.* doi: 10.1111/j.1467-9221.2012.00893.x.

Zisser, Eyal. 1995. "The Maronites, Lebanon and the State of Israel: Early Contacts." *Middle Eastern Studies* 31: 889–918.

YOUTH SURVEY IN EGYPT AND SAUDI ARABIA, 2005

Hello! How are you? My name is_____. I am a researcher working for a research group at_____

This survey is part of an investigation of general opinion of youth concerning a variety of social issues. You will probably find that you *agree* with some of the statements, and *disagree* with others, to varying extents. There is no right or wrong answer.

Please note that your answers to these questions will be kept anonymously. We record no names, identifies, or information that can be used by the people seeing the completed survey questionnaires to identify any of the respondents at any time. Please also note that your participation, while is greatly appreciated, is totally voluntary and that you can withdraw at any time during the interview.

This questionnaire consists of several parts. Here, I would like to begin by asking your opinion on some matters concerning family life around the world. I will read you some statements, and I would like you to tell me if you strongly agree, agree, disagree, or strongly disagree. These are:

			Strongly agree	Agree	Disagree	Strongly disagree
SA E ☒ ☒	v1.	Usually the age people marry is higher in rich, educated countries than in poor, uneducated countries. Would you say you strongly agree, agree, disagree, or strongly disagree?	1	2	3	4
☒ ☒	v2.	On average, families have more children in rich, educated countries than in poor, uneducated countries.	1	2	3	4
☒ ☒	v3.	Usually, women in countries that are richer are treated with more respect than in poor, uneducated countries. Would you say you strongly agree, agree, disagree, or strongly disagree?	1	2	3	4

			Strongly agree	Agree	Disagree	Strongly disagree
☒	☒	v4. The chance for choosing a life partner for people decreases/is less in countries that are rich and educated compared to poor, uneducated countries.	1	2	3	4
☒	☒	v5. In general, it is more popular for married children to live with their parents in countries that are rich and educated than in poor and uneducated countries.	1	2	3	4
☒	☒	v6. Having multiple wives are more popular in countries that are rich and educated than in countries that are poor and uneducated.	1	2	3	4

Now we would like you to consider how developed different places in the world are. Here is a scale of development—with the least developed places in the world marked 1 at the left and the most developed places in the world marked ten at the right. And, moderately developed places marked 5 in the middle. I will read to you a list of countries that includes Saudi Arabia, China, Yemen, and the United States and ask you to rate the level of development in each country.

SA	E	Country	Least developed							Most developed		
☒	☒	v7. Saudi Arabia	1	2	3	4	5	6	7	8	9	10
☒	☒	v8. Egypt	1	2	3	4	5	6	7	8	9	10
☒	☒	v9. Iran	1	2	3	4	5	6	7	8	9	10
☒	☒	v10. China	1	2	3	4	5	6	7	8	9	10
☒	☒	v11. Yemen	1	2	3	4	5	6	7	8	9	10
☒	☒	v12. The U.S.	1	2	3	4	5	6	7	8	9	10
☒	☒	v13. Somalia	1	2	3	4	5	6	7	8	9	10
☒	☒	v14. France	1	2	3	4	5	6	7	8	9	10
☒	☒	v15. UAE	1	2	3	4	5	6	7	8	9	10

I will ask you to rate all the countries that were sited in the previous question on a different scale that is related to specifying the level of individual freedom where (1) means the country gives less individual freedom while (10) means a country in which the individual enjoys more freedom:

SA	E	Country	Low level of freedom							High level of freedom		
☒	☒	v16. Saudi Arabia	1	2	3	4	5	6	7	8	9	10
☒	☒	v17. Egypt	1	2	3	4	5	6	7	8	9	10
☒	☒	v18. Iran	1	2	3	4	5	6	7	8	9	10
☒	☒	v19. China	1	2	3	4	5	6	7	8	9	10
☒	☒	v20. Yemen	1	2	3	4	5	6	7	8	9	10
☒	☒	v21. The U.S.	1	2	3	4	5	6	7	8	9	10
☒	☒	v22. Somalia	1	2	3	4	5	6	7	8	9	10
☒	☒	v23. France	1	2	3	4	5	6	7	8	9	10
☒	☒	v24. UAE	1	2	3	4	5	6	7	8	9	10

For each of the following statements I read out, can you tell me how much you agree with each. Do you agree strongly, agree, disagree, or disagree strongly?

SA	E	Attitudes toward women	Agree strongly	Agree	Disagree	Strongly disagree	DK
☒	☒	v25. On the whole, men make better political leaders than women do	1	2	3	4	9
☒	☒	v26. University education is more important for a boy than for a girl	1	2	3	4	9
☒	☒	v27. When jobs are scarce, men should have more right to a job than women	1	2	3	4	9
☒	☒	v28. Male and female university students should not attend classes together	1	2	3	4	9
☒	☒	v29. It is up to a woman to dress which ever way she wants to	1	2	3	4	9
☒	☒	v30. It is acceptable for a man to have more than one wife.	1	2	4	5	9
☒	☒	v31. A wife must always obey her husband.	1	2	4	5	9

SE E

☒ ☒ v32.   In your view, which of the following is the more important foundation
              for marriage:
              1. Parental approval
              2. Love
              3. DK

Now I'd like you to tell me your views on various issues. How would you place
your views on this scale? 1 means you agree completely with the statement on the
left; 10 means you agree completely with the statement on the right; and if your
views fall somewhere in between, you can choose any number in between.

SA E

☒ ☒ v33.   Incomes should be   We need larger income differences
              made more equal   as incentives for individuals
              1   2   3   4   5   6   7   8   9   10
              DK=99

SA E

☒ ☒ v34.   Private ownership of   Government ownership of business
              business and industry   and industry should be increased
              should be increased
              1   2   3   4   5   6   7   8   9   10
              DK=99

SA E

☒ ☒ v35.   The government   People should take more
              should take more   responsibility to provide
              responsibility to   for themselves
              ensure that everyone
              is provided for
              1   2   3   4   5   6   7   8   9   10
              DK=99

SA E

☒ ☒ v36. (People have different views about public sector in this country, by using this scale from 10 'steps' where the number (1) means very bad, and (10) means very good. What is the 'step' that you shall choose to express (your opinion) about the public sector.

1	2	3	4	5	6	7	8	9	10
Very bad									Very good

I'm going to describe various types of political systems and ask what you think about each as a way of governing this country. For each one, would you say it is a very good, fairly good, fairly bad or very bad way of governing this country?

SA	E		Very good	Fairly good	Fairly bad	Very bad	DK
☐	☒	v37. Having a strong head of government who does not have to bother with parliament and elections	1	2	3	4	9
☒	☒	v38. Having a democratic political system	1	2	3	4	9
☒	☒	v39. Having an Islamic government, where religious authorities have absolute power	1	2	3	4	9

I'm going to read off some things that people sometimes say about a democratic political system. Could you please tell me if you agree strongly, agree, disagree or disagree strongly, after I read each one of them?

SA	E		Agree strongly	Agree	Disagree	Strongly disagree	DK
☒	☒	v40. In democracy, the economy runs badly	1	2	3	4	9
☒	☒	v41. Democracies are indecisive and have too much quibbling	1	2	3	4	9
☒	☒	v42. Democracies aren't good at maintaining order	1	2	3	4	9
☒	☒	v43. Democracy may have problems but it's better than any other form of government	1	2	3	4	9
☐	☒	v44. Religious leaders should not interfere in politics	1	2	3	4	9
☐	☒	v45. Politicians who do not believe in God, should not run for public office	1	2	3	4	9

SA E

⊠ ⊠ v46. Generally speaking, would you say that this country's economy is run by a few big interests looking out for themselves or that it is run for the benefit of all the people?
  1 Run by a few big interests
  2 Run for all the people
  9 Don't know [DO NOT READ OUT]

Foreign threat: Every country faces a number of regional and international problems. Among the following, which problems do you consider very important (very serious), important, somewhat important, least important, or not important for Saudi Arabia?

SA	E		Very important	important	Somewhat important	Not very important	Not at all important	DK
⊠	⊠	v47. Aggression from a neighboring country	1	2	3	4	5	9
⊠	⊠	v48. The exploitation of this country's natural resources by powerful countries	1	2	3	4	5	9
⊠	⊠	v49. Cultural invasion by the West	1	2	3	4	5	9

Thinking about what should change to make your country a better place to live, and please tell us if you agree strongly, agree, disagree, or disagree strongly with the following:

SA	E	Saudi Arabia will be a better society	Agree strongly	Agree	Disagree	Disagree strongly	DK
⊠	⊠	v50. If women are treated with more respect than they are now. Would you say you strongly agree, agree, disagree, or strongly disagree?	1	2	3	4	9
⊠	⊠	v51. If religion and politics are separated.	1	2	3	4	9
⊠	⊠	v52. If its government was similar to Western (American or European) governments.	1	2	3	4	9

SA E	Saudi Arabia will be a better society	Agree strongly	Agree	Disagree	Disagree strongly	DK
☒ ☒	v53. If age at marriage increased.	1	2	3	4	9
☐ ☒ / ☒ ☐	v54. v54e (Egypt) If there was a small number of men that married more than one wife v54s (Saudi Arabia) If the number of men that married more than one wife decreased.	1	2	3	4	9
☒ ☒	v55. If more young people chose their spouses.	1	2	3	4	9
☒ ☒	v56. If the number of children born to families declined.	1	2	3	4	9
☒ ☒	v57. If people had more freedom to mix with the opposite sex.	1	2	3	4	9
☒ ☒	v58. If it had the technology of the West	1	2	3	4	9
☐ ☒	v59. If it had the sexual freedom available in the West	1	2	3	4	9
☒ ☒	v60. It had the entertainment options available in the West	1	2	3	4	9

The following are questions about religion and religious issues. Please tell us if you strongly agree, agree, disagree, or strongly disagree with the following statements.

SA E		Strongly agree	Agree	Disagree	Strongly disagree	DK
☒ ☒	v61. God has given humanity a complete, unfailing guide to happiness and salvation, which must be totally followed.	1	2	3	4	9
☒ ☒	v62. The basic cause of evil in this world is Satan, who is still constantly and ferociously fighting against God.	1	2	3	4	9
☒ ☒	v63. It is more important to be a good person than to believe in God and the right religion.	1	2	3	4	9

SA	E			Strongly agree	Agree	Disagree	Strongly disagree	DK
☒	☒	v64.	There is a particular set of religious teachings in this world that are so true, you can't go any "deeper" because they are the basic, bedrock message that God has given humanity.	1	2	3	4	9
☒	☒	v65.	When you get right down to it, there are basically only two kinds of people in the world: the Righteous, who will be rewarded by God; and the rest, who will not.	1	2	3	4	9
☐	☒	v66.	The Quran may have general facts, but the truth doesn't have to agree with it from beginning to end.	1	2	3	4	9
☒	☒	v67.	To lead the best, most meaningful life, one must belong to the one, fundamentally true religion.	1	2	3	4	9
☒	☒	v68.	Whenever science and religion conflict, *religion* is always right.	1	2	3	4	9
☒	☒	v69.	The fundamentals of God's religion should never be tampered with, or compromised with others' beliefs.	1	2	3	4	9
☒	☒	v70.	The only acceptable religion to God is Islam.	1	2	3	4	9
☒	☒	v71.	God will punish most severely those who abandon his true religion.	1	2	3	4	9
☒	☒	v72.	Islam is the only religion on this earth that teaches, without error, God's truth.	1	2	3	4	9

Now I would like to get your opinion on some matters concerning economic development. I will read you some statements, and I would like you to tell me if you strongly agree, agree, disagree, or strongly disagree.

SA E			Strongly agree	Agree	Disagree	Strongly disagree	DK
☒ ☒	v73.	As countries undergo economic development there will be a tendency for people to marry at older ages.	1	2	3	4	9
☒ ☒	v74.	As countries undergo economic development families will have fewer children.	1	2	3	4	9
☒ ☒	v75.	As countries undergo economic development the status of women will, in general, decline.	1	2	3	4	9
	v76.		1	2	3	4	9
☐ ☒		v76e (Egypt) With economic growth, some young adults will have the right to choose their husband/wife					
☒ ☐		v76s (Saudi Arabia) With economic growth the number of young people choosing their mates themselves decreases.					
☒ ☒	v77.	As countries undergo economic development, it will become more common for married children to live away from their older parents.	1	2	3	4	9
☒ ☒	v78.	The percentage of men having more than one wife increases with economic development.	1	2	3	4	9
☐ ☒	v79.	As societies become more developed pursuing of the opposite sex before marriage increases.	1	2	3	4	9

The following questions about Islam and non-Islamic religions and Muslims versus non-Muslims. Please tell us if you strongly agree, agree, disagree, strongly disagree. DKs are either 9 or 99.

SA E			Strongly agree	Agree	Disagree	Strongly disagree
☒ ☒	v80.	Islam should be the only religion taught in our public schools.	1	2	3	4
☒ ☒	v81.	I would *not* mind to have teachers who are not religious.	1	2	3	4
☒ ☒	v82.	Muslims are the only ones who will go to heaven, and the rest of the people from other religions will not go no matter how good they are.	1	2	3	4
☒ ☒	v83.	Non-Muslim religions have a lot of strange beliefs and pagan ways.	1	2	3	4
☒ ☒	v84.	People who belong to different religions are probably just as nice and moral as those who belong to mine	1	2	3	4
☒ ☒	v85.	I would like my religious leaders to meet with the leaders of other religions.	1	2	3	4
☒ ☒	v86.	If it were possible, I'd rather have a job where I worked with people with the same religious views I have rather than with people with different views.	1	2	3	4

Now, I would like you to rate several countries on a scale of morality (in Egypt, "a scale of morality and manners"), where "1" means that society is culturally decadent with a very low level of morality, where "10" means that people in that society have a high level of morality, and 5 means a middle level of morality. Where would you rate Saudi Arabia?

SA	E		Country	Low morality								High morality	
☒	☒	v87.	Saudi Arabia	1	2	3	4	5	6	7	8	9	10
☒	☒	v88.	Egypt	1	2	3	4	5	6	7	8	9	10
☒	☒	v89.	Iran	1	2	3	4	5	6	7	8	9	10
☒	☒	v90.	China	1	2	3	4	5	6	7	8	9	10
☒	☒	v91.	Yemen	1	2	3	4	5	6	7	8	9	10
☒	☒	v92.	The U.S.	1	2	3	4	5	6	7	8	9	10
☒	☒	v93.	Somalia	1	2	3	4	5	6	7	8	9	10
☒	☒	v94.	France	1	2	3	4	5	6	7	8	9	10
☒	☒	v95.	UAE	1	2	3	4	5	6	7	8	9	10

SA E
☒ ☒ v96. How often, if at all, do you think about the meaning and purpose of life?
(READ OUT IN REVERSE ORDER FOR ALTERNATE CONTACTS)
1 Often
2 Sometimes
3 Rarely
4 Never
9 Don't know [DO NOT READ OUT]

SA E
☒ ☒ v97. Apart from funerals, about how often do you go to a mosque these days?
1 More than once a week
2 Once a week
3 Once a month
4 Only on special holy days
5 Once a year
6 Less often
7 Never, practically never

SA E

☒ ☒ v98.   How often do you pray?
    1. five times a day
    2. once or twice a week
    3. once or twice a month
    4. at no time
    9. DK

SA E

☒ ☒ v99.   Independently of whether you go to religious services or not, would you
    say you are...(READ OUT)
    1. A religious person
    2. Not a religious person
    3. A convinced atheist (not believing in God)
    9 Don't know [DO NOT READ OUT]

Generally speaking, do you think that the religious authorities in this country are giving adequate answers to ... (Read out and code one answer for each)

SA E

			Yes	No	DK
☒ ☒	v100.	The moral problems and needs of the individual	1	2	9
☒ ☒	v101.	The problems of family life	1	2	9
☒ ☒	v102.	People's spiritual needs	1	2	9
☒ ☒	v103.	The social problems facing your country today	1	2	9

Please forgive me for asking these questions. I know that answers to some or all these questions may be obvious. But since we compare the results of this study with many other countries, and since some people in other countries may have much weaker religious beliefs than people in your country, we ask these questions for the sake of comparison. Which, if any, of the following do you believe in? (READ OUT AND CODE ONE ANSWER FOR EACH)

SA E

			Yes	No	DK
☒ ☒	v104.	Do you believe in God?	1	2	9
☒ ☒	v105.	Do you believe in life after death?	1	2	9
☒ ☒	v106.	Do you believe people have a soul?	1	2	9
☒ ☒	v107.	Do you believe in hell?	1	2	9
☒ ☒	v108.	Do you believe in heaven?	1	2	9

SA E

☒ ☒ v109. How important is God in your life? Please use this scale to indicate: 10 means very important and 1 means not at all important.

Not at all   Very

| 1 | 2 | 3 | 4 | 5 | 6 | 7 | 8 | 9 | 10 |

SA E

☒ ☒ v110. Do you find that you get comfort and strength from religion?

    1 Yes

    2 No

Now, I would like to know your views about a good government. Which of these traits a good government should have?

SA E		Very important	Important	Somewhat important*	Least important	Not important	DK
☒ ☒	v111. It should make laws according to the people's wishes	1	2	3	4	5	9
☒ ☒	v112. It should implement only the laws of the shari'a	1	2	3	4	5	9

Somewhat important was not available as a response category in Egypt

SA E

☒ ☒ v113. How proud are you to be a Saudi (Egyptian, etc.)?

    1 Very proud

    2 Quite proud

    3 Not very proud

    4 Not at all proud

    9. Don't know [DO NOT READ OUT]

SA E

☒ ☒ v114. Which of the following best describes you?

    1 Above all, I am a Saudi [Egyptian]

    2 Above all, I am a Muslim

    3 Above all, I am an Arab

    4 Other

Now I would like to get your opinion on some matters concerning family change. I will read you some statements, and I would like you to tell me if you strongly agree, agree, disagree, or strongly disagree. The first is:

SA	E		Strongly agree	Agree	Disagree	Strongly disagree
☒	☒	v115. In order for an underdeveloped country to achieve economic development its people should marry at older ages.	1	2	3	4
☒	☒	v116. In order for an underdeveloped country to achieve economic development its families should have more children.	1	2	3	4
☒	☒	v117. In order for an underdeveloped country to achieve economic development, it should increase the status of women.	1	2	3	4
☒	☒	v118. In order for an underdeveloped country to achieve economic development, more young people should choose their own spouse.	1	2	3	4
☒	☒	v119. In order for an underdeveloped country to achieve economic development, it should decrease the number of men having more than one wife.	1	2	3	4
☒	☒	v120. In order for an underdeveloped country to achieve economic development, it should allow young people more freedom to mix with the opposite sex.	1	2	3	4

SA	E			Strongly agree	Agree	Disagree	Strongly disagree
☒	☒	v121.	There are conspiracies against Muslim nations by Jews and Americans.	1	2	3	4
☐	☒	v122.	v122e. There is no peaceful way to establish a completely independent country.	1	2	3	4
☒	☐		v122s. There is a peaceful way to establish a completely independent country.				
☒	☒	v123.	Peaceful means are more effective to establish a truly Islamic state.	1	2	3	4
☒	☐	v124.	Armed struggle often leads to fitneh (trouble), even though it may cause injury to the enemy	1	2	3	4
☐	☒	v125.	v125e (Egypt) I desire my government to promote living or getting closer to nonbelievers	1	2	3	4
☒	☐		v125s (Saudi Arabia) I yearn for a way to improve our society so we can live with other societies				
☐	☒	126.	The enemies of our nation should be dealt with through military action.	1	2	3	4
☐	☒	v127.	v127e (Egypt) War is often necessary.	1	2	3	4
☒	☐		v127s (Saudi Arabia) War is always necessary.				
☒	☒	v128.	Killing of civilians is is acceptable if it helps defeats the enemy and win the war.	1	2	3	4

SA	E			Strongly agree	Agree	Disagree	Strongly disagree
☐	☒	v129.	It is necessary for our nation to manufacture weapons.	1	2	3	4
☐	☒	v130.	Killing foreigners can be justified if their government was doing things that hurt the sons of our nation even if these foreigners were not responsible for the actions of their governments	1	2	3	4

SA	E			Strongly agree	Agree	Disagree	Strongly disagree
☒	☒	v131.	For the realization of a truly ideal society, people must be ready for self-sacrifice.	1	2	3	4
☒	☒	v132.	The best way to persuade the enemy to change its actions is dealing with him thru peaceful methods.	1	2	3	4
☐	☒	v133.	Our society needs more social scientists to help us live a better life.	1	2	3	4
		v134.		1	2	3	4
☐	☒		v134e (Egypt) It is not possible to live happily in this world.				
☒	☐		v134s (Saudi Arabia) It is not possible to live very happily in this world				

SA E

☒ ☒ V135. Some people feel they have completely free choice and control over their lives, while other people feel that what they do has no real effect on what happens to them. Please use this scale where 1 means "none at all" and 10 means "a great deal" to indicate how much freedom of choice and control you feel you have over the way your life turns out.

None at all   A great deal

1   2   3   4   5   6   7   8   9   10

SA E

☒ ☒ V136. To what extent are you optimistic/pessimistic about your future?

Highly pessimistic   Highly Optimistic

1   2   3   4   5   6   7   8   9   10

SA E

☒ ☒ V137. Do you strongly agree, agree, disagree, or strongly disagree that in your country these days, life is unpredictable and dangerous?

Agree strongly	Agree	Disagree	Strongly disagree	DK
1	2	3	4	9

To what extent do you rely on, that is, do you believe and trust, what the following people tell you about the following subjects?"

SA	E	The role of women in society and politics		Do not rely	Generally do not rely	Sometimes rely and sometimes not	Generally rely	Rely completely
☒	☒	v138.	Parents	1	2	3	4	5
☒	☒	v139.	Teachers of religion at school or university	1	2	3	4	5
☒	☒	v140.	Other (secular) teachers	1	2	3	4	5
☒	☒	v141.	Friends	1	2	3	4	5
☒	☒	v142.	Religious leaders	1	2	3	4	5
☒	☒	v143.	Media-domestic TV and newspapers	1	2	3	4	5
☒	☒	v144.	Satellite TV and internet	1	2	3	4	5

SA	E	Politics and forms of government	Do not rely	Generally do not rely	Sometimes rely and sometimes not	Generally rely	Rely completely
☒	☒	v145. Parents	1	2	3	4	5
☒	☒	v146. Teachers of religion at school or university	1	2	3	4	5
☒	☒	v147. Other (secular) teachers	1	2	3	4	5
☒	☒	v148. Friends	1	2	3	4	5
☒	☒	v149. Religious Leaders	1	2	3	4	5
☒	☒	v150. Media-domestic TV and newspapers	1	2	3	4	5
☒	☒	v151. Satellite TV and internet	1	2	3	4	5

SA	E	Your education and career choice	Do not rely	Generally do not rely	Sometimes rely and sometimes not	Generally rely	Rely completely
☒	☒	v152. Parents	1	2	3	4	5
☒	☒	v153. Teachers of religion at school or university	1	2	3	4	5
☒	☒	v154. Other (secular) teachers	1	2	3	4	5
☒	☒	v155. Friends	1	2	3	4	5
☒	☒	v156. Religious Leaders	1	2	3	4	5
☒	☒	v157. Media-domestic TV and newspapers	1	2	3	4	5
☒	☒	v158. Satellite TV and internet	1	2	3	4	5

SA	E	Evolution: explanation of how plants and animals have evolved	Do not rely	Generally do not rely	Sometimes rely and sometimes not	Generally rely	Rely completely
☒	☒	v159. Parents	1	2	3	4	5
☒	☒	v160. Teachers of religion at school or university	1	2	3	4	5
☒	☒	v161. Other (secular) teachers	1	2	3	4	5
☒	☒	v162. Friends	1	2	3	4	5
☒	☒	v163. Religious Leaders	1	2	3	4	5
☒	☒	v164. Media-domestic TV and newspapers	1	2	3	4	5
☒	☒	v165. Satellite TV and internet	1	2	3	4	5

SA	E	Western societies and foreign culture	Do not rely	Generally do not rely	Sometimes rely and sometimes not	Generally rely	Rely completely
☒	☒	v166. Parents	1	2	3	4	5
☒	☒	v167. Teachers of religion at school or university	1	2	3	4	5
☒	☒	v168. Other (secular) teachers	1	2	3	4	5
☒	☒	v169. Friends	1	2	3	4	5
☒	☒	v170. Religious Leaders	1	2	3	4	5
☒	☒	v171. Media-domestic TV and newspapers	1	2	3	4	5
☒	☒	v172. Satellite TV and internet	1	2	3	4	5

SA	E	(Egypt) The role in which religion plays in politics and society	Do not rely	Generally do not rely	Sometimes rely and sometimes not	Generally rely	Rely completely
☐	☒	v173e Parents	1	2	3	4	5
☐	☒	v174e Teachers of religion at school or university	1	2	3	4	5
☐	☒	v175e Other (secular) teachers	1	2	3	4	5
☐	☒	v176e Friends	1	2	3	4	5
☐	☒	v177e Religious Leaders	1	2	3	4	5
☐	☒	v178e Media-domestic TV and newspapers	1	2	3	4	5
☐	☒	v179e Satellite TV and internet	1	2	3	4	5

SA	E	(Saudi Arabia) The role of religion and politics in society	Do not rely	Generally do not rely	Sometimes rely and sometimes not	Generally rely	Rely completely
☒	☐	v173s Parents	1	2	3	4	5
☒	☐	v174s Teachers of religion at school or university	1	2	3	4	5
☒	☐	v175s Other (secular) teachers	1	2	3	4	5
☒	☐	v176s Friends	1	2	3	4	5
☒	☐	v177s Religious Leaders	1	2	3	4	5
☒	☐	v178s Media-domestic TV and newspapers	1	2	3	4	5
☒	☐	v179s Satellite TV and internet	1	2	3	4	5

SA	E			Strongly agree	Agree	Disagree	Strongly disagree
☒	☒	v180.	A person can just accept answers from experts without question.	1	2	3	4
		v181.					
☒	☒		v181e (Egypt) What are considered scientific truths can change with time	1	2	3	4
☒	☐		v181s (Saudi Arabia) Scientific truths can usually be taken into account although they change with time				
		v182.					
☐	☒		v182e (Egypt) If people read about anything in an educational book they are confident in its correctness	1	2	3	4
☒	☐		v182s (Saudi Arabia) If people read something that was in a scientific book then they definitely trust what is written.				
☒	☒	v183.	Even in science, it is important to critically evaluate what experts tell us.	1	2	3	4
☒	☒	v184.	Scientific truths don't change	1	2	3	4
☒	☒	v185.	People can accept knowledge from scientific sources without discussion	1	2	3	4

SA E

☒ ☒ v186. What is the importance of (how important is) exercise (*sport*) in your life?

1. Very important
2. Important
3. Somewhat important
4. Not very important
5. Not at all important

SA E DEMOGRAPHICS

☒ ☒ v187. Sex of respondent:

1. Male
2. Female

SA E

☒ ☒ v188. Can you tell me your year of birth, please? 19____

☒ ☒ v189. This means you are __ __ years old.

☒ ☒ v190. What is the highest level of education your father has completed:

    1. No formal education

    2. Incomplete primary school

    3. Complete primary school

    4. Incomplete secondary school: technical/vocational type

    5. Complete secondary school: technical/vocational type

    6. Incomplete secondary: university-preparatory type

    7. Complete secondary: university-preparatory type

    8. Some university-level education, without degree

    9. University-level education, with degree

SA E

☒ ☒ v191. Have you attended school at all in the past 6 months?

    1. Yes

    2. No

SA E

☒ ☒ v192. What is the highest level of education your father has completed?

    1. No formal education

    2. Incomplete primary school

    3. Complete primary school

    4. Incomplete secondary school: technical/vocational type

    5. Complete secondary school: technical/vocational type

    6. Incomplete secondary: university-preparatory type

    7. Complete secondary: university-preparatory type

    8. Some university-level education, without degree

    9. University-level education, with degree

SA E

☒ ☒ v193. What is the highest level of education your mother has completed?

    1. No formal education

    2. Incomplete primary school

    3. Complete primary school

    4. Incomplete secondary school: technical/vocational type

    5. Complete secondary school: technical/vocational type

    6. Incomplete secondary: university-preparatory type

SA E
☒   ☒

      7. Complete secondary: university-preparatory type

      8. Some university-level education, without degree

      9. University-level education, with degree

SA E
☒   ☒ v194. During the time that you were between the ages of 12 and 16 did you live longest on a farm, in a village, in a town, in a small city, or in a large city?

      1. Farm

      2. Village

      3. Town

      4. Small City

      5. Large City

SA E
☒   ☒ v195. During the time that your father was between the ages of 15 and 25 did he live longest on a farm, in a village, in a town, in a small city, or in a large city?

      1. Farm

      2. Village

      3. Town

      4. Small City

      5. Large City

SA E
☒   ☒ v196. During the time that your mother was between the ages of 15 and 25 did she live longest on a farm, in a village, in a town, in a small city, or in a large city?

      1. Farm

      2. Village

      3. Town

      4. Small City

      5. Large City

SA E
☒   ☒ v197. In which profession/occupation do you work? If more than one job: the main job.

      1 Employer/manager of establishment with 10 or more employees

      2 Employer/manager of establishment with less than 10 employees

SA   E

☒   ☒   3 Professional worker lawyer, accountant, teacher, etc
                       4 Supervisory - office worker: supervises others.
                       5 non-manual - office worker: non-supervisory
                       6 Foreman and supervisor
                       7 Skilled manual worker
                       8 Semi-skilled manual worker
                       9 Unskilled manual worker
                      10 Farmer: has own farm
                      11 Agricultural worker
                      12 Member of armed forces, security personnel
                      13 Has no occupation

SA   E

☒   ☒   v198. In which profession/occupation does your father work? If more than one
                       job: the main job.
                       1 Employer/manager of establishment with 10 or more employees
                       2 Employer/manager of establishment with less than 10 employees
                       3 Professional worker lawyer, accountant, teacher, etc
                       4 Supervisory - office worker: supervises others.
                       5 non-manual - office worker: non-supervisory
                       6 Foreman and supervisor
                       7 Skilled manual worker
                       8 Semi-skilled manual worker
                       9 Unskilled manual worker
                      10 Farmer: has own farm
                      11 Agricultural worker
                      12 Member of armed forces, security personnel
                      13 Has no occupation

SA   E

☒   ☒   v199. People sometimes describe themselves as belonging to the working
                       class, the middle class, or the upper or lower class. Would you describe
                       yourself as belonging to the:
                       1. Upper class
                       2. Upper middle class
                       3. Lower middle class
                       4. Working class
                       5. Lower class
                       9. Don't know [DO NOT READ OUT]

SA E

☒   ☒   v200. Here is a scale of incomes. We would like to know in what group your household is, counting all wages, salaries, pensions and other incomes that come in. Just give the letter of the group your household falls into, before taxes and other deductions.

1	2	3	4	5	6	7	8	9	10
C	D	E	F	G	H	I	J	K	L

No answer = 99

[CODE INCOME CATEGORIES BY DECILES FOR YOUR SOCIETY, 1=LOWEST DECILE, 10=HIGHEST DECILE]

SA E

☒   ☒   v201. Do you ever watch television? IF YES: How much time do you usually spend watching television on an average weekday (NOT WEEKENDS)?

    1. Do not watch TV or do not have access to TV

    2. 1 - 2 hours per day

    3. 2 - 3 hours per day

    4. More than 3 hours per day

SA E

☒   ☒   v202. Total length of interview: ____ Minutes

SA E

☒   ☒   v203. During the interview the respondent was ....

    1 Very interested

    2 Somewhat interested

    3 Not very interested

SA E

☒   ☒   v204. Size of town

    1. Under 2,000

    2. 2,000 - 5,000

    3. 5,000 - 10,000

    4. 10,000 - 20,000

    5. 20,000 - 50,000

    6. 50,000 - 100,000

    7. 100,000 - 500,000

    8. 500,000 and more

SA E

☐ ☒ v205.   Ethnic group [code by observation}

       1. Native Egyptian

       2. Arab (non-Egyptian) living in Egypt

       3. non-Arab

       4. Other (specify)_____

SA E

☒ ☒ v206.   Region where the interview conducted

       1. Cairo

       2. Alexandria

       3. El-Menya

       4. Jeddah

       5. Riyadh

       6. Damman/Khobar

WORLD VALUES SURVEY IN IRAN, 2005

V1. Survey wave number(*write in constant*): 5
V2. Country code (*write in 3-digit code from list below*): 91 (Iran)
V3. Interview number (*write in 4-digit number identifying each respondent*): _____

(*Introduction by interviewer*):
Hello. I am from the _____ (*mention name of the interview organization*). We are carrying out a global study of what people value in life. This study will interview samples representing most of the world's people. Your name has been selected at random as part of a representative sample of the people in _____
(*mention country in which interview is conducted*). I'd like to ask your views on a number of different subjects. Your input will be treated strictly confidential but it will contribute to a better understanding of what people all over the world believe and want out of life.
(*Show Card A*)
For each of the following, indicate how important it is in your life. Would you say it is (*read out and code one answer for each*):

		Very important	Rather important	Not very important	Not at all important
4	Family	1	2	3	4
5	Friends	1	2	3	4
6	Leisure time	1	2	3	4
7	Politics	1	2	3	4
8	Work	1	2	3	4
9	Religion	1	2	3	4

(*NOTE: Code but do not read out– here and throughout the interview*):
-1 Don't know, -2 No answer, -3 Not applicable

10   Taking all things together, would you say you are (*read out and code one answer*):
   1   Very happy
   2   Rather happy
   3   Not very happy
   4   Not at all happy

11   All in all, how would you describe your state of health these days?
Would you say it is (*read out*):

1   Very good
2   Good
3   Fair
4   Poor

(*Show Card B*)
Here is a list of qualities that children can be encouraged to learn at home. Which,
if any, do you consider to be especially important? Please choose up to five! (*Code
five mentions at the maximum*):

		Mentioned	Not mentioned
12	Independence	1	2
13	Hard work	1	2
14	Feeling of responsibility	1	2
15	Imagination	1	2
16	Tolerance and respect for other people	1	2
17	Thrift, saving money and things	1	2
18	Determination, perseverance	1	2
19	Religious faith	1	2
20	Unselfishness	1	2
21	Obedience	1	2

(*Show Card C*)
22   All things considered, how satisfied are you with your life as a whole
these days? Using this card on which 1 means you are "completely dissatisfied" and 10 means you are "completely satisfied" where would you
put your satisfaction with your life as a whole? (*Code one number*):

Completely dissatisfied   Completely satisfied

1   2   3   4   5   6   7   8   9   10

23   Generally speaking, would you say that most people can be trusted or
that you need to be very careful in dealing with people? (*Code one
answer*):

1   Most people can be trusted.
2   Need to be very careful.

Now I am going to read off a list of voluntary organizations. For each one, could you tell me whether you are an active member, an inactive member or not a member of that type of organization? (*Read out and code one answer for each organization*):

		Active member	Inactive member	Don't belong
24	Church or religious organization	2	1	0
25	Sport or recreational organization	2	1	0
26	Art, music or educational organization	2	1	0
27	Labor Union	2	1	0
28	Political party	2	1	0
29	Environmental organization	2	1	0
30	Professional association	2	1	0
31	Humanitarian or charitable organization	2	1	0
32	Consumer organization	2	1	0

(*Show Card D*)
On this list are various groups of people. Could you please mention any that you would not like to have as neighbors? (*Code an answer for each group*):

		Mentioned	Not mentioned
33	Drug addicts	1	2
34	People of a different race	1	2
35	People who have AIDS	1	2
36	Immigrants/foreign workers	1	2
37	Homosexuals	1	2
38	People of a different religion	1	2
39	Heavy drinkers	1	2
40	Unmarried couples living together	1	2
41	Jews	1	2
42	Christians		

Do you agree, disagree or neither agree nor disagree with the following statements? (*Read out and code one answer for each statement*):

		Strongly Agree	Agree	Disagree	Strongly Disagree
43	When jobs are scarce, men should have more right to a job than women.	1	2	3	4
44	When jobs are scarce, employers should give priority to Iranian people over immigrants.	1	2	3	4

(*Show Card E*)

45 Some people feel they have completely free choice and control over their lives, while other people feel that what they do has no real effect on what happens to them. Please use this scale where 1 means "none at all" and 10 means "a great deal" to indicate how much freedom of choice and control you feel you have over the way your life turns out (*code one number*):

None at all   A great deal

1   2   3   4   5   6   7   8   9   10

(*Show Card F*)

46 Do you think most people would try to take advantage of you if they got a chance, or would they try to be fair? Please show your response on this card, where 1 means that "people would try to take advantage of you," and 10 means that "people would try to be fair" (*code one number*):

People would try to   People would
take advantage of you   try to be fair

1   2   3   4   5   6   7   8   9   10

47 To what extent are you optimistic/pessimistic about your future (1=highly pessimistic... 10=highly optimistic)

1   2   3   4   5   6   7   8   9   10

48 Now I would like to ask you something about the things which would seem to you, personally, most important if you were looking for a job. Here are some of the things many people take into account in relation to their work. Regardless of whether you're actually looking for a job, which one would you, personally, place first if you were looking for a job (*read out and code one answer*):

1   A good income so that you do not have any worries about money
2   A safe job with no risk of closing down or unemployment
3   Working with people you like
4   Doing an important job that gives you a feeling of accomplishment

49 And what would be your second choice (*code one answer*):
1   A good income so that you do not have any worries about money
2   A safe job with no risk of closing down or unemployment
3   Working with people you like
4   Doing an important job that gives you a feeling of accomplishment

(*Show Card G*)

50 Are you currently (*read out and code one answer only*):
1   Married
2   Living together as married
3   Divorced
4   Separated
5   Widowed
6   Single

51 What do you think is the ideal size of the family - how many children, if any?
0   None
1   1 child
2   2 children
3   3 children
4   4 children
5   5 children
6   6 children
7   7 children
8   8 or more children
9   DK, no answer

52   Have you had any children? (*Code 0 if no, and respective number if yes*):
     0   No children
     1   One child
     2   Two children
     3   Three children
     4   Four children
     5   Five children
     6   Six children
     7   Seven children
     8   Eight or more children

53   If someone says a child needs a home with both a father and a mother
     to grow up happily, would you tend to agree or disagree? (*Code one
     answer*):
     1   Tend to agree
     2   Tend to disagree

54   Do you agree or disagree with the following statement (*read out*):
     "Marriage is an out-dated institution." (*Code one answer*):
     1   Agree
     2   Disagree

55   If a woman wants to have a child as a single parent but she doesn't want
     to have a stable relationship with a man, do you approve or disapprove?
     (*Code one answer*):
     1   Approve
     2   Disapprove
     3   Depends (*do not read out, code only if volunteered*)

For each of the following statements I read out, can you tell me how strongly you
agree or disagree with each. Do you strongly agree, agree, disagree, or strongly
disagree? (*Read out and code one answer for each statement*):

		Strongly agree	Agree	Disagree	Strongly disagree
56	On the whole, men make better political leaders than women do.	1	2	3	4
57	A university education is more important for a boy than for a girl.	1	2	3	4
58	On the whole, men make better business executives than women do.	1	2	3	4

People pursue different goals in life. For each of the following goals, can you tell me if you strongly agree, agree, disagree or strongly disagree with it? (*Read out and code one answer for each statement*):

		Strongly agree	Agree	Disagree	Strongly disagree
59	One of my main goals in life has been to make my parents proud.	1	2	3	4
60	I make a lot of effort to live up to what my friends expect.	1	2	3	4

(*Show Card H*)

61 How satisfied are you with the financial situation of your household? Please use this card again to help with your answer (*code one number*):

Completely dissatisfied   Completely satisfied

1   2   3   4   5   6   7   8   9   10

(*Show Card I*)

62.1 People sometimes talk about what the aims of this country should be for the next ten years. On this card are listed some of the goals which different people would give top priority. Would you please say which one of these you, yourself, consider the most important? (*Code one answer only under "first choice"*)

62.2 And which would be the next most important? (*Code one answer only under "second choice"*)

	First choice	Second choice
A high level of economic growth	1	1
Making sure this country has strong defense forces	2	2
Seeing that people have more say about how things are done at their jobs and in their communities	3	3
Trying to make our cities and countryside more beautiful	4	4

(*Show Card J*)

    63.1   If you had to choose, which one of the things on this card would you say is most important? (*Code one answer only under "first choice"*):

    63.2   And which would be the next most important? (*Code one answer only under "second choice"*):

	First choice	Second choice
Maintaining order in the nation	1	1
Giving people more say in important government decisions	2	2
Fighting rising prices	3	3
Protecting freedom of speech	4	4

(*Show Card K*)

    64.1   Here is another list. In your opinion, which one of these is most important? (*Code one answer only under "first choice"*):

    64.2   And what would be the next most important? (*Code one answer only under "second choice"*):

	First choice	Second choice
A stable economy	1	1
Progress toward a less impersonal and more humane society	2	2
Progress toward a society in which ideas count more than money	3	3
The fight against crime	4	4

    65.   Of course, we all hope that there will not be another war, but if it were to come to that, would you be willing to fight for your country? (*Code one answer*):

      1   Yes

      2   No

I'm going to read out a list of various changes in our way of life that might take place in the near future. Please tell me for each one, if it were to happen, whether you think it would be a good thing, a bad thing, or don't you mind? (*Code one answer for each*):

		Good	Don't mind	Bad
66	Less importance placed on work in our lives	1	2	3
67	More emphasis on the development of technology	1	2	3
68	Greater respect for authority	1	2	3
69	More emphasis on family life	1	2	3

(*Show Card L*)

Now I will briefly describe some people. Using this card, would you please indicate for each description whether that person is very much like you, like you, somewhat like you, not like you, or not at all like you? (*Code one answer for each description*):

		Very much like me	Like me	Some-what like me	A little like me	Not like me	Not at all like me
70	It is important to this person to think up new ideas and be creative; to do things one's own way.	1	2	3	4	5	6
71	It is important to this person to be rich; to have a lot of money and expensive things.	1	2	3	4	5	6
72	Living in secure surroundings is important to this person; to avoid anything that might be dangerous.	1	2	3	4	5	6
73	It is important to this person to have a good time; to "spoil" oneself.	1	2	3	4	5	6
74	It is important to this person to help the people nearby; to care for their well-being.	1	2	3	4	5	6
75	Being very successful is important to this person; to have people recognize one's achievements.	1	2	3	4	5	6
76	Adventure and taking risks are important to this person; to have an exciting life.	1	2	3	4	5	6
77	It is important to this person to always behave properly; to avoid doing anything people would say is wrong.	1	2	3	4	5	6
78	Looking after the environment is important to this person; to care for nature.	1	2	3	4	5	6
79	Tradition is important to this person; to follow the customs handed down by one's religion or family.	1	2	3	4	5	6

(*Show Card O*)

How interested would you say you are in politics? Are you (*read out and code one answer*):

1   Very interested
2   Somewhat interested
3   Not very interested
4   Not at all interested

(*Show Card M*)

Here are two statements people sometimes make when discussing the environment and economic growth. Which of them comes closer to your own point of view? (*Read out and code one answer*):

1   Protecting the environment should be given priority, even if it causes slower economic growth and some loss of jobs.
2   Economic growth and creating jobs should be the top priority, even if the environment suffers to some extent.

(*Show Card N*)

I am going to read out some statements about the environment. For each one, can you tell me whether you strongly agree, agree, disagree or strongly disagree? (*Read out and code one answer for each*):

		Strongly agree	Agree	Disagree	Strongly disagree
80	I would give part of my income if I were certain that the money would be used to prevent environmental pollution.	1	2	3	4
81	I would agree to an increase in taxes if the extra money were used to prevent environmental pollution.	1	2	3	4
82	The Government should reduce environmental pollution, but it should not cost me any money.	1	2	3	4

I am going to read out a list of environmental problems facing many communities. Please, tell me how serious you consider each one to be here in your own community. Is it very serious, somewhat serious, not very serious or not serious at all? (*Read out and code one answer for each problem*):

		Very serious	Somewhat serious	Not very serious	Not serious at all
83	Poor water quality.	1	2	3	4
84	Poor air quality.	1	2	3	4
85	Poor sewage and sanitation.	1	2	3	4

Now let's consider environmental problems in the world as a whole. Please, tell me how serious you consider each of the following to be for the world as a whole. Is it very serious, somewhat serious, not very serious or not serious at all? (*Read out and code one answer for each problem*):

		Very serious	Somewhat serious	Not very serious	Not serious at all
86	Global warming or the greenhouse effect.	1	2	3	4
87	Loss of plant or animal species or biodiversity.	1	2	3	4
88	Pollution of rivers, lakes and oceans.	1	2	3	4

(*Show Card P*)

Imagine two secretaries, of the same age, doing practically the same job. One finds out that the other earns considerably more than she does. The better paid secretary, however, is quicker, more efficient and more reliable at her job. In your opinion, is it fair or not fair that one secretary is paid more than the other? (*Code one answer*):

1   Fair
2   Not fair

(*Show Card Q*)

89   Now I'd like you to tell me your views on various issues. How would you place your views on this scale? 1 means you agree completely with the statement on the left; 10 means you agree completely with the statement on the right; and if your views fall somewhere in between, you can choose any number in between. (*Code one number for each issue*):

Incomes should be made more equal						We need larger income differences as incentives for individual effort			
1	2	3	4	5	6	7	8	9	10

90 | Private ownership of business and industry should be increased | | | | | | Government ownership of business and industry should be increased | | | |
|---|---|---|---|---|---|---|---|---|---|
| 1 | 2 | 3 | 4 | 5 | 6 | 7 | 8 | 9 | 10 |

91 | The government should take more responsibility to ensure that everyone is provided for | | | | | | People should take more responsibility to provide for themselves | | | |
|---|---|---|---|---|---|---|---|---|---|
| 1 | 2 | 3 | 4 | 5 | 6 | 7 | 8 | 9 | 10 |

92 | Competition is good. It stimulates people to work hard and develop new ideas | | | | | | Competition is harmful. It brings out the worst in people | | | |
|---|---|---|---|---|---|---|---|---|---|
| 1 | 2 | 3 | 4 | 5 | 6 | 7 | 8 | 9 | 10 |

93 | In the long run, hard work usually brings a better life | | | | | | Hard work doesn't generally bring success—it's more a matter of luck and connections | | | |
|---|---|---|---|---|---|---|---|---|---|
| 1 | 2 | 3 | 4 | 5 | 6 | 7 | 8 | 9 | 10 |

94 | People can only get rich at the expense of others | | | | | | Wealth can grow so there's enough for everyone | | | |
|---|---|---|---|---|---|---|---|---|---|
| 1 | 2 | 3 | 4 | 5 | 6 | 7 | 8 | 9 | 10 |

(*Show Card R*)

95   Some people believe that individuals can decide their own destiny, while others think that it is impossible to escape a predetermined fate. Please tell me which comes closest to your view on this scale on which 1 means "everything in life is determined by fate," and 10 means that "people shape their fate themselves." (*Code one number*):

Everything is determined by fate							People shape their fate themselves		
1	2	3	4	5	6	7	8	9	10

(*Show Card S*)

96   How about people from other countries coming here to work. Which one of the following do you think the government should do? (*Read out and code one answer*):
1   Let anyone come who wants to?
2   Let people come as long as there are jobs available?
3   Place strict limits on the number of foreigners who can come here?
4   Prohibit people coming here from other countries?

I am going to name a number of organizations. For each one, could you tell me how much confidence you have in them: is it a great deal of confidence, quite a lot of confidence, not very much confidence or none at all? (*Read out and code one answer for each*):

		A great deal	Quite a lot	Not very much	None at all
97	The religious leaders	1	2	3	4
98	The armed forces	1	2	3	4
99	The press	1	2	3	4
100	Television	1	2	3	4
101	Labor unions	1	2	3	4
102	The police	1	2	3	4
103	The courts	1	2	3	4
104	The government (in your nation's capital)	1	2	3	4
105	Political parties	1	2	3	4
106	Parliament	1	2	3	4
107	The Civil service	1	2	3	4
108	Major Companies	1	2	3	4
109	Environmental organizations	1	2	3	4
110	Women's organizations	1	2	3	4
111	Charitable or humanitarian organizations	1	2	3	4
112	The United Nations	1	2	3	4

I'm going to describe various types of political systems and ask what you think about each as a way of governing this country. For each one, would you say it is a very good, fairly good, fairly bad or very bad way of governing this country? (*Read out and code one answer for each*):

		Very good	Fairly good	Fairly bad	Very bad
113	Having a strong leader who does not have to bother with parliament and elections	1	2	3	4
114	Having experts, not government, make decisions according to what they think is best for the country	1	2	3	4
115	Having the army rule	1	2	3	4
116	Having a democratic political system	1	2	3	4

(*Show Card T*)
Many things may be desirable, but not all of them are essential characteristics of democracy. Please tell me for each of the following things how essential you think it is as a characteristic of democracy. Use this scale where 1 means "not at all an essential characteristic of democracy" and 10 means it definitely is "an essential characteristic of democracy" (*read out and code one answer for each*):

		Not an essential characteristic of democracy					An essential characteristic of democracy			
117	Governments tax the rich and subsidize the poor.	1	2	3	4	5	6	7	8	9	10
118	Religious authorities interpret the laws.	1	2	3	4	5	6	7	8	9	10
119	People choose their leaders in free elections.	1	2	3	4	5	6	7	8	9	10
120	People receive state aid for unemployment.	1	2	3	4	5	6	7	8	9	10
121	The army takes over when government is incompetent.	1	2	3	4	5	6	7	8	9	10
122	Civil rights protect people's liberty against oppression.	1	2	3	4	5	6	7	8	9	10
123	The economy is prospering.	1	2	3	4	5	6	7	8	9	10

		Not an essential characteristic of democracy						An essential characteristic of democracy			
124	Criminals are severely punished.	1	2	3	4	5	6	7	8	9	10
125	People can change the laws in referendums.	1	2	3	4	5	6	7	8	9	10
126	Women have the same rights as men.	1	2	3	4	5	6	7	8	9	10
127	The political leader should stay in power only for a limited number of years	1	2	3	4	5	6	7	8	9	10
128	People should be free to recall their political leaders, if they fail to perform	1	2	3	4	5	6	7	8	9	10

129   Do you think that a woman has to have children in order to be fulfilled or is this not necessary?
  1   Needs children
  2   Not necessary
  9   Don't know [DO NOT READ OUT]

130   In you view, what is the basis for marriage:
  1.   parental approval
  2.   Love
  3.   DK

In your opinion, how important are each of the following traits in a woman?

		Very important	Important	Somewhat important	Not very important	Not at all important	DK
131	Wearing a veil in public places	1	2	3	4	5	9
132	Being a good mother	1	2	3	4	5	9
133	Being a good wife	1	2	3	4	5	9
134	Being religious	1	2	3	4	5	9
135	Being educated	1	2	3	4	5	9
136	Having a job outside the home	1	2	3	4	5	9
137	It is up to a woman to dress as she wishes	1	2	3	4	5	9

I would like to ask your personal opinion about the following issues related to relationships between men and women. To what extent do you agree or disagree with men having more than one wife? Do you strongly agree, agree, disagree, or strongly disagree?

INTERVIEWER: This same style should be used in asking both questions.

		Strongly agree	Agree	Neither agree or disagree	Disagree	Strongly disagree	DK
138	It is acceptable for a man to have more than one wife.	1	2	3	4	5	9
139	A wife must always obey her husband.	1	2	3	4	5	9

140 People have different views about the system for governing this country. Here is a scale for rating how well the government is doing: 1 means very bad; 10 means very good.

What point on this scale would you choose to describe how well the government is doing?

1	2	3	4	5	6	7	8	9	10	99
Bad								Very good	Dk

141 On the whole are you very satisfied, rather satisfied, not very satisfied or not at all satisfied with the way democracy is developing in our country?
1   Very satisfied
2   Satisfied
3   To some extent satisfied
4   Not very satisfied
5   Not at all satisfied
9   DK

I'm going to read off some things that people sometimes say about a democratic political system. Could you please tell me if you agree strongly, agree, disagree or disagree strongly, after I read each one of them?

		Agree strongly	Agree	Disagree	Strongly disagree	DK
142	Democracy may have problems but it's better than any other form of government	1	2	3	4	9

143 How satisfied are you with the way the government is handling the
     country's affairs? Would you say you are very satisfied, fairly satisfied,
     fairly dissatisfied or very dissatisfied?
     1. Very satisfied
     2. Fairly satisfied
     3. Fairly dissatisfied
     4. Very dissatisfied
     9. DK

144 Generally speaking, would you say that this country's economy is run
     by a few big interests looking out for themselves or that it is run for the
     benefit of all the people?
     1   Run by a few big interests
     2   Run for all the people
     9   Don't know [DO NOT READ OUT]

(*Show Card U*)
145 How important is it for you to live in a country that is governed demo-
     cratically? On this scale where 1 means it is "not at all important" and
     10 means "absolutely important" what position would you choose?
     (*Code one number*):

     Not at all important   Absolutely important
     1   2   3   4   5   6   7   8   9   10

(*Show Card V*)
146 And how democratically is this country being governed today? Again
     using a scale from 1 to 10, where 1 means that it is "not at all demo-
     cratic" and 10 means that it is "completely democratic," what position
     would you choose? (*Code one number*):

     Not at all democratic   Completely democratic
     1   2   3   4   5   6   7   8   9   10

147 How much respect is there for individual human rights nowadays in
     this country? Do you feel there is (*read out and code one answer*):
     1   A great deal of respect for individual human rights
     2   Fairly much respect
     3   Not much respect
     4   No respect at all

151.1   Which is the first andsecond most serious problem for the world as a
        whole? (*Code one answer under "next most serious for the world"*):

	Most serious in the world	Second most serious in the world
People living in poverty and need.	1	1
Discrimination against girls and women.	2	2
Poor sanitation and infectious diseases.	3	3
Inadequate education.	4	4
Environmental pollution.	5	5

151.2   And which is the first and second most serious problem for the world
        as a whole? (*Code one answer under "next most serious for the world"*):

152.1   Which of these problems do you consider the most serious one **in
        your own country?** (*Code one answer under "most serious for own
        country"*):

152.2   And which is the next most serious **for your own country?** (*Code one
        answer under "next most serious for own country"*):

	Most serious in own country	Next most serious in own country
People living in poverty and need.	1	1
Discrimination of girls and women.	2	2
Poor sanitation and infectious diseases.	3	3
Inadequate education.	4	4
Environmental pollution.	5	5

153   Thinking at your own country's problems, should your country's lead-
        ers give top priority to help reducing poverty in the world or should
        they give top priority to solve your own country's problems? Use this
        scale where 1 means "top priority to help reducing misery in the world"
        and 10 means "top priority to solve my own country's problems." (*Code
        one answer*):

Top priority to help   Top priority to solve
reducing poverty in   my own country's
the world   problems

  1   2   3   4   5   6   7   8   9   10

Some people believe that certain kinds of problems could be better handled by the United Nations or regional organizations, such as the European Union, rather than by each national government separately. Others think that these problems should be left entirely to the national governments. I'm going to mention some problems. For each one, would you tell me whether you think that policies in this area should be decided by the national governments, by regional organizations, or by the United Nations? (*Read out and code one answer for each problem*):

		National governments	Regional organizations	United Nations
154	Peacekeeping	1	2	3
155	Protection of the environment	1	2	3
156	Aid to developing countries	1	2	3
157	Refugees	1	2	3
158	Human Rights	1	2	3

159   Now let's turn to another topic. How often, if at all, do you think about the meaning and purpose of life? (*Read out and code one answer!*)
   1   Often
   2   Sometimes
   3   Rarely
   4   Never

160   Do you belong to a religion or religious denomination? If yes, which one? (*Code answer due to list below. Code 0, if respondent answers to have no denomination!*)

No:	do not belong to a denomination	0
Yes:	Shi'i	1
	Sunni	2
	Zoroastrian	3
	Armenian (Christian)	4
	Christian non-Armenian	5
	Jew	6
	Other (*write in*):_____	66

(*NOTE: If your own society does not fit into this coding system, please devise an alternative, following this as closely as possible; for example, in Islamic countries, ask about Sunni, Shia, etc. Send a list of the categories used here along with your data.*)

161   How often do you pray daily?
  1.   five times a day
  2.   every day
  3.   once or twice a week
  4.   once or twice a month
  5.   at no time
  9.   DK

Which, if any, of the following do you believe in? (READ OUT AND CODE ONE
ANSWER FOR EACH)

		YES	NO	DK
162	Do you believe in God?	1	2	9
163	Do you believe in life after death?	1	2	9
164	Do you believe people have a soul?	1	2	9
165	Do you believe in hell?	1	2	9
166	Do you believe in heaven?	1	2	9

167   Do you find that you get comfort and strength from religion?
  1   Yes
  2   No
  9   Don't know [DO NOT READ OUT]

Now, I would like to know your views about a good government. Which of these
traits a good government should have?

		Very important	Important	Somewhat important	Least important	Not important	DK
168	It should make laws according to the people's wishes	1	2	3	4	5	9
169	It should implement only the laws of the shari'a	1	2	3	4	5	9

(*Show Card X*)

170 Apart from weddings and funerals, about how often do you attend religious services these days? (*Code one answer*):

    1 More than once a week
    2 Once a week
    3 Once a month
    4 Only on special holy days
    5 Once a year
    6 Less often
    7 Never, practically never

171 Independently of whether you attend religious services or not, would you say you are (*read out and code one answer*):

    1 A religious person
    2 Not a religious person
    3 An atheist

Generally speaking, do you think that the religious authorities in your country are giving adequate answers to (*read out and code one answer for each*):

		Yes	No
172	The moral problems and needs of the individual	1	2
173	The problems of family life	1	2
174	People's spiritual needs	1	2
175	The social problems facing our society	1	2

(*Show Card Y*)

176 How important is God in your life? Please use this scale to indicate. 10 means "very important" and 1 means "not at all important." (*Code one number*):

Not at all important   Very important

  1   2   3   4   5   6   7   8   9   10

177 Do you take some moments of prayer, meditation or contemplation or something like that?

    1 Yes
    2 No

(*Show Card Z*)

How strongly do you agree or disagree with each of the following statements? (*Read out and code one answer for each statement*):

		Strongly agree	Agree	Neither agree nor disagree	Disagree	Strongly disagree
178	Politicians who do not believe in God are unfit for public office.	1	2	3	4	5
179	Religious leaders should not influence how people vote in elections.	1	2	3	4	5
180	It would be better for Iran if more people with strong religious beliefs held public office.	1	2	3	4	5
181	Religious leaders should not influence government decisions.	1	2	3	4	5

(*Show Card AA*)

Please tell me for each of the following statements whether you think it can always be justified, never be justified, or something in between, using this card. (*Read out and code one answer for each statement*):

	Never justifiable	Always justifiable								
182	Claiming government benefits to which you are not entitled	1	2	3	4	5	6	7	8	9	10
183	Avoiding a fare on public transport	1	2	3	4	5	6	7	8	9	10
184	Cheating on taxes if you have a chance	1	2	3	4	5	6	7	8	9	10
185	Someone accepting a bribe in the course of their duties	1	2	3	4	5	6	7	8	9	10
186	Homosexuality	1	2	3	4	5	6	7	8	9	10
187	Prostitution	1	2	3	4	5	6	7	8	9	10
188	Abortion	1	2	3	4	5	6	7	8	9	10
189	Divorce	1	2	3	4	5	6	7	8	9	10
190	Euthanasia—ending of the life of the incurable sick	1	2	3	4	5	6	7	8	9	10
191	Suicide	1	2	3	4	5	6	7	8	9	10
192	For a man to beat his wife	1	2	3	4	5	6	7	8	9	10

193   How proud are you to be Iranian (*Read out and code one answer*):
    1   Very proud
    2   Quite proud
    3   Not very proud
    4   Not at all proud
    5   I am not Iranian (*do not read out! Code only if volunteered!*)
    *   [*Substitute your own nationality for "French"*]

194   To which of these geographical groups would you say you belong first of all?

Locality or town where you live	1
State or region of country where you live	2
Iran as a whole	3
The Middle East or Islamic world (Rahmat: One or the other not both)	4
The world as a whole	5
Don't know [DO NOT READ OUT]	9

195   Which of the following best describes you?
    1   Above all, I am an Iranian
    2   Above all, I am a Muslim
    3   Above all, I am an Turk
    4   Above all, I am a Kurd
    5   Other

Every country faces a number of regional and international problems. Among the following, which problems do you consider very important (very serious), important, somewhat important, least important, or not important?

		Very important	Important	Somewhat important	Least important	Not important	DK
196	Aggression from a neighboring country	1	2	3	4	5	9
197	The exploitation of this country's natural resources by powerful countries	1	2	3	4	5	9
198	Cultural invasion by the West	1	2	3	4	5	9

199   Do you agree strongly, agree, disagree or disagree strongly with the following statement:
      "Television is my most important form of entertainment."
      1. Agree strongly
      2. Agree
      3. Disagree
      4. Disagree Strongly
      9. DK

Please tell us if you agree strongly, agree, disagree, or disagree strongly with the following:

		Agree strongly	Agree	Disagree	Disagree strongly	DK
200	Iran will be a better society if women are treated with more respect than they are now.	1	2	3	4	9
201	Iran will be a better society if religion and politics are separated.	1	2	3	4	9
202	Iran will be a better society if its government was similar to Western (American or European) governments	1	2	3	4	9

Where would you place the following countries on a scale of morality, where "1" means that society is culturally decadent and people have a very low level of morality, and where "10" means that people in that society have a high level of morality? 99-DK

	Country	Low morality								High morality	
203	Iraq	1	2	3	4	5	6	7	8	9	10
204	Saudi Arabia	1	2	3	4	5	6	7	8	9	10
205	France	1	2	3	4	5	6	7	8	9	10
206	UAE	1	2	3	4	5	6	7	8	9	10
207	Iran	1	2	3	4	5	6	7	8	9	10
208	The U.S.	1	2	3	4	5	6	7	8	9	10
209	Kuwait	1	2	3	4	5	6	7	8	9	10

Where would you place these countries on a scale that measures individual freedom? 99-DK

	Country	Low level of freedom								High level of freedom	
210	Iraq	1	2	3	4	5	6	7	8	9	10
211	Saudi Arabia	1	2	3	4	5	6	7	8	9	10
212	France	1	2	3	4	5	6	7	8	9	10
213	UAE	1	2	3	4	5	6	7	8	9	10
214	Iran	1	2	3	4	5	6	7	8	9	10
215	The U.S.	1	2	3	4	5	6	7	8	9	10
216	Kuwait	1	2	3	4	5	6	7	8	9	10

		Strongly agree	Agree	Disagree	Strongly disagree
217	Islam should be the only religion taught in our public schools.	1	2	3	4
218	I would *not* mind to have teachers who are not religious. *	1	2	3	4
219	Only good Muslims will go to heaven. Non Muslims will not, no matter how good they are. *	1	2	3	4
220	Non-Muslim religions have a lot of weird beliefs and pagan ways. *	1	2	3	4
221	People who belong to different religions are probably just as nice and moral as those who belong to mine	1	2	3	4
222	The religion of Islam is closer to God than other religions.	1	2	3	4
223	It is more important to be a good person than to be a religious person.	1	2	3	4
224	Whenever there is a conflict between science and religion, religion is probably right	1	2	3	4

(*Show Card AB*)

People have different views about themselves and how they relate to the world. Using this card, would you tell me how strongly you agree or disagree with each of the following statements about how you see yourself? (*Read out and code one answer for each statement*):

		Strongly agree	Agree	Disagree	Strongly disagree
225	I see myself as a world citizen.	1	2	3	4
226	I see myself as member of my local community.	1	2	3	4
227	I see myself as citizen of **Iran**	1	2	3	4
228	I see myself as citizen of the Islamic world	1	2	3	4
229	I see myself as an autonomous individual.	1	2	3	4

(*Show Card AC*)

230   What language do you normally speak at home? (*Code one answer!*)

  1   Persian
  2   Azari (Turkish)
  3   Kurdish
  4   Arabic
  6   Other

[*NOTE: modify the list of languages to fit your own society. Optional if only one language is spoken!*]

People use different sources to learn what is going on in their country and the world. For each of the following sources, please indicate whether you used it last week or did not use it last week to obtain information (*read out and code one answer for each*):

		Used it last week	Did not use it last week
231	Daily newspaper	1	2
232	News broadcasts on radio or TV	1	2
233	Books	1	2
234	Internet, Email	1	2
235	Talk with friends or colleagues	1	2

236   How often, if ever, do you use a personal computer? (*Read out and code one answer*):
      1   Never
      2   Occasionally
      3   Frequently
      4   Don't know what a computer is (*do not read out, code only if volunteered!*)

(*Show Card AD*)
237   If there were a national election tomorrow, for which party on this list would you vote? Just call out the number on this card. If you are uncertain, which party appeals to you most? (*Code one answer*):
      01   Fundamentalists
      02   Reformists
      03   Independents
      06   etc.
      [*NOTE: use two-digit code to cover the major parties in given society!*]

238   And which party would be your second choice? If you are uncertain, which one appeals you second most? (*Code one answer*):
      01   Fundamentalists
      02   Reformists
      03   Independents
      06   etc.

239   And is there a party that you would never vote for? (*Code one answer*):
      01   Fundamentalists
      02   Reformists
      03   Independents
      06   etc.

[OPTIONAL]

240   Did you vote in the seventh parliamentary elections? (*Code one answer*):
      1   Yes
      2   No

241   Did you in the 2005 presidential elections?
      1   Yes
      2   No

242 If yes, for which of the candidates did you vote?
  1. Mr. Ahmadinejad
  2. Mr. Karroubi
  3. Mr. Hashemi-Rafsanjani
  4. Mr. Mehralizadeh
  5. Moeen
  6. Qalibaf
  7. Larijani

243 Did you vote in the second round of presidential elections?
  1 Yes
  2 No

244 If yes, to which of the two candidates did you vote? (*Code one answer*):
  1 Mr. Ahmadinejad
  2 Mr. Hashemi-Rafsanjani

DEMOGRAPHICS
245 (*Code respondent's sex by observation*):
  1 Male
  2 Female

246 Can you tell me your year of birth, please? 19___ (*write in last two digits*)

247 This means you are ___ years old (*write in age in two digits*).

248 What is the highest educational level that you have attained? [*NOTE: if respondent indicates to be a student, code highest level s/he expects to complete*]:
  1 No formal education
  2 Incomplete primary school
  3 Complete primary school
  4 Incomplete secondary school: technical/vocational type
  5 Complete secondary school: technical/vocational type
  6 Incomplete secondary: university-preparatory type
  7 Complete secondary: university-preparatory type
  8 Some university-level education, without degree
  9 University-level education, with degree

249 At what age did you (or will you) complete your full time education, either at school or at an institution of higher education? Please exclude apprenticeships [*NOTE: if respondent indicates to be a student, code highest level s/he expects to complete*]:
  _____ (*write in age in two digits*)

250   Do you live with your parents? (*Code one answer*):
      1   Yes
      2   No

251   Are you employed now or not? If yes, about how many hours a week?
      If more than one job: only for the main job (*code one answer*):

      Yes, has paid employment:

      Full time employee (30 hours a week or more)   1
      Part time employee (less than 30 hours a week)   2
      Self employed   3

      No, no paid employment:

      Retired/pensioned   4
      Housewife not otherwise employed   5
      Student   6
      Unemployed   7
      Other (*write in*):_____   8

**(NOTE: If answer is "yes" and respondent has a job, continue with next question.
If no, continue with V249!)**

252   In which profession/occupation do you work? If more than one job,
      the main job? What is/was your job there?
      _____ (*write in and code due to list below but do not
      read out list!*)
      1   Employer/manager of establishment with 10 or more employees
      2   Employer/manager of establishment with less than 10 employees
      3   Professional worker lawyer, accountant, teacher, etc
      4   Supervisory - office worker: supervises others.
      5   Non-manual - office worker: non-supervisory
      6   Foreman and supervisor
      7   Skilled manual worker
      8   Semi-skilled manual worker
      9   Unskilled manual worker
      10   Farmer: has own farm
      11   Agricultural worker
      12   Member of armed forces, security personnel
      13   Never had a job

253   Are you working for the government or for a private business or indus-
      try? (*read out and code one answer*):
      1   Government or public organization
      2   Private businessor industry
      3   Private non-profit organization (if volunteered)

254 Are the tasks you perform at work mostly manual or non-manual? Use this scale where 1 means "mostly manual tasks" and 10 means "mostly non-manual tasks" (*code one answer*):

Mostly manual   Mostly non-manual tasks
tasks

| 1 | 2 | 3 | 4 | 5 | 6 | 7 | 8 | 9 | 10 |

255 Are the tasks you perform at work mostly routine tasks or mostly not routine? Use this scale where 1 means "mostly routine tasks" and 10 means "mostly not routine tasks" (*code one answer*):

Mostly routine tasks   Mostly not routine tasks

| 1 | 2 | 3 | 4 | 5 | 6 | 7 | 8 | 9 | 10 |

256 How much independence do you have in performing your tasks at work? Use this scale to indicate your degree of independence where 1 means "no independence at all" and 10 means "complete independence" (*code one answer*):

No independence at all   Complete independence

| 1 | 2 | 3 | 4 | 5 | 6 | 7 | 8 | 9 | 10 |

257 Do you supervise other people at work? (*Code one answer*):
1 Yes
2 No

258 Are you the chief wage earner in your household? (*Code one answer*):
1 Yes (*in this case skip next two questions and continue with V250*)
2 No (*in this case continue with next question*)

259 Is the chief wage earner of your household employed now or not? (*Code one answer*):
1 Yes
2 No

260 In which profession/occupation does he/she work (or did work)? If more than one job, the main job? What is/was his/her job there?
_____ (*write in and code due to list below but do not read out list!*)
1 Employer/manager of establishment with 10 or more employees
2 Employer/manager of establishment with less than 10 employees
3 Professional worker lawyer, accountant, teacher, etc
4 Supervisory - office worker: supervises others.
5 Non-manual - office worker: non-supervisory

6   Foreman and supervisor
7   Skilled manual worker
8   Semi-skilled manual worker
9   Unskilled manual worker
10 Farmer: has own farm
11 Agricultural worker
12 Member of armed forces, security personnel
13 Never had a job

261 During the past year, did your family (*read out and code one answer*):
1   Save money
2   Just get by
3   Spent some savings
4   Spent savings and borrowed money

262 People sometimes describe themselves as belonging to the working class, the middle class, or the upper or lower class. Would you describe yourself as belonging to the (*read out and code one answer*):
1   Upper class
2   Upper middle class
3   Lower middle class
4   Working class
5   Lower class

(*Show Card AE*)

263 On this card is a scale of incomes on which 1 indicates the "lowest income decile" and 10 the "highest income decile" in your country. We would like to know in what group your household is. Please, specify the appropriate number, counting all wages, salaries, pensions and other incomes that come in. (*Code one number*):

Lowest deciles   Highest deciles

1   2   3   4   5   6   7   8   9   10

264 The ethnicity of the respondents.
1. Fars
2. Turk
3. Kurd
4. Arab
5. Baluch
6. Lor
7. Gilak
66. _____

265   The language of interview
1.   Persian
2.   Turkish
3.   Kurdish
4.   Arabic
5.   Gilaki
6.   Lori
66.   _____

266   (*Code size of town*):
1   Under 2,000
2   2,000 - 5,000
3   5 - 10,000
4   10 - 20,000
5   20 - 50,000
6   50 - 100,000
7   100 - 500,000
8   500,000 and more

Please tell us your view about the following:

267   Stealing other people's property

Not necessarily immoral   totally immoral

1   2   3   4   5   6   7   8   9   10

268   Violence against other people

Not necessarily immoral   totally immoral

1   2   3   4   5   6   7   8   9   10

269   Premarital sex between boys and girls.

Not necessarily immoral   totally immoral

1   2   3   4   5   6   7   8   9   10

270   (*Code how interested the respondent was during the interview*):
1   Respondent was very interested
2   Respondent was somewhat interested
3   Respondent was not interested

271   (*Code region where the interview was conducted*):
Province of Iran   1
[*NOTE: use 2-digit regional code appropriate to your own society*]

272 Weight variable (*Provide a 4-digit weight variable to correct your sample to reflect national distributions of key variables. If no weighting is necessary, simply code each case as "1." It is especially important to correct for education. For example, if your sample contains 10 percent more university-educated respondents as there are in the adult population, members of this group should be downweighted by 10 percent, giving them a weight of .9, coded as "90"*).

WORLD VALUES SURVEY IN LEBANON, 2008

Questionnaire ID, four digit: _____

Kaza: _____   Area: _____

Interviewer: _____   Date: _____

INTRODUCTION BY INTERVIEWER:

Hello. I am from the [NAME OF ORGANIZATION]. We are carrying out a study of what people value in life. This study will interview samples of the adult population of Lebanon. Your name has been selected at random as part of a representative sample of the Lebanese public. I'd like to ask your views on a number of different subjects. You are under no obligation to respond, but your help will contribute to a better understanding of what Lebanese people believe and want out of life. There is no right or wrong answer. Your answers will be completely confidential.

For each of the following, indicate how important it is in your life. Would you say it is?

		Very important	Rather important	Not very important	Not at all important	DK
v1.	Family	1	2	3	4	9
v2.	Friends	1	2	3	4	9
v3.	Leisure time	1	2	3	4	9
v4.	Politics	1	2	3	4	9
v5.	Work	1	2	3	4	9
v6.	Religion	1	2	3	4	9

v7. Taking all things together, would you say you are: [READ OUT]
   1. Very happy
   2. Quite happy
   3. Not very happy
   4. Not at all happy
   9 Don't know [DO NOT READ OUT]

v8. All in all, how would you describe your state of health these days? Would you say it is...? (READ OUT REVERSING ORDER FOR ALTERNATE CONTACTS)
  1. Very Good
  2. Good
  3. Fair
  4. Poor
  9 Don't know [DO NOT READ OUT]

Here is a list of qualities that children can be encouraged to learn at home. Which, if any, do you consider to be especially important? Please choose up to five. (CODE FIVE ONLY)

		Important	Not important	Don't know
v9.	Independence	1	2	9
v10.	Hard work	1	2	9
v11.	Feeling of responsibility	1	2	9
v12.	Imagination	1	2	9
v13.	Tolerance and respect for other people	1	2	9
v14.	Thrift, saving money and things	1	2	9
v15.	Determination, perseverance	1	2	9
v16.	Religious faith	1	2	9
v17.	Unselfishness	1	2	9
v18.	Obedience	1	2	9
v19.	Among these top five important characteristics, which one is number one? ( )			

Now I am going to read off a list of voluntary organizations. For each one, could you tell me whether you are an active member, an inactive member or not a member of that type of organization? (*Read out and code one answer for each organization*):

		Active member	Inactive member	Don't belong
v20.	Religious organization	2	1	0
v21.	Sport or recreational organization	2	1	0
v22.	Art, music or educational organization	2	1	0
v23.	Labor Union	2	1	0

		Active member	Inactive member	Don't belong
v24.	Political party	2	1	0
v25.	Environmental organization	2	1	0
v26.	Professional association	2	1	0
v27.	Humanitarian or charitable organization	2	1	0
v28.	Consumer organization	2	1	0

v29. Generally speaking, would you say that most people can be trusted or that you need to be very careful in dealing with people?
   1 Most people can be trusted.
   2 Need to be very careful.
   9 Don't know [DO NOT READ OUT]

v30. Do you think most people would try to take advantage of you if they got a chance, or would they try to be fair? Please show your response, where 1 means that "people would try to take advantage of you," and 10 means that "people would try to be fair" (code one number):

People would try to take advantage of you								People would try to be fair	
1	2	3	4	5	6	7	8	9	10

v31. Do you think most men would try to take advantage of women if they got a chance, or would they try to be fair? Please show your response, where 1 means that "men would try to take advantage of women," and 10 means that "men would try to be fair" (code one number):

Men would try to take advantage of women								Men would try to be fair toward women	
1	2	3	4	5	6	7	8	9	10

v32. When you get together with your friends or relatives, would you say you discuss political matters frequently, occasionally or never?
   1. Frequently
   2. Occasionally
   3. Never
   9 Don't know [DO NOT READ OUT]

I'd like to ask you how much you trust people from various groups: Could you tell me for each whether you trust people from this group completely, somewhat, not very much or not at all? (Read out and code one answer for each):

		Trust completely	Trust somewhat	Do not trust very much	Do not trust at all
v33.	Your family	1	2	3	4
v34.	Your neighborhood	1	2	3	4
v35.	People you know personally	1	2	3	4
v36.	People you meet for the first time	1	2	3	4
v37.	People of another religion	1	2	3	4
v38.	People of another nationality	1	2	3	4

On this list are various groups of people. Could you please sort out any that you would not like to have as neighbors? (CODE AN ANSWER FOR EACH)

		Don't like	Like
v39.	Sunnis	1	2
v40.	Christians	1	2
v41.	Shi'as	1	2
v42.	Druze	1	2
v43.	French	1	2
v44.	Saudis	1	2
v45.	Jews	1	2
v46.	Iranians	1	2
v47.	Syrians	1	2
v48.	Palestinians	1	2
v49.	Americans	1	2

Do you agree, disagree or neither agree nor disagree with the following statements? (*Read out and code one answer for each statement*):

		Strongly agree	Agree	Disagree	Strongly disagree	DK
v50.	When jobs are scarce, men should have more right to a job than women	1	2	3	4	99
v51.	When jobs are scarce, employers should give priority to **Lebanese** people over immigrants.	1	2	3	4	99

v52. How satisfied are you with the financial situation of your household? If "1" means you are completely dissatisfied on this scale, and "10" means you are completely satisfied, where would you put your satisfaction with your household's financial situation?

Completely Dissatisfied   Completely Satisfied

   1   2   3   4   5   6   7   8   9   10

v53. All things considered, how satisfied are you with your life as a whole these days? Please use the following scale from one to ten to answer.

Completely Dissatisfied   Completely Satisfied

   1   2   3   4   5   6   7   8   9   10

v54. Some people feel they have completely free choice and control over their lives, while other people feel that what they do has no real effect on what happens to them. Please use this scale where 1 means "none at all" and 10 means "a great deal" to indicate how much freedom of choice and control you feel you have over the way your life turns out.

None at all   A great deal

   1   2   3   4   5   6   7   8   9   10

v55. To what extent are you optimistic/pessimistic about your future?

Highly pessimistic   Highly Optimistic

   1   2   3   4   5   6   7   8   9   10

v56. Do you strongly agree, agree, disagree, or strongly disagree that in Lebanon these days, life is unpredictable and dangerous?

Agree strongly	Agree	Disagree	Strongly disagree	DK
1	2	3	4	9

v57. Are you currently (READ OUT AND CODE ONE ONLY)
  1   Married
  2   Living together as married
  3   Divorced
  4   Separated
  5   Widowed
  6   Single

  IF not single:
v58. Where did you live during the first year after the marriage?
  1.   With your own parents
  2.   With your spouse's parents (in-laws)
  3.   In a separate house
  4.   With your brother
  97. Other _____

  ASK ALL RESPONDENTS:
v59. Have you had any children? How many?
  0   No child
  1   1 child
  2   2 children
  3   3 children
  4   4 children
  5   5 children
  6   6 children
  7   7 children
  8   8 or more children
  9   No answer

v60. If someone says a child needs a home with both a father and a mother to grow up happily, would you tend to agree or disagree? (*Code one answer*):
  1.   Tend to agree
  2.   Tend to disagree

v61. Do you agree or disagree with the following statement (*read out*):
  "Marriage is an out-dated institution." (*Code one answer*):
  1.   Agree
  2.   Disagree

v62. If a woman wants to have a child as a single parent but she doesn't want to have a stable relationship with a man, do you approve or disapprove? (*Code one answer*):
  1. Approve
  2. Disapprove
  3. Depends (*do not read out, code only if volunteered*)

v63. What do you think is the ideal size of the family – how many children, if any?
  0   None
  1   1 child
  2   2 children
  3   3 children
  4   4 children
  5   5 children
  6   6 children
  7   7 children
  8   8 or more children
  9   DK, no answer

v64. Do you think that a woman has to have children in order to be fulfilled or is this not necessary?
  1   Needs children
  2   Not necessary
  9   Don't know [DO NOT READ OUT]

For each of the following statements I read out, can you tell me how much you agree with each. Do you agree strongly, agree, disagree, or disagree strongly?

		Agree strongly	Agree	Disagree	Strongly disagree	DK
v65.	One of my main goals in life has been to make my parents proud	1	2	3	4	9
v66.	On the whole, men make better political leaders than women do	1	2	3	4	9
v67.	A university education is more important for a boy than for a girl	1	2	3	4	9
v68.	On the whole, men make better business executives than women do	1	2	3	4	9

v69. In your view, which of the following is the more important basis for marriage:

1. Parental approval
2. Love
3. DK

In your opinion, how important are each of the following traits in a woman?

		Very important	Important	Somewhat important	Not very important	Not at all important	DK
v70.	a) (*For Muslim respondents*): Wearing a veil in public places b) (*For Christian respondents*): Dressing modestly in public	1	2	3	4	5	9
v71.	Being a good mother	1	2	3	4	5	9
v72.	Being a good wife	1	2	3	4	5	9
v73.	Being religious	1	2	3	4	5	9
v74.	Being educated	1	2	3	4	5	9
v75.	Having a job outside the home	1	2	3	4	5	9

There are different Islamic countries. And in each country people have different understanding of their religion and issues facing their faith. We would like to know how you feel about the following issue:

		Strongly agree	Agree	Disagree	Strongly disagree	DK
v76.	It is up to a woman to dress whichever way she wants to	1	2	3	4	9

I would like to ask your personal opinion about the following issues related to relationships between men and women.
INTERVIEWER: This same style should be used in asking both questions.

		Strongly agree	Agree	Neither agree or disagree	Disagree	DK
v77.	It is acceptable for a man to have more than one wife	1	2	3	5	9
v78.	A wife must always obey her husband.	1	2	3	5	9

v79. If you had to choose, which of the following statements would you say is most important?

Code one answer only

	First choice
Maintaining order in the nation	1
Giving people more say in important government decisions	2
Fighting rising prices	3
Protecting freedom of speech	4
Don't know [DO NOT READ OUT]	9

v80. And, which one is the second most important

	Second choice
Maintaining order in the nation	1
Giving people more say in important government decisions	2
Fighting rising prices	3
Protecting freedom of speech	4
Don't know [DO NOT READ OUT]	9

v81. People sometimes talk about what the aims of this country should be for the next ten years. Different people would give top priority to the following goals: Would you please say which one of these you would consider the most important? (*Code one answer only under "first choice"*)

	First choice
A high level of economic growth	1
Making sure this country has strong defense forces	2
Seeing that people have more say about how things are done at their jobs and in their communities	3
Trying to make our cities and countryside more beautiful	4

v82. And which would be the next most important? (*Code one answer only under "second choice"*)

	Second choice
A high level of economic growth	1
Making sure this country has strong defense forces	2
Seeing that people have more say about how things are done at their jobs and in their communities	3
Trying to make our cities and countryside more beautiful	4

v83. In your opinion, which one of these is most important? (*Code one answer only under "first choice"*):

	First choice
A stable economy	1
Progress toward a less impersonal and more humane society	2
Progress toward a society in which Ideas count more than money	3
The fight against crime	4

v84. And what would be the next most important? (*Code one answer only under "second choice"*):

	Second choice
A stable economy	1
Progress toward a less impersonal and more humane society	2
Progress toward a society in which Ideas count more than money	3
The fight against crime	4

v85. Some people feel that there are so many rules and regulations in society that sometime overwhelm the individuals and undermine their freedom of choice. Other people feel that there are no regulations at all, society is affected and people are disoriented. Now, on the scale of one to ten, one being "too few regulations and rules" and ten being "too many regulations and rules" how do you rank your society on this scale?

Too few regulations and rules   Too many regulations and rules

1   2   3   4   5   6   7   8   9   10

v86. Of course, we all hope that there will not be another war, but if it were to come to that, would you be willing to fight for your country? (*Code one answer*):
1. Yes
2. No

v87. How interested would you say you are in politics?
1   Very interested
2   Somewhat interested
3   Not very interested
4   Not at all interested
9   Don't know [DO NOT READ OUT]

Now I'd like you to tell me your views on various issues. How would you place your views on this scale? 1 means you agree completely with the statement on the left; 10 means you agree completely with the statement on the right; and if your views fall somewhere in between, you can choose any number in between.

v88.   Incomes should be   We need larger income differences
        made more equal   as incentives for individuals

        1   2   3   4   5   6   7   8   9   10
        DK=99

v89.   Private ownership of   Government ownership of
        business and industry   business and industry should
        should be increased   be increased

        1   2   3   4   5   6   7   8   9   10
        DK=99

v90.   In the long run, hard   Hard work doesn't generally
        work usually brings a   bring success—it's more a
        better life   matter of luck and
                                            connections

        1   2   3   4   5   6   7   8   9   10
        DK=99

v91.   People can only get rich at   Wealth can grow so there's
        the expense of others   enough for everyone

        1   2   3   4   5   6   7   8   9   10
        DK=99

v92.   Competition is good. It   Competition is
        stimulates people to work   harmful. It brings out
        hard and develop new ideas   the worst in people

        1   2   3   4   5   6   7   8   9   10
        DK=99

v93.   The government should take   People should take
        more responsibility to ensure   more responsibility to
        that everyone is provided for   provide for
                                            themselves

        1   2   3   4   5   6   7   8   9   10
        DK=99

v94. Some people believe that individuals can decide their own destiny, while others think that it is impossible to escape a predetermined fate. Please tell me which comes closest to your view on this scale on which 1 means "everything in life is determined by fate," and 10 means that "people shape their fate themselves." (*Code one number*):

Everything is determined by fate							People shape their fate themselves		
1	2	3	4	5	6	7	8	9	10

I'm going to read out a list of various changes in our way of life that might take place in the near future. Please tell me for each one, if it were to happen, whether you think it would be a good thing, a bad thing, or don't you mind? (*Code one answer for each*):

		Good	Don't mind	Bad
v95.	Less importance placed on work in our lives	1	2	3
v96.	More emphasis on the development of technology	1	2	3
v97.	Greater respect for authority	1	2	3
v98.	More emphasis on family life	1	2	3

I am going to name a number of groups and organizations. For each one, could you tell me how much confidence you have in them: is it a great deal of confidence, quite a lot of confidence, not very much confidence or none at all?

		A great deal	Quite a lot	Not very much	None at all	DK
v99.	Religious institutions	1	2	3	4	9
v100.	The Lebanese armed forces	1	2	3	4	9
v101.	The press	1	2	3	4	9
v102.	Lebanese television	1	2	3	4	9
v103.	Non-Lebanese television	1	2	3	4	9
v104.	Labor unions	1	2	3	4	9
v105.	The police	1	2	3	4	9
v106.	The courts	1	2	3	4	9
v107.	The government	1	2	3	4	9
v108.	Political parties	1	2	3	4	9
v109.	Parliament	1	2	3	4	9
v110.	The Civil service	1	2	3	4	9
v111.	Major Companies	1	2	3	4	9

		A great deal	Quite a lot	Not very much	None at all	DK
v112.	Environmental organizations	1	2	3	4	9
v113.	Women's organizations	1	2	3	4	9
v114.	Charitable or humanitarian organizations	1	2	3	4	9
v115.	The Arab League	1	2	3	4	9
v116.	The United Nations	1	2	3	4	9

v117. People have different views about the ideal way of governing this country. Here is a scale for rating how well the government is doing: 1 means very bad; 10 means very good.
What point on this scale would you choose to describe how well the government is doing?

1 2 3 4 5 6 7 8 9 10
Very bad   Very good

v118. How satisfied are you with the way the government is handling the country's affairs? Would you say you are very satisfied, fairly satisfied, fairly dissatisfied or very dissatisfied?
1. Very satisfied
2. Fairly satisfied
3. Fairly dissatisfied
4. Very dissatisfied
9. DK

v119. How important is it for you to live in a country that is governed democratically? On this scale where 1 means it is "not at all important" and 10 means "absolutely important" what position would you choose? (*Code one number*):

Not at all   Absolutely
important   important
1 2 3 4 5 6 7 8 9 10

v120. And how democratically is this country being governed today? Again using a scale from 1 to 10, where 1 means that it is "not at all democratic" and 10 means that it is "completely democratic," what position would you choose? (*Code one number*):

Completely   Completely
authoritarian   democratic
1 2 3 4 5 6 7 8 9 10

v121. Which of these problems do you consider the most serious one in your **own country**? (*Code one answer under "most serious for own country"*):

	Most serious in Lebanon
– People living in poverty and need.	1
– Discrimination against female.	2
– Poor sanitation and infectious diseases.	3
– Inadequate education.	4
– Environmental pollution.	5

v122. And which is the next most serious **for your own country**? (*Code one answer under "next most serious for own country"*):

	Next most serious Lebanon
– People living in poverty and need.	1
– Discrimination of female.	2
– Poor sanitation and infectious diseases.	3
– Inadequate education.	4
– Environmental pollution.	5

v123. Thinking at your own country's problems, should your country's leaders give top priority to help reducing poverty in the world or should they give top priority to solve your own country's problems? Use this scale where 1 means "top priority to help reducing misery in the world" and 10 means "top priority to solve my own country's problems." (*Code one answer*):

Top priority to help reducing poverty in the world							Top priority to solve my own country's problems		
1	2	3	4	5	6	7	8	9	10

I'm going to describe various types of political systems and ask what you think about each as a way of governing this country. For each one, would you say it is a very good, fairly good, fairly bad or very bad way of governing this country?

		Very good	Fairly good	Fairly bad	Very bad	DK
v124.	Having a strong head of government who does not have to bother with parliament and elections	1	2	3	4	9
v125.	Having technocrats, not government, make decisions according to what they think is best for the country	1	2	3	4	9

		Very good	Fairly good	Fairly bad	Very bad	DK
v126.	Having the army rule	1	2	3	4	9
v127.	Having a democratic political system	1	2	3	4	9
v128.	a) For Muslim respondents: Having an Islamic government, where religious authorities have absolute power b) For Christian respondents: Having a Christian government, where religious authorities have absolute power	1	2	3	4	9

Some people say that democracy may have problems but it's better than any other form of government system. Could you please tell me if you agree strongly, agree, disagree or disagree strongly, with this statement?

		Agree strongly	Agree	Disagree	Strongly disagree	DK
v129.	Democracy may have problems but it's better than any other form of government	1	2	3	4	9

Many things may be desirable, but not all of them are essential characteristics of democracy. Please tell me for each of the following things how essential you think it is as a characteristic of democracy. Use this scale where 1 means "not at all an essential characteristic of democracy" and 10 means it definitely is "an essential characteristic of democracy" (*read out and code one answer for each*):

		Not essential									Essential
		1	2	3	4	5	6	7	8	9	10
v130.	Governments tax the rich and subsidize the poor.	1	2	3	4	5	6	7	8	9	10
v131.	Religious authorities interpret the laws.	1	2	3	4	5	6	7	8	9	10
v132.	People choose their leaders in free elections.	1	2	3	4	5	6	7	8	9	10
v133.	People receive state aid for unemployment.	1	2	3	4	5	6	7	8	9	10
v134.	The army takes over when government is incompetent.	1	2	3	4	5	6	7	8	9	10
v135.	Civil rights protect people's liberty against oppression.	1	2	3	4	5	6	7	8	9	10

		Not essential									Essential
v136.	The economy is prospering.	1	2	3	4	5	6	7	8	9	10
v137.	Criminals are severely punished.	1	2	3	4	5	6	7	8	9	10
v138.	People can change the laws in referendums.	1	2	3	4	5	6	7	8	9	10
v139.	Women have the same rights as men.	1	2	3	4	5	6	7	8	9	10
v140.	The political leader should stay in power only for a limited number of years	1	2	3	4	5	6	7	8	9	10
v141.	People should be free to recall their political leaders, if they fail to perform	1	2	3	4	5	6	7	8	9	10

I'm going to read out some forms of political action that people can take, and I'd like you to tell me, for each one, whether you have done any of these things, whether you might do it or would never under any circumstances do it (*read out and code one answer for each action*):

	Have done	Might do	Would never do
v142. Signing a petition	1	2	3
v143. Joining in boycotts	1	2	3
v144. Attending peaceful demonstrations	1	2	3

Now I will briefly describe some people. Using the following statements, would you please indicate for each description whether that person is very much like you, like you, somewhat like you, not like you, or not at all like you? (*Code one answer for each description*):

	Very much like me	Like me	Some-what like me	A little like me	Not like me	Not at all like me
v145. It is important to this person to think up new ideas and be creative; to do things one's own way.	1	2	3	4	5	6
v146. It is important to this person to be rich; to have a lot of money and expensive things.	1	2	3	4	5	6
v147. Living in secure surroundings is important to this person; to avoid anything that might be dangerous.	1	2	3	4	5	6

	Very much like me	Like me	Some-what like me	A little like me	Not like me	Not at all like me
v148. It is important to this person to have a good time; to "spoil" oneself.	1	2	3	4	5	6
v149. It is important to this person to help the people nearby; to care for their well-being.	1	2	3	4	5	6
v150. Being very successful is important to this person; to have people recognize one's achievements.	1	2	3	4	5	6
v151. Adventure and taking risks are important to this person; to have an exciting life.	1	2	3	4	5	6
v152. It is important to this person to always behave properly; to avoid doing anything people would say is wrong.	1	2	3	4	5	6
v153. Looking after the environment is important to this person; to care for nature.	1	2	3	4	5	6
v154. Tradition is important to this person; to follow the customs handed down by one's religion or family.	1	2	3	4	5	6

v155. Generally speaking, would you say that this country's economy is run by a
few big influential people and organizations that are looking out for
themselves only or that it is run for the benefit of all the people?
1   Run by a few big interests
2   Run for all the people
9   Don't know [DO NOT READ OUT]

v156. How often, if at all, do you think about the meaning and purpose of life?
(READ OUT IN REVERSE ORDER FOR ALTERNATE CONTACTS)
1   Often
2   Sometimes
3   Rarely
4   Never

v157. If I asked you about your religion, what do you prefer your answer to be?
1. Shi'a
2. Sunni
3. Druze
4. Maronite
5. Greek Orthodox
6. Melkite Catholic
7. Roman Catholic
8. Armenian Orthodox
9. Armenian Catholic
10. Protestant
11. Syrian Catholic
12. Syrian Orthodox
13. Chaldean
14. Assyrian
15. Copt
16. Isma'ilite
17. Alawite
18. Nusayri
19. Other

v158. Apart from funerals, about how often do you go to a mosque/church these days?
1 More than once a week
2 Once a week
3 Once a month
4 Only on special holy days
5 Once a year
6 Rarely
7 I do not go to mosque/church

v159. How often do you pray?
1. five times a day
2. every day
3. once or twice a week
4. once or twice a month
5. Never

v160. Independently of whether you go to religious services or not, would you say you are...
1. Religious
2. Not religious
3. Atheist

Generally speaking, do you think that the religious authorities in this country are giving adequate answers to (Read out and code one answer for each)

		Yes	No	DK
v161.	The moral problems and needs of the individual	1	2	9
v162.	The problems of family life	1	2	9
v163.	People's spiritual needs	1	2	9
v164.	The social problems facing your country today	1	2	9

Please forgive for asking these questions. I know that answers to some or all these questions may be obvious. But since we compare the results of this study with many other countries, and since some people in other countries may have much weaker religious beliefs than Lebanese, we ask these questions for the sake of comparison. Which, if any, of the following do you believe in?
(*READ OUT AND CODE ONE ANSWER FOR EACH*)

		Yes	No	DK
v165.	Do you believe in God?	1	2	9
v166.	Do you believe in life after death?	1	2	9
v167.	Do you believe people have a soul?	1	2	9
v168.	Do you believe in hell?	1	2	9
v169.	Do you believe in heaven?	1	2	9

v170. How important is God in your life? Please use this scale to indicate: 10 means very important and 1 means not at all important.

Not at all important   Very important

    1   2   3   4   5   6   7   8   9   10

v171. Do you find that you get comfort and strength from religion?

    1   Yes
    2   No
    9   Don't know [DO NOT READ OUT]

How much do you agree or disagree with each of the following statements?

		Agree Strongly	Agree	Neither agree nor disagree	Disagree	Strongly disagree	DK
v172.	Politicians who do not believe in God are unfit to work for the government in high offices	1	2	3	4	5	9
v173.	Religious leaders should not interfere in politics	1	2	3	4	5	9
v174.	It would be better for Lebanon if more people with strong religious beliefs held public office	1	2	3	4	5	9

Now, I would like to know your views about a good government. How important is each of the following traits for a good government?

		Very important	Important	Somewhat important	Least important	Not important	DK
v175.	It should make laws according to the people's wishes	1	2	3	4	5	9
v176.	a) (For Muslim respondents): It should implement only the laws of the shari'a b) (For Christian respondents): It should adopt only the laws inspired by Christian values	1	2	3	4	5	9

I am going to name a number of groups. For each one, could you tell me how much trust, in general, you have in them: is it a great deal of trust, some trust, not very much trust or none at all?

		A great deal	Some	Not very much	None at all	DK
v177.	Shi'a	1	2	3	4	9
v178.	Sunni	1	2	3	4	9
v179.	Druze	1	2	3	4	9
v180.	Maronites	1	2	3	4	9
v181.	Catholics	1	2	3	4	9
v182.	Orthodox	1	2	3	4	9

Thinking about what should change to make your country a better place to live, and please tell us if you agree strongly, agree, disagree, or disagree strongly with the following:

	Lebanon will be a better society ..	Agree strongly	Agree	Disagree	Disagree strongly	DK
v183.	If religion and politics are separated	1	2	3	4	9
v184.	If its government was similar to Western (American or European) governments	1	2	3	4	9
v185.	Lebanon will be a better place if people treat one another as Lebanese rather than on the basis of their confession	1	2	3	4	9

Where would you place the following countries on a scale of morality, where "1" means that society is culturally decadent and people have a very low level of morality, and where "10" means that people in that society have a high level of morality? 99-DK

	Country	Low morality							High morality		
v186.	Lebanon	1	2	3	4	5	6	7	8	9	10
v187.	Saudi Arabia	1	2	3	4	5	6	7	8	9	10
v188.	France	1	2	3	4	5	6	7	8	9	10
v189.	China	1	2	3	4	5	6	7	8	9	10
v190.	Iran	1	2	3	4	5	6	7	8	9	10
v191.	The U.S.	1	2	3	4	5	6	7	8	9	10
v192.	Syria	1	2	3	4	5	6	7	8	9	10

Where would you place these countries on a scale that measures individual freedom? 99-DK

	Country	Low level of freedom					High level of freedom				
v193.	Lebanon	1	2	3	4	5	6	7	8	9	10
v194.	Saudi Arabia	1	2	3	4	5	6	7	8	9	10
v195.	France	1	2	3	4	5	6	7	8	9	10
v196.	China	1	2	3	4	5	6	7	8	9	10
v197.	Iran	1	2	3	4	5	6	7	8	9	10
v198.	The U.S.	1	2	3	4	5	6	7	8	9	10
v199.	Syria	1	2	3	4	5	6	7	8	9	10

Now we would like you to consider how developed different places in the world are. Here is a scale of development—with the least developed places in the world marked 1 at the left and the most developed places in the world marked ten at the right. And, moderately developed places marked 5 in the middle. I will read to you a list of countries that includes Lebanon, Saudi Arabia, China and the United States and ask you to rate the level of development in each country.

	Country	Least developed							Most developed		
v200.	Lebanon	1	2	3	4	5	6	7	8	9	10
v201.	Saudi Arabia	1	2	3	4	5	6	7	8	9	10
v202.	France	1	2	3	4	5	6	7	8	9	10
v203.	China	1	2	3	4	5	6	7	8	9	10
v204.	Iran	1	2	3	4	5	6	7	8	9	10
v205.	The U.S.	1	2	3	4	5	6	7	8	9	10
v206.	Syria	1	2	3	4	5	6	7	8	9	10

Now, I would like to know your opinion about the following issues:

(Interviewers should distinguish between Muslim and Christian respondents and accordingly ask questions)	Strongly agree	Agree	Disagree	Strongly disagree
v207. Islam (Christianity) should be the only religion taught in our public schools.	1	2	3	4
v208. I would *not* mind to have teachers who are not religious.*	1	2	3	4
v209. Only good Muslims [Christians] will go to heaven. Non Muslims [Christians] will not, no matter how good they are.*	1	2	3	4
v210. Non-Muslim [Christians] religions have a lot of weird beliefs and pagan ways.*	1	2	3	4
v211. People who belong to different religions are probably just as nice and moral as those who belong to mine.	1	2	3	4
v212. The religion of Islam [Christianity] is closer to God than other religions.	1	2	3	4
v213. It is more important to be a good person than to be a religious person.	1	2	3	4
v214. Whenever there is a conflict between science and religion, religion is probably right	1	2	3	4

People have different views about themselves and how they relate to the world. Would you tell me how strongly you agree or disagree with each of the following statements about how you see yourself? (*Read out and code one answer for each statement*):

	Strongly agree	Agree	Disagree	Strongly disagree
v215. I see myself as a world citizen.	1	2	3	4
v216. I see myself as member of my local community.	1	2	3	4
v217. I see myself as citizen of **Lebanon**	1	2	3	4
v218. I see myself as citizen of the Islamic world.	1	2	3	4
v219. I see myself as an autonomous individual.	1	2	3	4
v220. I see myself as a citizen of the Arab world.	1	2	3	4

People use different sources to learn what is going on in their country and the world. For each of the following sources, please indicate whether you used it last week or did not use it last week to obtain information (*read out and code one answer for each*):

		Used it last week	Did not use it last week
v221.	Daily newspaper	1	2
v222.	News broadcasts on radio or TV	1	2
v223.	Books	1	2
v224.	Internet, Email	1	2
v225.	Talk with friends or colleagues	1	2

v226. How often, if ever, do you use a personal computer? (*Read out and code one answer*):
  5. Never
  6. Occasionally
  7. Frequently
  8. Don't know what a computer is (do not read out, code only if volunteered!)

Now let's consider environmental problems in the world as a whole. Please, tell me how serious you consider each of the following to be for the world as a whole. Is it very serious, somewhat serious, not very serious or not serious at all? (*Read out and code one answer for each problem*):

		Very serious	Somewhat serious	Not very serious	Not serious at all
v227.	Global warming or the greenhouse effect.	1	2	3	4
v228.	Loss of plant or animal species or biodiversity.	1	2	3	4
v229.	Pollution of rivers, lakes and oceans.	1	2	3	4

To what extent, if any, do you think each of the following would be an obstacle for the formation of an independent prosperous Lebanon?

		A great deal	Quite a lot	Not very much	None at all	DK
v230.	Syrian gains too much power in Lebanon.	1	2	3	4	9
v231.	The U.S. gains too much power in Lebanon.	1	2	3	4	9
v232.	Civil war breaks out in Lebanon.	1	2	3	4	9
v233.	Iran gains too much influence in Lebanon	1	2	3	4	9
v234.	Israel gains too much influence in Lebanon	1	2	3	4	9

Please tell me for each of the following statements whether you think it can always be justified, never be justified, or something in between. (*Read out and code one answer for each statement*):

		Never justifiable								Always justifiable	
v235.	Claiming government benefits to which you are not entitled	1	2	3	4	5	6	7	8	9	10
v236.	Cheating on taxes if you have a chance	1	2	3	4	5	6	7	8	9	10
v237.	Homosexuality	1	2	3	4	5	6	7	8	9	10
v238.	Prostitution	1	2	3	4	5	6	7	8	9	10
v239.	Euthanasia—ending of the life of the incurable sick	1	2	3	4	5	6	7	8	9	10
v240.	Suicide	1	2	3	4	5	6	7	8	9	10
v241.	For a man to beat his wife	1	2	3	4	5	6	7	8	9	10

Please tell me for each of the following statements whether you think it can always be justified, never be justified, or something in between. READ OUT STATEMENTS. CODE ONE ANSWER FOR EACH STATEMENT

v242. Someone accepting a bribe in the course of their duties
       Never   Always
       justifiable   justifiable
       1   2   3   4   5   6   7   8   9   10

v243. Abortion
       Never   Always
       justifiable   justifiable
       1   2   3   4   5   6   7   8   9   10

v244. Divorce
       Never   Always
       justifiable   justifiable
       1   2   3   4   5   6   7   8   9   10

v245. Drinking alcoholic beverages
       Never   Always
       justifiable   justifiable
       1   2   3   4   5   6   7   8   9   10

v246. Below are three types of behavior. Which of the three is the most immoral
       behavior?
       5.   Stealing other people's property
       6.   Violence against other people
       7.   Premarital sex between boys and girls.

v247. How proud are you to be Lebanese?
       7   Very proud
       8   Quite proud
       9   Not very proud
       10   Not at all proud
       9.   Don't know [DO NOT READ OUT]

v248. Which of the following best describes you?
       5.   Above all, I am a Lebanese
       6.   Above all, I am a Muslim
       7.   Above all, I am an Arab
       8.   Above all, I am a Christian
       9.   Other

v249. What language do you normally speak at home?
    1.   Arabic
    2.   English
    3.   French
    4.   Other

v250. If there were national elections in the near future, which party on this list would you vote for?

1.	Armenian Revolutionary Federation	حز ا بـلطشنق
2.	Democratic Left	حرآةا ليسا ر لدمقراطي
3.	Democratic Renewal	حرآةا لتجدا دلـدييموقرّاطي
4.	El Marada Movement	تيا ا ر لمرةد
5.	Free Patriotic Movement	التيا ر لوطني"الحر
6.	Free Shiite movement	النيا ر الشيعيّا لحر
7.	Future Movement	تيا ا ر لمستقبّل
8.	Hezbollah	حز ا بـالله
9.	Hope Movement or Amal Movement	حرآةأ مل
10.	Islamic Group	الجماعةا لإسلامية
11.	Lebanese Forces	القوا تـللبنانية
12.	National Liberal Party	حز ا بـلوطنيينا لأحررا
13.	North Metn Bloc (Murr Bloc)	تكتلا لمتنا لشمالي
14.	Phalanges Party	حز ا بـلكتائب للبّنانية
15.	Popular Bloc (Skaff Bloc)	التكّتلا لشعبي
16.	Progressive Socialist Party	التقدمي ا لحز آ بـلإشنر آلي
17.	Syrian Social Nationalist Party	الحزا تـلقومي ا لسوا ير لإجتماعي
18.	Tripoli Bloc	التكّتلا لطرابّلسي
19.	Other	غيره
20.	I have not voted	لما قترع

v251. If "Other", then which party or independent person appeals to you the most? (   )

v252. And is there any party on this list that you would never vote for? (   )
Use the same code from the list above

v253. Did you vote in the parliamentary elections in 2005?
Yes
No

v254. If yes, whom did you vote for? : (   )
    97.   Other

Some people believe that Lebanon is experiencing considerable political problems and violence nowadays, and some of these problems are caused by foreign countries. In your opinion, how do you rate the role of the following countries in affecting these conditions in Lebanon? "1" means very negative and "5" means very positive.

		Very negative			Very positive	
v255.	Iran	1	2	3	4	5
v256.	Syria	1	2	3	4	5
v257.	Saudi Arabia	1	2	3	4	5
v258.	the U.S.	1	2	3	4	5
v259.	Israel	1	2	3	4	5
v260.	France	1	2	3	4	5

DEMOGRAPHICS

v261. Sex of respondent:
1. Male
2. Female

v262. Can you tell me your year of birth, please? 19____
[ENTER ONLY THE LAST TWO DIGITS OF THE YEAR: "19" IS ASSUMED]

v263. This means you are __ __ years old.

v264. What is the highest educational level that you have attained?
10 No formal education
11 Incomplete primary school
12 Complete primary school
13 Incomplete secondary school: technical/vocational type
14 Complete secondary school: technical/vocational type
15 Incomplete secondary: university-preparatory type
16 Complete secondary: university-preparatory type
17 Some university-level education, without degree
18 University-level education, with degree

v265. [Asked in 2008] At what age *did you* complete your full time education, either at school or at an institution of higher education? Please exclude apprenticeships:
WRITE IN AGE IN YEARS _____

v266. [If student] [Asked in 2008] At what age *will you* complete your full time education, either at school or at an institution of higher education? Please exclude apprenticeships:
WRITE IN AGE IN YEARS _____

v267. Do you live with your parents?
    1 Yes
    2 No

v268. Are you employed now or not?
    1 Yes
    2 No
    IF YES:

v269. About how many hours do you work per week? If you have more than one job: specify only the main job
    Has paid employment

– Full time (30 hours a week or more)	1
– Part time (less than 30 hours a week)	2
– Self employed	3

    IF NO:

v270. Reason for unemployment
    IF no paid employment

– Retired/pensioned	1
– Housewife not otherwise employed	2
– Student	3
– Inability to find a job	4
– Disabled	5
– Lack of jobs	6
– Old age	7
– Lost job	8
– Other	97

v271. Are the tasks you perform at work mostly manual or non-manual? Use this scale where 1 means "mostly manual tasks" and 10 means "mostly non-manual tasks" (*code one answer*):

Mostly manual tasks   Mostly non-manual tasks
    1   2   3   4   5   6   7   8   9   10

v272. Are the tasks you perform at work mostly routine tasks or mostly not routine? Use this scale where 1 means "mostly routine tasks" and 10 means "mostly not routine tasks" (*code one answer*):

Mostly routine tasks   Mostly not routine tasks
    1   2   3   4   5   6   7   8   9   10

v273. How much independence do you have in performing your tasks at work?
Use this scale to indicate your degree of independence where 1 means "no
independence at all" and 10 means "complete independence" (*code one
answer*):

No independence at all   Complete independence

   1   2   3   4   5   6   7   8   9   10

v274. Are you the chief wage earner in your household?
    1- Yes   (skip v275-276)
    2- No go 275

v275. Is the chief wage earner employed now or not?
    1   Yes
    2   No

v276. In which profession/occupation does he/she work? (or did work) If more
than one job, the main job? What is/was his/her job there? *CODE BELOW*
    3. Employer/manager of establishment with 10 or more employees
    4. Employer/manager of establishment with less than 10 employees
    5. Professional worker lawyer, accountant, teacher, etc.
    6. Supervisory non-manual - office worker.
    7. Non-manual - office worker: non-supervisory
    8. Foreman and supervisor
    9. Skilled manual worker
  10. Semi-skilled manual worker
  11. Unskilled manual worker
  12. Farmer: has own farm
  13. Agricultural worker
  14. Member of armed forces, security personnel
  15. Never had a job

v277. During the past year, did your family:
    4. Save money
    5. Just get by
    6. Spent some savings
    7. Spent savings and borrowed money
  10. DK, NA

v278. People sometimes describe themselves as belonging to the working class, the middle class, or the upper or lower class. Would you describe yourself as belonging to the:
   3 Upper class
   4 Upper middle class
   5 Lower middle class
   6 Working class
   7 Lower class
   9. Don't know [DO NOT READ OUT]

v279. On a scale of incomes on which 1 indicates the "lowest income decile" and 10 the "highest income decile" in your country. We would like to know in what group your household is. Please, specify the appropriate number, counting all wages, salaries, pensions and other incomes that come in. (*Code one number*):

Lowest deciles   Highest deciles
   1   2   3   4   5   6   7   8   9   10

v280. Lebanon is experiencing a very difficult political stalemate, which may have affected the economic conditions of some people. On the scale of 1 to 10, to what extent this current political situation affected your economic conditions—"1" being none at all and "10" being a great deal.

None at all   A great deal
   1   2   3   4   5   6   7   8   9   10

v281. Do you ever watch television? IF YES: How much time do you usually spend watching television on an average weekday (NOT WEEKENDS)?
   4. Do not watch TV or do not have access to TV
   5. 1 - 2 hours per day
   6. 2 - 3 hours per day
   7. More than 3 hours per day

v282. Total length of interview: ____ Minutes:

v283. During the interview the respondent was ....
   5 Very interested
   6 Somewhat interested
   7 Not very interested

v284. Size of town:
     1 Under 2,000
     2 2,000 - 5,000
     3 5 - 10,000
     4 10 - 20,000
     5 20 - 50,000
     6 50 - 100,000
     7 100 - 500,000
     8 500,000 and more

v285. Ethnic group [code by observation]:
     1. Arab
     2. Armenian
     3. Other

v286. Region where the interview was conducted: [use 2-digit regional code appropriate to your own society]

v287. Language in which interview was conducted:

INDEX

Abbasids 42, 95
Abduh, Muhammad 50, 52, 55, 143
Addis Ababa 75
Afghanistan 68, 80, 200
Afterlife 108
Ahmad, Aziz 35
Ahmad, Hamza ibn Ali ibn 95–97
Ahmad, Jalal Ale (or Jalal Al-e Ahmad) 64, 66–67
Akhundzadah, Mirza Fath Ali 101
al-Afghani 52
al-Assad, Hafiz 57
Alavi Kurds 102
Alawites 90, 102, 132
al-Azhar 58
al-Banna, Hassan 20, 25, 58, 60–61, 63
al-Bustani, Butrus 84
Aleppo 96
Alexandria 93, 113
Algeria 7, 53, 55–57, 68, 73, 95
Algerian War of Independence (1954–1962) 56
al-Ghazali, Muhammad 20
al-Hakim, Abu Ali Mansur Tariq 95–97
al-Hasa (Oasis) 82
al-Hikmat al-Sharifa (the Noble Knowledge) 96
al-Husri, Sati' 203
Ali, Amir 52
Ali, Chiragh 52, 55, 142
Ali, Muhammad 76
Ali, Mumtaz 52, 143
Aligarh College 52
Aligarh intellectual movement 52
al-Islam wa Usul al-Hum (Islam and the Fundamentals of Authority) 89
Al-Khobar 82, 122
Allies (World War II) 77
al-Mawardi, Abu al-Hasan Ali 43
al-Mulk, Sitt 95
al-Nour Party 208
al-Qaddah, Abd Allah Ibn Maymun 95
al-Qaeda 33, 58, 64
al-Raziq, Ali Abd 52, 89
al-Sadat, Anwar 63, 74
al-Sahwa 80
al-Samuqi, Baha al-Din 95–96

al-Saudi, Abd al-Aziz Ibn Abd al-Rahman 79
al-Shidya, Ahmad Faris 84
al-Tahtawi, Rifa'a 52
al-Utaibi, Juhaiman 81
al-Wahhab, Muhammad Ibn Abd 35
al-Yaziji, Ibrahim 84
al-Zahir 95
American Druze Public Affairs Committee 97
Americas 97
Americatoxication (*Amrikazadegi*) 66
Amin, Qasim 52, 143
Anglo-Russian Agreement (1907) 76
Anomie 27
Anti-Western attitudes 4, 6, 31, 56, 59, 68, 86, 90, 143, 148, 173
Aql (Reason) 40–42
Arab Spring 16, 32, 206–208
Arabia 49, 62, 63, 79,
Arabic language 43, 93,
  as the sacred universal language of the *umma* 41, 43,
Aramaic language 91
Ardabil 101
Armenia 90, 103
Asabiyya (Particularistic tribal solidarity) 41
Asia Minor 44
Asir 79
Assyout 113
Assyrian 90
Assyrian Catholics 92
Assyrian Church of the East 90
Ataturk, Kemal 102
Augustine (Saint Augustine) 109
Australia 97
Authoritarianism 14, 19, 21, 30, 58, 65, 71, 75, 77, 79, 88, 106, 118, 122, 135, 196, 200, 204
  secular 14, 16, 21, 33, 58, 70, 77, 80, 122, 123, 134–135, 149, 179, 196, 200,
  religious 14, 19, 21, 79, 84, 122, 135, 149, 179, 200
Ayatollah Khomeini 25, 38, 65, 66–68
Ayatollah Motahhari 204
Ayatollah Na'ini 54
Ayatollahs 6, 12